GLASS HOUSE

Shattering the ~~Theory~~ *Myth* of Evolution

KEN HAM &
BODIE HODGE
General Editors

First printing: February 2019

ISBN: 978-1-68344-156-4
Digital ISBN: 978-1-61458-702-6
Library of Congress Number: 2018968229

Cover by Left Coast Design, Portland, OR

Please consider requesting that a copy of this volume be purchased by your local library system.

Printed in the United States of America

Please visit our website for other great titles:
www.masterbooks.com

For information regarding author interviews,
please contact the publicity department at (870) 438-5288.

Master Books®
A Division of New Leaf Publishing Group
www.masterbooks.com

Contents

The Big Four: Origin of Life, Natural Selection, Mutations, and Missing Links

More Science Arguments: Genetics and Anatomy

Implications of an Evolutionary Worldview?

Christians and the Big Picture

> "
>
> *Evolution is a model, hypothesis, idea, belief, or a worldview — it is not a theory, a law, a fact, or the truth (God's Word is truth).*
>
> "

PREFACE

The CEO and founder of Answers in Genesis-US (AiG), the highly acclaimed Creation Museum, and the world-renowned Ark Encounter, **KEN HAM**, is one of the most in-demand Christian speakers in North America. He has appeared on Fox's *The O'Reilly Factor* and *Fox and Friends*, CNN's *The Situation Room* with Wolf Blitzer, ABC's *Good Morning America*, the BBC, and more. His 2014 creation/evolution debate with Bill Nye "the Science Guy" was watched by an estimated 25 million people.

Author and speaker **BODIE HODGE** attended Southern Illinois University at Carbondale (SIUC) and received a BS and MS (in 1996 and 1998, respectively) in mechanical engineering. Currently, Hodge is a writer and researcher at Answers in Genesis and a consultant of the Editorial Review Board. He has been involved in several books and DVDs and is a regular speaker in the Creation Museum Speaker Series.

Evolution (molecules-to-man) is a glass house. When you analyze it honestly, you can see right through the facade. A glass house, as its name implies, is not a sturdy structure, and is ripe for shattering at a moment's notice.

In our culture, many have been deceived into believing that evolution is a solid foundation and is well-attested — after all, it's integrated into nearly all subject material in most schools. The evolutionary worldview consists of more than just biological evolution. There is:

- Cosmological evolution or big bang where all things supposedly came from nothing.
- Geological evolution or millions of years of supposed earth history.
- Chemical evolution or an abiogenesis event to supposedly cause life to arise from non-living matter. Chemical evolution is sometimes denoted as a subset of biological evolution.
- Biological evolution or Darwinian evolution, where that initial life supposedly evolves into all the different kinds we have today.

This book dives into answering evolutionary claims, putting them to the test, and watching how they shatter. Christians are commanded to test everything and hold fast what is good while abstaining from every form of evil (1 Thessalonians 5:21–22). We are also commanded to demolish arguments and false beliefs that are predicated on the opinions of man who oppose God's Word (2 Corinthians 10:5).

As we dive into the problems of an evolutionary worldview let us first examine a brief history of evolution thought:

- *Spontaneous Generation* or *Aristotelian Abiogenesis* (all sorts of life constantly arises from non-living matter almost daily) was believed by some ancient Greeks as the origin of living creatures in the mid-300s B.C.
- Epicureans, based on Epicurus' ideas, developed biological evolution in Ancient Greece about 300 B.C., arguing that all things are material and that everything evolves from tiny particles called atoms, hence their position of "atomists" or *Epicureanism*, one form of Greek mythology.
- Epicureanism took a hit after *Paul publicly refuted them* at Mars Hill in Acts 17 and Epicureanism essentially died until the A.D. 1500s.
- In the 1500s, a few people began *rethinking some atomistic positions.*

- In 1743, a French Historian, Benoît de Maillet, proposed *panspermia* — that life came from germs falling from outer space. This idea was rekindled several times.
- Frenchman Jean-Baptiste Pierre Antoine de Monet, Chevalier de Lamarck (Jean Lamarck) reinvented evolution in the late 1700s and early 1800s and it became known as *Lamarckian Evolution,* which proposed change through *use* or *disuse* (i.e., if a giraffe reaches up enough, its neck will get longer and pass that along to its offspring).
- *Erasmus Darwin* (Charles Darwin's grandfather) published a book called *Zoonomia* in 1794 that promoted Lamarckian Evolution in England.
- *Geological Evolution* began with precursor ideas by people like James Hutton in his book *Theory of the Earth* in 1795, that the past must be interpreted by what we can see in nature today (i.e., the *present is the key to understanding the past* as opposed to using the *past to understand the present*).
- Pierre-Simon Laplace proposed initial *Astronomical Evolution* in his book *Exposition of the Systems of the World* via nebular hypothesis in 1796.
- *Uniformitarianism in Geological Evolution* was solidified by Charles Lyell in his three-volume set *Principles of Geology* in the 1830s which argues that geological deposits were laid down slowly and gradually (uniformly) over long periods of time, presuming that catastrophes had NO major impact on geology in the past.
- Charles Darwin published his book *On the Origin of Species by Means of Natural Selection for the Preservation of Favored Races* and *The Descent of Man and Selection in Relation to Sex* in 1859 and 1871, respectively, promoting *Traditional Darwinism* where natural selection is popularized as a mechanism to supposedly lead to evolution.
- *Louis Pasteur* ultimately destroyed spontaneous generation with simple experiments in the 1850s–1860s, proving the Law of Biogenesis that life only comes from life, not non-life.
- Thomas Henry Huxley insisted on a specialized form of spontaneous generation called *Modern Abiogenesis or Chemical Evolution* to insist on a naturalistic chemical origin of life sometime in the past to give biological evolution a starting point so that biological evolution could finally proceed.

- *Neo Darwinism* developed in the early 20th century when people realized that natural selection doesn't develop the new information required for evolutionary changes — it only filters already-existing information. Thus, mutations (with natural selection) were proposed to generate new information for an organism (e.g., to go from an ameba to a dog, you need to add information for hair, lungs, circulatory system, nervous system, etc.). Observations show mutations are a detriment or nearly neutral, so those "in the know" are still looking for an actual mechanism for evolution.

- The *Scopes Trial* in 1925 unlocked a door to allow *human* evolution to be taught in classrooms (even though the evolutionists actually lost the case). This triggered a systematic removal of the Christian worldview in schools and the addition of the humanistic religion (i.e., atheism, naturalism, etc.) in state schools.

- In 1931, Georges Lemaître (with support from Edwin Hubble and Milton Humason, as well as George Gamow) developed what became known as the big bang or *Cosmological Evolution.*

- In their famous experiment regarding their primordial soup model, *Stanley Miller* and *Harold Urey* failed to make life in a test tube (a result we continue to see). It only produced some amino acids.

- In 1972, Niles Eldridge and Stephen Jay Gould proposed *Punctuated Equilibria* to explain why we don't observe gradual evolutionary changes in organisms in the fossil record (missing links). Essentially, the onward and upward changes in biological evolution must occur so quickly in spurts that we don't have a snapshot of them in the fossil record.

- Francis Crick (known for his co-discovery of DNA) with Leslie Orgel popularized *Directed Panspermia* in 1973 where it was proposed that aliens brought life to earth to seed it because the odds of naturalistic evolution are nearly impossible.

- Atheist and humanist John J. Dunphy insisted in 1983 that the *faith of humanism* must entirely replace the faith of Christianity in the classroom.

Much more could be stated, but this brief history leads us to the issues we find today permeating our culture surrounding evolution. This book dives into subjects like the origin of life (abiogenesis), natural selection, mutations, missing links, the religious nature of evolution, and many other topics that challenge the evolutionary worldview that has been imposed on most people.

Evolution is a model, hypothesis, idea, belief, or a worldview — it is *not* a theory, a law, a fact, or the truth (God's Word is truth). A "theory" in science is one step below a "law" and, accordingly, has no evidence against it. Since evolution has mountains of evidence against it, it doesn't even come close to being warranted a "theory."

Some may argue that naturalistic religions that incorporate evolution, such as atheism, agnosticism, humanism, secularism, and the like, are not religious. However, this is false. An easy test of religiousness is to see if these views oppose religious tenets like biblical Christianity. And, of course, the answer is "yes" — humanistic religions do conflict with Christianity. As one example, God created in six days and rested on the seventh, where a naturalistic evolutionary view doesn't have a God or a Creator but merely an accidental (naturalistic) beginning.

Another test is to see if these ideas are compatible with biblical Christianity's young earth creation. How can a big bang, millions of years, and evolution be mixed perfectly with 6 normal-length-day creation thousands of years ago, a global Flood (which accounts for most of the rock layers that have fossils), and the existence of the God of the Bible? It is absurd to think these two can mix without conflict.

Of course, this doesn't stop some Christians from trying to mix these beliefs, but they do so by giving up the Bible's plain teachings (e.g., "a day doesn't mean a day" in Genesis, the sun was created on day 1 as opposed to day 4, Adam and Eve didn't exist, and so on). These syncretistic religions (mixing humanism and Christianity) have so many problems. We discuss this in the book as well.

We want to encourage you to relax and enjoy the book and its challenges. For Christians, our hope is that this book will help give you answers for your faith and a means to defend the biblical position when it is challenged.

For the non-Christian, we trust this book challenges the religion of evolution that has been imposed upon you through state schools, secular media outlets, secular books, and secular museums. We do this book not to merely refute false arguments, but because we care about you. We want to see people understand the truth and not be misled into false religions.

> *Sadly, our culture is deteriorating into a wasteland of evil. Even the youth of today are really 'ticking time bombs' — repercussions of a secular worldview.*

INTRODUCTION: HAS EVOLUTION INFILTRATED THE CHURCH?

KEN HAM is heard daily on the radio feature *Answers with Ken Ham* (broadcast on more than 950 stations). Since the Creation Museum opened, he has been interviewed on *CBS News Sunday Morning, The NBC Nightly News* with Brian Williams, *The PBS News Hour* with Jim Lehrer, and many other outlets. Ken is also the founder of *Answers* magazine and writes articles for AiG's popular website. During his many speaking events, Ken's emphasis is on the relevance and authority of the Book of Genesis to the life of the average Christian, and how compromise on Genesis has changed how the culture and church view biblical authority. Ken also reflects on "hot button" topics of our day (e.g., the breakdown of the society, the attack by secularists on religious liberty, school violence, creation/evolution in public schools, abortion, lawlessness, and more).

Abortion, homosexual "marriage," transgender, school shootings, euthanasia, global warming, free-sex, illegal drug use, suicide, anti-Christian sentiment — what do these have to do with evolution? More than you may realize. They are the evil fruits of an evolutionary worldview that has been imposed on generations of people in the Western world.

Worse than that, many people sitting in the pews have adopted these anti-biblical positions. When the church gave up the absolute authority of the Bible, particularly in Genesis, we opened a door that let the world dictate their beliefs as superior, and the Bible was "tossed aside."

We need to *right* the ship of Christianity. But there is another problem. The ship of Christianity isn't just going in the wrong direction, it's sinking in our Western world. How do we right the sinking ship of Christianity? The first thing we need to do is get the water out and plug the leak. Then we need to get the ship turned to the proper course.

These fruits of evolution have their foundation in millions of years and naturalism (i.e., nature is all that there is, no God). This is part of the religion of humanism (where man is seen as the ultimate authority, not God) with denominations like secularism (no spiritual), agnosticism (can't know if God exists), and atheism (no God exists).

So why should Christians accept aspects of this other religion and mix it with their Christianity? They shouldn't. So now you know where the leak is on the ship! Now it's time to start fixing the leak.

A Good God and World of Suffering?

How is it that the world is full of death and suffering, and yet, at the same time, was called "good." Consider God's initial creation:

> And God saw every thing that he had made, and, behold, it was very good. And the evening and the morning were the sixth day (Genesis 1:31; KJV).

Try to imagine putting yourself in the position of a person who has no background knowledge of Christianity — a person who did not grow up in a Christian home, never attended church, and has been indoctrinated in evolutionary concepts through the education system. Most likely, this person has also been taught against Christianity by his/her parents, and by teachers in school and college.

Imagine a Christian who meets this person and tells him there is a God of infinite love who made the world and cares for us. After this non-Christian listens, it wouldn't be surprising to hear him respond with the following:

> I don't see any God of love. All I see are children suffering and dying. I see people killing and stealing. Disease and death seem to be everywhere. Nature is "red in tooth and claw" as a poet once stated. It's a horrible world. I don't see your God of love. If your God does exist, He must be a sadistic ogre.

The problem is that this non-Christian is looking at a fallen world. As Romans 8:22 states: "For we know that the whole creation has been groaning together in the pains of childbirth until now."[1]

When this person considers what is being told to him about the God of creation, he then, in a sense, blames God for the horrible world we live in. Without an understanding of Genesis and the account of the Fall, he won't comprehend at all how there can be a God of love amidst the groaning.

Now for a Christian, when a loved one dies or some tragedy strikes, it's understandable to ask God why these things happen. However, there are many Christians who also blame God and become angry at Him because they don't understand the real reason for the existence of death and suffering. I believe a major cause of this is that many Christians have been indoctrinated to believe that God "created" over billions of years, and that death, disease, and suffering are a part of this creative process. But this is not really the God of the Bible.

If we can believe Genesis 1:31, then we realize that God created everything very good. Every work of God is perfect in Deuteronomy 32:4. So we expected a perfect world, from a perfect God. So what happened to bring about this groaning world?

It's vital that Christians understand what occurred in the universe as a result of Adam's fall into sin. You see, the groaning, horrible world we now see around us (even though there's still a remnant of beauty from the original creation) exists because this is what we as human beings, in essence, have asked for!

In Colossians 1:17 and Hebrews 1:3, we learn that Jesus Christ, the Creator of all things, upholds all things by the Word of His power. As John Gill states in his commentary:

> The whole frame of nature would burst asunder and break in pieces, was it not held together by him; every created being has its

---

1. Unless otherwise noted, Scripture in this chapter is from the English Standard Version (ESV) of the Bible.

support from him, and its consistency in him; and all the affairs of Providence relating to all creatures are governed, directed, and managed by him, in conjunction with the Father and the blessed Spirit. . . . preserves every creature in its being, and supports it, and supplies it with the necessaries of life; rules and governs all, and providentially orders and disposes of all things in the world, and that by his all-powerful will.[2]

The reason for our very existence — even at this very moment — is because He holds us together by His power. What an awesome thought! No wonder the Psalmist in Psalm 139:6 exclaimed, "Such knowledge is too wonderful for me; it is high; I cannot attain it."

Personally, I believe what happened at the time of the Fall was this: God gave Adam a choice: choose God and His absolutes, or choose autonomy (i.e., man makes his own rules). Adam (and, as rebellious creatures, we in Adam) chose life without God. We didn't want God's rules; we wanted to determine truth for ourselves. As a result, God, as a righteous Judge, gave us, in a sense, what we wanted (and deserved). He has withdrawn some of His power so as to not uphold the world in a perfect state — and look what happened. Everything is running down and falling apart. We are now experiencing the judgment of a taste of what life would be like without God — this mess is really our fault.

In Deuteronomy 8:4, 29:5 and Nehemiah 9:21, we read how the Israelites, when they were in the wilderness for 40 years, didn't see their clothes or shoes wear out (and their feet didn't swell). This was obviously a miracle of preservation from the Lord. Imagine if God were to do this with everything in the entire universe — then nothing would wear out. There would be no disease or suffering. This, of course, is how it will be in the New Earth after the restoration.

When you think about it, God is so merciful to us. Even though we have a predisposition to want life without God because of our rebellion in Adam, our Creator has given us only a taste of what this is like. He still upholds things so we can live in this world. If God were to withdraw even more of the Word of His power, then things would become much worse. And the more God removes His restraining influence from the nations (remember it is God who raises up kings and destroys kingdoms), the more we would see the horrible sinful nature of man expressed in evil deeds.

---

2.   https://biblehub.com/commentaries/gill/colossians/1.htm and https://www.biblestudytools.com/commentaries/gills-exposition-of-the-bible/hebrews-1-3.html.

I believe we can see a practical example of this before our very eyes in America, the UK, Australia, and other countries. What happened? These nations were once more Christianized. God's laws were respected and, by and large, obeyed. But now we observe a nation full of fornication, wickedness, murder, deceit, haters of God, inventors of evil things, children disobedient to parents — and even a Church that, for the most part, has compromised the Word of God with the teachings of sinful, finite, and imperfect people.

More and more people are rejecting the God of the Bible. Evolutionary teaching is rampant. We see Western nations that seem to have lost a sense of right and wrong — there doesn't seem to be an understanding of God's absolutes. America appears to have lost its moral basis. Other once-Christianized countries (e.g., England) are even further along than America.

God has a warning for all nations. In Romans 1, we read that when people rejected God's Word, God gave them up and gave them over. Romans 1:25 states: "because they exchanged the truth about God for a lie and worshiped and served the creature rather than the Creator, who is blessed forever! Amen."

This, of course, is a very apt description of a naturalistic evolutionary worldview. And it is also an apt description of those Christians who compromise with evolution and/or millions of years teachings. They are in essence placing the word of sinful fallible people above God's Word — thus worshiping the creature more than the Creator.

I believe Romans 1 is describing what happens when God removes more of His restraining influence and Word of His power. Things will degenerate even more. And what will be the result? Paul describes it for us in Romans 1:28–32:

> And since they did not see fit to acknowledge God, God gave them up to a debased mind to do what ought not to be done. They were filled with all manner of unrighteousness, evil, covetousness, malice. They are full of envy, murder, strife, deceit, maliciousness. They are gossips, slanderers, haters of God, insolent, haughty, boastful, inventors of evil, disobedient to parents, foolish, faithless, heartless, ruthless. Though they know God's righteous decree that those who practice such things deserve to die, they not only do them but give approval to those who practice them.

Oh, America, and other once-great Christianized nations! "Return, O faithless sons; I will heal your faithlessness" (Jeremiah 3:22). "Let the wicked forsake his way, and the unrighteous man his thoughts; let him return to the LORD, that he may have compassion on him, and to our God, for he will abundantly pardon" (Isaiah 55:7).

Sadly, our culture is deteriorating into a wasteland of evil. Even the youth of today are really "ticking time bombs" — repercussions of a secular worldview.

Defusing Bombs in Public Schools

People are asking: "why?" Why do some teenagers have such a low view of human life that would lead them to shoot and kill their fellow students and attempt to kill and destroy them with bombs in a suicide attack? What's behind all this? Could it happen again?

The sad thing is that potential "bombs" are being built in public schools every day. The mayhem created by school shooters from the USA to Finland to Germany over the past few years is nothing compared to the "bombs" still waiting to explode in this culture. This nation needs to brace itself as these begin to explode across the nation.

Today, generations of young people appear to have an utter sense of purposelessness and hopelessness. Many have an obsession with death, with little or no sense of right and wrong. These are the "time bombs" in our culture, and many of them already have their "fuses" lit.

There will be more senseless killing, more violence, more bloodshed, and more sorrow and suffering. And for all the talk, and all the opinions, this nation and many others haven't learned the lesson. The real "disease" has not been dealt with.

Evolutionary Bombs

Just a couple of weeks after the horrible killings at Columbine High School in Colorado (one of the first major school shootings), students (including those who saw friends shot in front of their eyes) went back to school and sadly were given the ingredients to make more "bombs." You see, when millions of students have been told in their classes that there is no God, that man is just an animal, and that death, bloodshed, and violence (similar to what we observe in today's world) are a natural part of the evolutionary mechanisms that produced man, then let's be honest about the logical consequences!

In that worldview, who determines what are (or are not) "right" and "wrong" actions? If violence is a part of the evolutionary process, then why should we try to combat it? If man is just an animal, then who decides what "value" is placed upon human life? If death is nothingness, then what is the point of suffering in this present world?

Whose Values?

People are crying out asking why these students don't have the "values" of past generations. But what they mean by "values" in reality is Christian morality. It is only on the basis of an absolute authority (the God of the Bible) that one could insist on the morality of the Ten Commandments (e.g., Thou shalt not murder); otherwise, it's just an opinion. And who determines whose opinions are the right ones?

School students once went through the public education system learning Christian morality, understanding its foundation in an absolute authority — the Word of the Creator God to whom they were all accountable. Then there followed students who went through the education system learning Christian morality (but without its foundation), a time when the Bible, prayer, and God's Law were taken out of the system. Thus, they had a moral structure but with no foundation.

At the same time, students were being taught with ever-increasing fervor that man was an evolved animal. Shortly after, a new group of students went through this same education system, but not only were they taught evolution as fact, they also increasingly saw Christianity attacked and ridiculed. The more the foundation for Christian morality was attacked and removed, and the more students were taught there were no absolutes, the more their worldview reflected this change.

These are ingredients for powerful "bombs" to explode, resulting in hatred of Christians and the devaluing of human life, leading to killing one's fellow man and suicide. Now it's not that a student wakes up one morning and says, "There's no God, and I'm just an evolved animal, so there's nothing wrong with killing students and teachers." The longer that generations of young people grow up in a culture whose education system is devoid of Christianity and pervaded by evolutionary philosophy, the more possible that an increasingly large subset of these students will eventually act out in accord with the foundation they've been given for their understanding of life. It is not just the schools that are giving the ingredients for "bombs" to the students. Much of the Church has also contributed in this regard.

The Church's Compromise

The 1999 Templeton Prize for Progress in Religion ($1.24 million award) was given to scientist Ian Barbour who stated in an interview concerning his work for which he received this accolade, "You simply can't any longer say as traditional Christians that death was God's punishment for sin. Death was around long before human beings. Death is a necessary aspect of an evolutionary world."[3]

Sadly, much of the Church has accepted the view that millions of years of death (in the fossil record) preceded the arrival of man on this planet. Thus death, bloodshed, disease (there is evidence of much disease like cancer, arthritis, etc. in the fossil bones), and violence existed for millions of years leading up to man. After God finished creating man and the animals, the Bible states that "everything he had made . . . was very good." Thus, with this compromise with Scripture, death, bloodshed, disease, and violence would actually be seen as "very good" per Genesis 1:31.

How then can the Church give an answer to those asking "why?" in regard to these terrible school killings? Imagine a pastor who believes in millions of years sitting down with a student who says that he would like to commit violence to his classmates. The following could be the conversation:

> "Billy, you can't hurt your fellow classmates like that. You must love your fellow man as God loves. There is a God of love, Billy."
>
> "Pastor?"
>
> "Yes, Billy."
>
> "Pastor, do you believe in millions of years before man? Do you believe the fossil record is millions of years old?"
>
> "Yes, why, Billy?"
>
> "Well it's a record of death, disease, bloodshed, and violence, right?"
>
> "Yes, Billy — that's true."
>
> "Well, according to the Bible then, God described this as very good?"
>
> "Well — yes."
>
> "Well, pastor, I am loving as God loves. Death, bloodshed, violence, and suffering have always been a part of how God loves."

The point is, those in the Church who have added millions of years to the Bible have to admit that Billy — and not the pastor — is being the consistent one. It's only the Christian who believes in a literal Genesis and understands that death, bloodshed, violence, suffering, and disease are a consequence of sin (our sin because we are descendants of the first man Adam)

---

3. *Dayton Daily News*, Religion section, March 13, 1999.

who can talk about a real God of love (who provided His Son as a sacrifice for our sin to suffer death for us). He gives the answer as to why this is a groaning and violence-filled world.

As a ministry, we want to help defuse these "bombs" and provide these students (and teachers) in the public school system, secular media, secular museums, and so on with the truth about their origins so that they will understand that they are made in the image of God, are sinners separated from their Creator, but that they can be saved for eternity, and know purpose and meaning in life through Jesus Christ.

The Evolutionary Story Changes and Is Rewritten Over and Over Again

Where would you rather put your faith and trust: in the words of fallible, sinful men who don't know everything, who weren't there, and whose ideas and models change all the time — or the Word of the infallible God, who knows everything, has always been there, and whose Word changes not?

The Bible certainly makes it clear that God's Holy Word is forever "fixed in the heavens" (Psalm 119:89). Because the infallible Creator God is omniscient, omnipresent, and omnipotent, this of course is what we would expect of God's Word to us.

However, because human beings are fallible, sinful, and very limited in what they can know (e.g., "If anyone imagines that he knows something, he does not yet know as he ought to know" — 1 Corinthians 8:2), we should always keep this in perspective when listening to the claims of secular humanistic scientists concerning life and its origins.

Therefore, we shouldn't be surprised when it seems that evolutionists find new evidence almost daily that causes them to rewrite some aspect of evolution. But when is the public going to wake up? If one kept a file of what is happening in evolutionary thought, it would be an almost endless stream of articles where evolution changes daily!

It is incredible to see people putting their faith and trust in the ever-shifting sands of evolutionary ideas rather than in the changeless Word of God. The Word of God, however, declares many times, "It is written."

Where do you put your faith and trust? In "It is written" (God's Word — beginning with Genesis) or "It is rewritten" (man's word/humanism — evolutionary ideas)?

The church needs to get back to the authority of the Bible in the church — plug the hole in the ship. Training the next generation to stand on the authority of Scripture in Genesis in our culture is the next step at "righting the ship." So long as the church continues to give their children to the world for their training instead of training them up in righteousness of the Lord and teaching them to defend their faith with apologetics, then this spiral down into humanism will only worsen, as the ship will continue to sink.

To be certain, there is no straightforward way to read Genesis 1–2 and arrive at a history of the universe that approaches the evolutionary view held by so many Christians today.

1

WHAT IS EVOLUTION: THE THREE TYPES TO RECOGNIZE

ROGER PATTERSON earned his BS Ed degree in biology from Montana State University. Before coming to work at Answers in Genesis, he taught for eight years in Wyoming's public school system and assisted the Wyoming Department of Education in developing assessments and standards for children in public schools. He is a contributing author to *Answers Magazine*, and has served as general editor and contributing author in numerous books, including the multi-volume works *World Religions and Cults* and *How Do We Know the Bible Is True?* He helps to answer many difficult questions of faith, theology, and science, as well as serving as part of Answers in Genesis' editorial review board.

If we want to have a meaningful interaction with someone, it would be really helpful if we spoke the same language. But within the language, we must have a common understanding of the words that we are using. If you were from Wisconsin and flew to Florida and asked where the bubbler is in the airport, you would probably get a confused look.

In the discussions around origins, defining our terms is extremely important. If we don't start with common definitions for words like science, evolution, religion, faith, and theory, we will be talking past one another. When most people use the word *evolution*, they have the idea of biological evolution in mind — molecules turned into minnows which turned into mice and men. But there are several forms and senses of evolution that could create confusion.

Evolution comes from a Latin word that means "to unroll." With that in mind, we can use the sense of "change over time" as the broadest meaning of the word. Someone's taste in music or ability to paint can evolve. But in the origins debate, we can't just use the word in a loose sense. It must be clearly defined.

Two Main Senses

From a biblical worldview, the idea that all life on earth shares a common ancestor must be rejected. God has revealed in the opening chapter of Genesis how he created living things according to their kinds — one kind did not come from another. A Christian should not agree with the naturalist that life gradually evolved from a common universal ancestor billions of years ago.

But Christians can agree that there is change among dogs over time. Some people use the term *microevolution* to talk about the small changes that we can observe in living things (e.g., new dog breeds, antibiotic resistance in bacteria, etc.). The same people may refer to the supposed change from amphibians into reptiles — a much larger change — as *macroevolution*. They would argue that the same type of processes that produce the small changes in dogs can eventually produce the extreme changes needed to go from fish to amphibian. Thus, microevolution eventually leads to macroevolution . . . or so they believe.

But to argue for both ideas with the same definition of "evolution" introduces the logical fallacy called *equivocation* (or bait-and-switch fallacy). The types of changes that result in a new breed of dog are not the same types of changes needed to turn fins into legs or gills into lungs. The first is selecting from traits and information already present; the second requires the addition of traits and the new genetic information that codes for those traits. Thus, the terms *microevolution* and *macroevolution* should be avoided — they are misleading terms.

Three Main Types

The idea of evolutionary changes in both living and nonliving things is not a new idea. We know from the writings of ancient Greek thinkers that evolutionary views were common. The Epicureans promoted a form of spontaneous evolution that rejected the need of gods to bring about forms of life from basic elements they called atoms.[1] Earlier, Anaximander of Miletus promoted a view of the first life emerging in an ancient wet period of earth and amphibious forms coming later, with humans eventually arriving. While these and other thinkers proposed various views of evolution, these ideas are not what we think of as evolution today.

Among these early Greek explanations, we see an emphasis on chemical elements turning into living things and those lifeforms changing over time. In Eastern thought, there are also forms of evolutionary thinking. Taoist, Buddhist, and Hindu traditions also extend to the formation of the physical elements of our universe. It is apparent that the idea of evolution has expanded through time and across both the physical and biological realms.

With that as background, naturalistic evolution encompasses these key points:

- The universe is approximately 14 billion years old.
- The big bang explains the origin of the universe.
- Stars and galaxies formed gradually over billions of years.
- Our solar system, including our planet, formed gradually about 4.5 billion years ago.
- Life evolved on the earth as chemicals interacted to form the first "living" organism.
- The landscape of the earth has been gradually shaped by natural forces through uniformitarian processes.
- Organisms increased in complexity over time with all life on earth sharing a common ancestor.

To simplify, we can break this into three categories that can be easily remembered.

---

1. Bodie Hodge, "If Paul Were Around Today, Would He Argue Against Evolutionists?" Answers in Genesis, http://answersingenesis.org/apologetics/if-paul-were-around-today-would-he-argue-against-evolutionists.

1. **Cosmological Evolution:** From the singularity of the big bang, all space, matter, and energy gradually formed the universe and all the galaxies, stars, and planets in it. (Cosmic Evolution is another term that could be used here.)

2. **Geological Evolution:** The earth formed from the debris spinning around our sun as it gathered into a ball. Over time, the earth cooled, the atmosphere formed, and the seas accumulated. The surface of the earth was shaped and reshaped over billions of years.

3. **Biological Evolution:** The first life formed as chemicals spontaneously formed every component needed for life. From this first organism, all life on earth has gradually developed into the variety we see today. (**Chemical Evolution** is another term included in this category, denoting specifically when nonliving matter supposedly gave rise to life.)

While we can divide these into three categories, those with an evolutionary worldview (whether they are Christian, atheist, deist, or any other religious group)[2] view this overall process as a continuum. These ongoing, natural processes overlap one another and flow into one another. For example, the formation of stars could be included in cosmological evolution, but the planets that supposedly formed from the spinning disks of stars is on the line between cosmological and geological. Likewise, the alleged assembling of chemicals to form the first life is a precursor to biological evolution, but must happen for the evolution of living things. So, some would separate chemical evolution as a fourth category.

Cosmological Evolution

Cosmogony and cosmology are the fields of study that deal with the origin and formation of the universe, including the galaxies and the stars they are made of. The dominant view of the origin of the universe is known as the big bang model. While it has undergone many changes (and will surely undergo more), the basic idea is that the universe came into existence 13.7 billion years ago. The entire universe was contained in an infinitely small point known as a singularity. This singularity began to expand slowly, then extremely rapidly, and then slowly again, though there is no reason for such changes in rate.

---

2. Roger Patterson, "What About Theistic Evolution?" Answers in Genesis, http://answersin-genesis.org/theistic-evolution/what-about-theistic-evolution.

Cosmological models propose that over time stars and galaxies began to form through natural processes, as basic elements like hydrogen, helium, and lithium formed and collected into clouds called nebulae. These clouds of gas coalesced to form the first stars (specifically *astronomical evolution*). Stars grouped together as galaxies were born. These galaxies continued to move away from one another as the universe continued to expand.

Later, galaxies began to interact and collide. As stars were born, aged, and died, heavier elements like carbon, nitrogen, and iron were formed. As stars exploded at the end of their lives, they spread these elements into space, and they were collected in new stars. Eventually, all of the elements that we see were created through this gradual process over many generations of star formation.

While many people will reject that this is a form of evolution, the evolutionists themselves use the language. You can take classes taught from textbooks like *Introduction to the Theory of Stellar Structure and Evolution, Stellar Evolution, Cosmology: The Origin and Evolution of Cosmic Structure.* Terms like galactic evolution, stellar evolution, and cosmic evolution are common in scientific literature. Based on this, it is a significant part of the larger evolutionary worldview. People who believe the universe came about as described in the big bang model can rightly be called evolutionists, even if they reject Darwin's ideas regarding biological evolution.

But can any of these events be verified? Are there other ways to interpret the things we observe in the universe around us? Why has the model changed so much? Are there other models to consider?

Biblical and Scientific Concerns

The many scientific problems with the big bang model and other aspects of cosmological evolution have been written about in great detail by both scientists who are biblical creationists and secular scientists who will honestly criticize their fellow scientists. How the first stars formed, where the singularity came from, how the laws of physics operated in the singularity, the relatively smooth nature of the cosmic background, and the horizon problem are just a few.[3]

To resolve the horizon problem, big bang supporters have suggested that there was a period of inflation, or a burst of expansion, in the first fractions of a second after the universe began to expand. The problem is that there is no evidence or reason to suggest there was an inflationary period other than

---

3.   Danny Faulkner, "Problems with the Big Bang," Answers in Genesis, http://answersingenesis.org/big-bang/problems-with-the-big-bang.

to avoid the horizon problem. One textbook refers to this as a "correction . . . needed to allow for the fact that the expansion was more rapid at the beginning."[4]

The inflation solution to the horizon problem is nothing more than a story to support a belief about the past. To add to the problem, there is no well-established reason for the inflationary period to have occurred and no explanation of how it slowed itself down in a smooth fashion. Despite these observational shortcomings, most big bang supporters adhere to the "fact" of the inflationary phase. The same type of flawed explanation is given to prop up other aspects of the story without any substantial evidence.

From a biblical perspective, the big bang and the description of creation given in Genesis 1 are absolutely incompatible — there is no way to marry the two. One major problem is the order of events. To be certain, there is no straightforward way to read Genesis 1–2 and arrive at a history of the universe that approaches the evolutionary view held by so many Christians today.

In fact, there are many blatant contradictions in the order of events described in Genesis and the evolutionary accounting of the events that formed the universe as known today. To reconcile these differences, it seems that much dismissal or twisting of the text must be performed to accommodate the various evolutionary processes.[5]

The table on the following page presents a few of the differences with biblical text that must be reconciled if an evolutionary view is embraced (including geological and biological elements that will be discussed later). Many people have not considered these contradictions, and this is a great point of discussion as biblical creationists dialog with believers who hold evolutionary views.

There are clear biblical and scientific refutations of the ideas within cosmological evolution. Examining these makes it clear that anyone who holds onto these ideas has a shaky foundation for their worldview.

Geological Evolution

At some point during this cosmological evolution, the earth and our solar system had to form. The dominant model in the evolutionary view is called the nebular hypothesis. The basic idea proposes that a cloud of dust and gasses from previously exploded stars gathered together and began spinning.

4. F.S. Hess et al., *Earth Science: Geology, the Environment, and the Universe* (Teacher Wraparound Edition), (New York: Glencoe/ McGraw Hill, 2005).
5. Terry Mortenson, "Evolution vs. Creation: The Order of Events Matters!" Answers in Genesis, http://www.answersingenesis.org/articles/2006/04/04/order-of-events-matters.

Evolutionary History	Genesis Account
The sun forms before the earth	The earth is present before the sun
Earth forms at the same time as other planets	The earth is formed before the other planets
The earth begins as a molten mass of rock without any water	The earth begins with water
Reptiles evolve before birds	Birds are formed before reptiles
Thorns and thistles evolve before man	Thorns and thistles are a result of man's sin

A star formed in the center, and the remnants collected together based on their relative densities (the inner planets are rocky, and the outer planets are gaseous) to form planets and their satellites. The earth began as a molten ball that eventually cooled. The atmosphere eventually formed, and water was available to form the oceans. Once there was water, life could develop.

Along with this, the plates that make up the earth's crust were in constant motion. They shifted up and down as well as horizontally over the billions of years of earth's history. The plate tectonics model we know today was not developed and broadly accepted until the 1960s. Adopting the standards of uniformitarian thinking, evolutionists teach that the plates move at an incredibly slow rate today, so they must have done so in the past.

Likewise, the layers that we can see as part of the geologic column are supposed to be a record of slow and gradual deposition and erosion over billions of years. The formation and erosion of mountains that formed as plates collided and volcanoes erupted, as well as the rift valleys that formed and flooded to form seas, represent a slow and steady process in the evolutionary models.[6]

Since these models speak of "change over time" in the surface of the earth, the layers in the crust, the atmosphere, and other aspects, these models can rightly be called forms of geological evolution. While the term may not be common, textbooks like *Historical Geology: Evolution of Earth*

---

6. John Whitmore, "Aren't Millions of Years Required for Geological Processes?" Answers in Genesis, http://answersingenesis.org/geology/arent-millions-of-years-required-for-geological-processes.

and Life Through Time and thousands of journal articles include geological evolution in their titles.

Biblical and Scientific Concerns

The nebular hypothesis is not something that has been observed, nor have the smaller theoretical ideas that make up the model. For example, gas clouds do not naturally collapse on themselves. As the density of the gas increases, it naturally wants to expand, not contract into a star. Likewise, the particles floating through space would not clump together to form planets, but bounce off one another.

The date of 4.5 billion years assigned to the earth does not actually come from measurements of earth rocks, but of meteorites. This only makes sense if you assume that the nebular hypothesis is true and that meteors in our solar system formed at the same time as the earth.

On top of that are many assumptions that must be accepted to calculate the age of a rock. While the evolutionary view proposes that the rock layers were laid down gradually, there is virtually no erosion between many layers where millions of years are supposed to have passed. There is also no convincing explanation for how an ice age would be sustained, let alone many of them, through history.

The Bible gives us a date for the age of the earth, and it is thousands, not billions, of years old. The Bible also gives us a simple explanation for explaining the rapid formation of layers of sediment without any erosion between them. Further, the Bible gives us a superior mechanism to explain the ice age as a result of the Flood of Noah's day. These explanations, based on both biblical data and scientific observations and models, are rejected without consideration by naturalistic evolutionists.

Biological Evolution (Including Chemical Evolution)

In the naturalistic view, all life on earth today came from some unknown collection of nonliving substances. There have been many models proposed for how this happened, but the general term applied to all of them is chemical evolution. Another term is abiogenesis — the genesis of life (*bio*) from non-life.

Once life got started, the first cell must have had all of the parts that would allow it to be separate from its environment, gather and process food, eliminate waste, store information to replicate itself, repair damage to itself, have a process to duplicate itself, and many other functions. And all of this happened through random interactions of chemicals acting under natural laws . . . or so they believe.

Once this first cell evolved, it would then need to continue to duplicate itself. Variations by mutations would be needed so that natural selection could work to bring about survival of the fittest in various environments. From there, the single-celled organisms supposedly developed into various forms (e.g., eukaryotes and prokaryotes), some of which remained as single cells while others began to develop into multiple cells working together.

It was these multicellular organisms that then developed into more and more complex organisms like worms. Worms became fish, fish became amphibians, which became reptiles. Other cells developed into algae and plants, which eventually moved onto the land.[7]

Once the plants and animals moved onto land, they continued diversifying through mutations, natural selection, and other natural processes. From the original single-celled organism that was the first living thing, all life supposedly diversified through a branching process that would resemble a giant bush with branches of varying lengths. This "tree of life" concept is the heart of biological evolution.

Most evolutionists today would hold to the neo-Darwinian evolutionary ideas. Based on the proposal of Charles Darwin, primarily in his book *Origin of Species* in 1859, all life evolved from a single organism, diversifying over time. Though Darwin had no notion of DNA and genetics as we understand them today, his basic idea of traits that were inherited and passed on with variations to offspring still stands as the foundation for evolutionary views today. While there is new data used to support the evolutionary explanation of life, the *grand theory of evolution* has become so flexible it seems that any idea can fit into it regardless of how it may contradict other aspects.

Biblical and Scientific Concerns

If this all sounds like a lovely story, that is exactly what it is. While there are fossils and traces of life in the rock record, these pieces of scientific data must all be interpreted. While they can be used to attempt to support the ideas of evolution, they can also be used to support the biblical model of origins. No one has ever observed these processes happening. In fact, the type of transformation necessary to turn a fish's gills into the lungs of an amphibian are only ideas in the minds of evolutionists, not facts that can be examined.

---

7.   Elizabeth Mitchell, " '600 Million-Year-Old' Sponge Said To Show When Multicellular Animals Evolved," Answers in Genesis, http://answersingenesis.org/origin-of-life/600-million-year-old-sponge-said-show-when-multicellular-animals-evolved.

The biggest hurdle to chemical evolution is the origin of information. The code found in DNA is very complex. There is no known natural mechanism that can create such a code from natural interactions of chemical substances. To accept that DNA formed spontaneously is to accept something that cannot be demonstrated scientifically — yet it must be true in the evolutionary worldview. And many who hold to evolution will actively deny that chemical evolution is part of biological evolution. While that is technically correct, how did biological evolution get started if chemical evolution didn't happen?

There are several chicken-and-egg problems with this theory of evolution. For example: DNA needs to be transcribed into RNA to make proteins; proteins are needed to duplicate DNA, but DNA provides the code to make the proteins; proteins spontaneously fall apart in water, but water was needed for the first life to form. The challenges to chemical evolution are so numerous that to accept that it happened by chance is to accept odds that can only be accepted by faith — faith in unobservable events and chance.

While the odds of chemical evolution bringing about the first cell are astronomically high, there is a bigger problem. To accept this idea is to contradict what God has revealed in the Bible. Genesis 1 clearly describes how God supernaturally created the world and all of the living things in it. Rather than natural processes over billions of years, God created the living things over the course of a few days. There is no way to reconcile these two views without doing great harm to one or the other. Either the Bible is true and God created the plants and animals according to their kinds, or life evolved gradually from the same kind of organism. These two worldviews are not compatible.

Chain of Assumptions

If we were to draw a diagram of the naturalistic evolutionary view of the universe, it would have the big bang at the center and move out to the evolution of the organisms living today. In between would be the formation of stars, planetary formation, gradual deposition and erosion, chemical evolution, the first cells, multicellular life, and then the diversity of life we see today.

If we use the analogy of a chain, we can examine naturalism as it applies to evolution to see if it is a reliable foundation to build a worldview upon. If one truth claim is dependent upon another claim, if we can prove the first is faulty, then the second is faulty also. And if all of these ideas have flowed through time in a great chain, then the support for the entire model crashes to the ground if any of the links is shown to be flawed. Biological evolution can't be true if chemical evolution (abiogenesis) didn't happen in the first place. And stars can't form if the big bang didn't create the matter needed for the first stars.

When we start from a biblical perspective, we can demonstrate on the authority of the Bible that these evolutionary ideas are false. But if we do an internal critique of the naturalistic evolutionary worldview by accepting (for the sake of argument) the assumptions of naturalism, we can examine whether the system can stand on its own merits.

The links in the chain could be arranged in different ways, but let's think about the "highest" lifeforms we see today as the top link, stretching down (backward through evolutionary time) to the formation of the earth, and eventually the big bang. For the moment, we will grant the billions of years and the laws of nature needed to allow evolutionary processes to happen. So all we have is the observed evidence, the laws of nature, time, and chance occurrences (since there is no "guide" or "intelligence" in the naturalistic worldview).

But First . . .

- Before you tell me how humans and gorillas evolved from an ape-like creature (the top of the evolutionary chain), you have to be able to explain how a trait like sexual reproduction came to exist.
- And before you tell me how sexual reproduction happened, you have to tell me how the first organisms that were sexually different came to be without going extinct (a male and a female would have to accidentally evolve simultaneously).
- And how did the first multicellular organism have the genetic information to develop different cell types?
- And before you tell me that the first living thing diversified into many types, you have to prove to me that chemicals can assemble themselves into complex integrated systems (despite the fact that it is not happening today).
- And you will have to demonstrate how specific, coded information came to exist in the DNA from simple interactions of chemicals in an environment in the past.

These are just some of the assumptions in the links of biological evolution and abiogenesis. If any of these links fail to be proven, especially the earliest links, the chain cannot hold the weight of the worldview it is supposedly supporting.

The same types of issues come with geological evolution.

- Biological evolution requires billions of years for the random interactions to produce complex life.
- But to support the story of biological evolution, you have to assume that the layers of rock were deposited gradually over billions of years.
- You have to explain how there are many layers where millions of years are supposed to have passed, yet there is virtually no erosion.
- You have to assume that a tree trunk can be fossilized standing upright through layers that supposedly span millions of years without rotting away.
- You have to prove how fossilized crabs from "millions of years ago" look identical to crabs walking the beach today.
- You have to assume that the dates calculated from radiometric isotopes are not impacted by the assumptions involved in the calculations.
- You have to accept that the extrapolation of measured rates of radiometric decay can be extrapolated backward for millions or billions of years.
- You must prove that the current rate of movement of the continents has always been the same.
- You have to explain how those layers formed from a cooling molten earth as an atmosphere was forming to provide the water for life to begin.
- And you have to assume that the dust particles floating around the nebula would actually stick together to form clumps large enough to make a planet, not to mention what caused the nebula to spin in the first place.

And if you are still holding onto the chain after the assumptions of geological evolution, you have to assume that heavy elements were forged in the hearts of ancient stars billions of years ago, exploding to provide those elements to form our sun and earth.

- But how did those first stars form if gas clouds tend to spread out, not collapse into extremely dense spheres (of which our sun is a fairly small specimen).
- And you must also assume that the stars we see in the galaxy around us represent stars in their various stages of development, which

means you have to first assume stars develop over time, passing through stages.

- And this matter had to come from an exquisitely fine-tuned process responding to highly specific physical laws that just happen to be the way they are without a lawgiver to set them in place. This includes the apparently smooth period of rapid expansion and then slowing down of that expansion . . . for some reason.
- And what exactly was the singularity that initiated the big bang?
- And where did it come from?

There are many places along the naturalistic chain that the only answer to why you would accept these ideas is a blind faith (accepting a claim without scientific evidence) in naturalism — it must have happened that way, because here we are. Biblical creationists don't have every detail worked out as far as how things happened in the past, but the restraints of naturalism make the acceptance of immaterial things like the laws of nature, laws of logic, and information impossible to account for. Only the God of the Bible can explain how these laws came into existence, how the information in the first living things was programmed into the DNA, and how the universe we see around us was formed.

Are you really going to put your faith in this chain to hold up your worldview?

Who Do You Trust?

When it comes to evaluating the evolutionary worldview, there is a lot to try to understand. But all of this ultimately comes down to a matter of authority. Are you going to trust man's word based on the assumption that everything we see came from an impersonal source that defies the laws of nature? Or are you going to trust the intelligent God who has revealed Himself to us in His creation, the pages of Scripture, and the person of Jesus Christ?

While I have argued in broad, general statements, the specifics of each point I have raised have been examined by qualified scientists from both a naturalistic evolutionary and a biblical creation worldview. Are you going to place your trust in the evolutionary view or the biblical view? One view paints you as an animal who is a consequence of random chance collisions of particles with no future beyond this life and no standard of right and wrong.

The other tells you that a loving God created you in His image with purpose and that there is hope of an eternity of joy with Him after you die.

So, were you once a worm who is just going to die and become worm food? Or are you a special creation of a God who cares for you? Those are the consequences of the worldview you trust in.

> *Evolution is an example of an idea which is not observable, measurable, or repeatable.*

2   WHAT IS AND ISN'T SCIENCE?

DR. JENNIFER HALL RIVERA, is a forensic science educator, speaker, and author. She has educated high school students in the study of forensic science for over five years. Dr. Rivera has been published in the *Journal of Forensic Identification* and has been a guest speaker at the Georgia Division of the International Association for Identification state conference in both 2015 and 2016, as well as the International Association for Identification 2017 world conference. Prior to teaching, Dr. Rivera was employed as a fingerprint examiner in a crime scene unit, where she received extensive training in the field of forensics.

Have you ever heard the statement, "Science disproves the Bible!" or "How can you believe the Bible in this scientific age?" If so, you are not alone.

In today's culture, there is an attack on the truthfulness of Scripture and far too many people have bought into this idea that the Bible is not trustworthy in its teachings because of "science." But is it? Are science and the Bible in conflict? Some may mistakenly think so, because they have misunderstandings about what science is and what science is not. This brings us to the discussion over *operational* science vs. *origins* science — more on this in a moment.

What Is Science?

"What is science?" is a simple question that has "evolved" into a variety of definitions over the last two centuries. The study of science originated in a quest to understand the structure and function of God's creation to utilize the resources for the good of mankind. The majority of early scientists acknowledged the one true God of the Bible as the Creator and designer of the universe (Genesis 1) and that it was God who put into motion the fundamental laws of nature at creation.[1]

But over the past 200 years, evolutionary models, a survival-of-the-fittest mentality, and the idea that man is his own god, have greatly influenced science and academia. A majority of scientists today have disregarded the Creator God as the originator and designer of the universe and of the scientific principles that govern it.

Instead, secular scientists have distorted what science is capable of proving by upholding scientific discoveries as the only source of "truth" and defaulting to an evolutionary belief system which does not include God. Further, these same scientists acknowledge their scientific "truths" may fluctuate and change under the influence of the societal and cultural beliefs of the era. Consider what this writer said in *New Scientist* as far back as 1979:

> Science is but one special and actually rather small part of knowledge, whose truths depend on the social beliefs of the time and the cultural atmosphere in which they are created.[2]

This should make a person question how "true" is science if it can be easily modified or disregarded by the climate of the culture?

---

1. R. Patterson, "Evolution Exposed: Biology," Answers in Genesis, 2009.
2. R. Clarke, *New Scientist* (1979), 81, 1049.

When scientists elevate scientific "truths" as a form of religious dogma, they are exercising a form of blind faith. Their faith lies in the objective "truths" of science. Richard Dawkins, prominent atheist and evolutionary biologist, stated, "Science is committed to objective truth."[3] Interestingly, objective truth is defined as truth that exists outside of a scientist's bias or worldview. In Dawkins view, objective truth is only found in science and this truth is "universal," which is inconsistent.

Ultimately, Dawkins is proposing that regardless of what you believe, think, or feel, science is the only source of what is true, and that this truth exists outside of individuals and resides in the natural world. It is interesting to note that a materialistic atheist like Dr. Dawkins would appeal to an immaterial entity like truth and agree it exists! At least Dawkins is correct in stating that "science works," but he does not differentiate between observational science (observable, testable, repeatable) and historical science (not observable, testable, or repeatable).

Observational science uses observable, repeatable experiments to understand how things function so that we can produce new technology, find cures for disease, etc. Creationists and evolutionists love and do observational science and use its fruits all the time. In contrast, historical science studies observable evidence in the present to reconstruct the unobservable, unrepeatable past events that produced the evidence we see. Since past events are "in the past," they cannot be observed or measured directly in the present, and present processes are not necessarily the same as they were in the past.

When reliable eyewitness testimony about those past events is available, that can be used to interpret the physical evidence we see. But those interpretations are very dependent on assumptions we make about the past processes that could have produced the evidence in the present. The difference between creationists and evolutionists involved in historical science is that they have different assumptions about past processes. Creationists believe the Bible is the eyewitness testimony of the God who saw all the events of history and use that testimony to interpret the physical evidence, whereas evolutionists reject that testimony as irrelevant to the interpretation of the evidence.

God designed the world with a near-limitless supply of diversity and complexity. Not only did He design His creation to demonstrate His glory and power (Psalm 19:1; Romans 1:20), but also for mankind to study

---

3. R. Dawkins, 2018, http://bigthink.com/videos/richard-dawkins-why-science-must-embrace-imagination-intuition-and-evidence,

through orderly processes to satisfy our curiosity, enjoyment, and innate desire to discover the unknown (Psalm 111:2) and to rule (under God's sovereignty as stewards) over the creation (Genesis 1:28), harnessing its resources for the good of man and the glory of God. Therefore, it is important to be able to differentiate between what science actually is and is not and how to correctly address this topic with God's Word as the foundation.

The term *science* is derived from the Latin term *scientia* which means "to know." Dictionary.com defines science as "the knowledge of the physical (natural) world gained through observation and experimentation." There are basically two broad categories of science: observational (also called experimental or operational) science and historical science (also called origins science).[4]

The definition of *science* has changed throughout the past. As mentioned, science literally means "knowledge" and is derived from Latin. For example, *scientia* and *scientiae* are used respectively in the Latin Vulgate by Jerome in the early A.D. 400s for Daniel 1:4 and 1 Timothy 6:20.

In the 1600s, the practice of scientific study was very subjective. A prominent creation scientist named Francis Bacon recognized that the orderly processes evident in the world allowed for a method of operational science through direct observation and testing. This methodology allowed for repeatable testing and verification of results. With the advent of Francis Bacon's new definition of scientific methodology (Baconian Method) in the 1600s, that method became an additional entry for the definition of science in dictionaries. The Baconian method was a precursor to modern scientific methods.

But dictionaries change. One significant change can be seen in Webster's dictionary of 1828 which openly affirmed that *the knowledge of God must be perfect* in its definition of "science."[5] This is because God has all knowledge (e.g., Psalm 139:1–3; Job 21:22, 37:16, Colossians 2:2-3). And this is why He is the standard of knowledge or omniscience (*omni* = all and *science* = knowledge).

But current dictionaries no longer retain that God has all knowledge.[6] Instead, secularists retain and expand on phrases like "such activities

---

4. K. Ham and T. Mortenson, "Science or the Bible?" 2007, https://answersingenesis.org/what-is-science/science-or-the-bible/.

5. Webster's 1828 Dictionary, Entry: "Science," http://webstersdictionary1828.com/Dictionary/science, accessed August 3, 2018.

6. The American Heritage College Dictionary, Third Edition (Boston, MA: Houghton Mifflin Company, 2000), p. 1221.

restricted to a class of natural phenomena" — naturalism. The modern definition of science has essentially become the religion of naturalism (nature is all that there is), while God has been removed from any semblance of the definition of science.

Worse yet, many people today are baited with one definition of science being the good observable and repeatable experimentation (operational science) and then switched to the religion of naturalism. The God of the Bible is God over both the natural and the supernatural. To leave God out of the subject because of one's adherence to the religion of naturalism, is to limit God and place oneself in the position above God. Furthermore, it is an equivocation fallacy (illogical) to equate the two different definitions of science.

Evolution is an example of an idea which is not observable, measurable, or repeatable. The word *evolution* in this context refers to belief that a slow, gradual naturalistic process of change produced the first single-cell organism from non-living matter, which was then changed over millions of years of natural processes to become all the complex forms of life we see today and in the fossil record. Since no scientists have observed the long process of chemical and biological evolution over millions of years, the hypothesis requires a set of assumptions or starting points by which the physical evidence in the present is interpreted to reconstruct that unobservable past.[7]

These assumptions (or presuppositions) stem from the scientists' personal beliefs and worldview. Consider forensic science, which along with examination of any eyewitnesses, is part of a criminal investigation — a form of historical science — to reconstruct the unobservable, unrepeatable past. It is not unusual for artifacts left at a crime scene to lead investigators to draw different conclusions due to their personal bias, experience, and viewpoints. Investigators will often disagree on items such as point of entry, location and distance, and methodology of the suspect.

This is also true for issues concerning origins. Both creationists and evolutionists are presented with the same evidence (e.g., rock layers, fossils, DNA, radioactive isotopes), they just come to different conclusions based on their philosophical/religious starting points. Creationists start with the inerrant word of our holy God (the eyewitness testimony) to interpret physical evidence, whereas evolutionists rely on the fallible ideas of sinful man (naturalistic assumptions) to interpret the same evidence.

7.   W. Gitt, 2012, https://answersingenesis.org/theory-of-evolution/11-the-principles-of-science-theory/.

What method do scientists use for testable, observable, repeatable results? It was a method developed by Francis Bacon, a creationist, who believed God upheld the world in a particular state, which makes observable and repeatable science possible. This logical, orderly process should sound familiar, because it is called the scientific method.

The Stanford Encyclopedia provides a criterion to recognize when activities are science by stating they are "enterprises which employ some canonical form of the scientific method" and that only processes that use the scientific method "should be considered science."[8] The scientific method assumes that experimental results can be duplicated, under the same conditions, at another time or location.[9] The scientific method includes basic fundamental steps:

- Identify a problem or question based on observation.
- Develop a hypothesis to predict the results of the experiment.
- Design a controlled experiment to test the hypothesis.
- Observe, measure, and collect the results.
- Interpret the results by either accepting, modifying, or rejecting the hypothesis.
- [repeat]

Take note that the scientific process will never yield an absolute proof. It is always probabilistic and suggestive at best. It is a *process* to help us continually modify or falsify a hypothesis. When someone says they have proved something scientifically, then it shows they are not utilizing the scientific method properly.

Let's take a closer look at each step in the scientific method by relating the process to a popular topic in mainstream culture — forensic investigation. It is important to recognize that forensic science uses observational science techniques (such as observation, collection, and testing) to make assumptions on past events. So it is a mixture of operational / experimental / observational science with historical / origins science. The forensic investigator was not present when the crime occurred. Therefore, they use the evidence gathered, by utilizing the scientific method, to make an educated guess on what may have happened in the past.

8. Stanford Encyclopedia of Philosophy, Scientific Method, 2015, https://plato.stanford.edu/entries/scientific-method/.

9. John F. Ashton, *On the Seventh Day: 40 Scientists and Academics explain Why They Believe in God*, J. De Laeter, "Physics," (Green Forest, AR: Master Books, 2002).

Imagine a wallet has been stolen from a coffee shop. Eyewitnesses' testimonies provide police with clues to the location of the suspect in the restaurant, and on the table is an empty coffee cup.

When the forensic investigator arrives on the scene, they will begin by analyzing the problem, to uncover evidence to aid in the identification of the person who stole the wallet. Once the problem is identified, a forensic scientist is able to develop a set of ideas or hypotheses to solve the problem, usually asking "how" or "why." Many important scientific advances were discovered because someone asked a simple question like "how" or "why."

But it is important to remember that for observational science to be effective, the question must be testable through an observable, measurable, and repeatable process. A scientist cannot use the scientific method to answer the question "What is moral or good?" Nor can he/she use this (experimental) scientific method to answer the question, "What happened in the unobservable unrepeatable past to produce the Grand Canyon or the first dog or Saturn?" This requires a different method.

Secondly, the investigator develops a hypothesis. A standard hypothesis includes an if-then statement. For example, "If I process the coffee cup for fingerprints, then I will uncover a latent print for comparison." A hypothesis is fundamentally an educated guess developed by the scientist. Initially, a hypothesis is not required to be accurate, it just needs to be testable.

The hypothesis is influenced by the expertise, viewpoint, and bias of the scientist. It is impossible to eliminate bias in scientific research. Every scientist begins with a preconceived set of ideals, or starting points, which influence their experimental process.[10] If a scientist believes there is no God, their hypotheses, observations, and analysis will reflect this starting point. The same is true of a scientist who starts with God's Word. This scientist recognizes that the inerrant truth of God's Word is superior to man's imperfect ideas.

The third step in the scientific method is a form of experimentation or measurable observation. This involves using one or more of the five senses for direct observations. The scientist will also try to eliminate extraneous variables by creating a controlled environment. In this case, the investigator attempts to protect the environment from contagions by sectioning off the area to be examined with crime scene tape. This allows the forensic scientist time to process the area for fingerprints in an environment where careful,

---

10. J. Ioannidis, "Studies of Scientific Bias Targeting the Right Problems," 2017, Stanford University Medical Center, Proceedings of the National Academy of Sciences.

methodical forensic procedures can be performed on the crime scene without the influence of extraneous variables.[11]

Theoretically, a controlled experiment reduces the possibility of outside variables influencing or contaminating the research, but not every experiment is examined within a controlled environment. A true controlled environment or experiment is very difficult to achieve, and should always be scrutinized due to the difficulty in effectively attaining a 100% controlled environment.

The fourth step is collection of experimental results. Once the investigator has retrieved viable latent fingerprints, they will be submitted into the database for comparison. Once the computer completes the comparison, the investigator will gather the results and form an analysis. The goal of gathering results is to compare them to the original hypothesis for confirmation.

Subsequently, scientific results are only as accurate as the experimental data. Results are also influenced by the scientist's starting assumptions, which have the ability to lead to errors. This error occurs in crime scene investigation. The National Registry of Exonerations has been tracking individuals who were found guilty at trial, but later exonerated due to advances in technology or the discovery of investigator error. Currently, they have documented over 2,263 exonerations. This is just one example of how assumptions influence interpretations of evidence.[12]

Since the forensic scientist was an eyewitness to the evidence left behind at a crime scene and not to the crime, the assumptions about what may have occurred in the past have the potential to be flawed and may result in an inaccurate analysis.

The investigator now completes the final step in the scientific method by analyzing and interpreting the results and applying the results to the criminal act. The analysis should include the rejection or acceptance of the original hypothesis. Often in scientific discovery, rejection of the hypothesis is just as important as the acceptance of it, because it leads the scientist in a new direction or area needing further study.

Ideally, the forensic investigator identifies the suspect, but ultimately the interpretation of experimental results lies in the value of the evidence and the bias of the scientist conducting the research.

---

11. L. Carmack, "Working a Crime Scene," 2017, https://www.county.org/magazine/features/Pages/2017July/Working-a-Crime-Scene.aspx.
12. The National Registry of Exonerations, 2018, http://www.law.umich.edu/special/exoneration/Pages/about.aspx.

Geddes, in her article about flaws in forensic science, stated, "Research has shown that the same fingerprint expert can reach a different conclusion about the same fingerprints depending on the context they're given about a case."[13] It is important to point out, the forensic investigator did not directly observe the criminal act, therefore their analysis applies to a historical event. This means that the investigator cannot prove anything, but only establish facts.

Though the process described above is simplified, it provides a big picture overview of the methodology behind the scientific method. When the process is followed (by both Christians and non-Christians), the scientific method provides a framework upon which scientists are able to find cures for disease, develop satellite technology, and analyze the microscopic world of DNA.

But have you ever considered how a logical, orderly process such as the scientific method could exist without a logical, orderly Creator? If everything that exists is a product of random evolutionary processes, then why is there a logical, orderly systematic method of scientific discovery? If the world is the result of random processes, then observational results could not be trusted. Random crime scene evidence producing arbitrary results would never be upheld in a courtroom.

A rational person would never look at an instrument like a microscope and assume that all the parts assembled themselves by random chance. He would recognize that the complexity of a microscope requires a designer and Creator — the God of the Bible. A courtroom recognizes that orderly crime scene procedures must have occurred for evidence to be accepted by the court system. The only logical answer is there must be a perfect eyewitness, an intelligent Creator who started the fundamental process of discovery at the beginning of creation and provided us the details in the Bible (Hebrews 3:4).

What Isn't Science?

There is no denying that observational science is capable of providing doctors with new treatments for disease or engineers with new technology for cell phone and computer capabilities. But both observational and historical science have limitations:

1. To be observational science it must be observable, repeatable, and experimental in the present. This is not possible with historical science.

---

13. L. Geddes, "The Troubling Flaws in Forensic Science," 2015, http://www.bbc.com/future/story/20150512-can-we-trust-forensic-science.

2. A scientist is influenced by their belief system.
3. Science cannot establish absolute truth.

Because mainstream culture chooses to overlook these factors, what is considered "science" by definition continues to evolve, change, and morph with the imagination of the scientists. It seems odd to see the words *science* and *imagination* used in the same sentence, but well-known scientists like Richard Dawkins have stated that real science requires "imagination."[14] Dawkins states, "Science proceeds on intuitive leaps of the imagination, building an idea of what might be true." To some extent, this statement holds merit. Many scientific discoveries are the result of an idea (hypothesis) which, after experimentation, was found to be valid. But the problem arises after the experimentation when the results do not support the scientist's idea or hypothesis.

When experimental results do not support their assumptions, there is no other option than to use imaginative applications to support conclusions. This is not the correct application of observational science. As one UCLA professor stated, when disagreeing with those who do not believe in evolution, "The problem with those who don't see evolution, is they don't have imaginations."[15] But is this really science or more like science fiction?

Science is not the measuring stick for morality, good or evil, or other cultural values. Similar to the definition of "science" or what is considered "science," what is acceptable in our day and age regarding values changes with the moral climate of the culture. A society's values are driven by bias, influenced by one's worldview or starting point. Our modern society often claims that everyone is inherently good, but this is contrary to the Bible. In Matthew 15:19, it describes humans, "For out of the heart come evil thoughts, murder, adultery, sexual immorality, theft, false witness, slander."[16] Romans 3:23 says, "For all have sinned and fall short of the glory of God."

God's Word shows us that people are incapable of measuring morality by our own autonomous standard, since we are born sinners. What is right or wrong and good or evil require a measuring stick not found in the realm of science. This measuring stick is found only in Jesus Christ, revealed to us through his Holy Word the Bible.

Additionally, observational science is not capable of determining the origin of life. The only eyewitness historical record of the origin of life is

14. R. Dawkins, 2018, http://bigthink.com/videos/richard-dawkins-why-science-must-embrace-imagination-intuition-and-evidence.
15. "Evolution vs. God," 2013. https://www.youtube.com/watch?v=U0u3-2CGOMQ.
16. Scripture in this chapter is from the English Standard Version (ESV) of the Bible.

found in the inspired Word of God. The perfect eyewitness, Jesus Christ, the Creator Himself, gave us a description of the origin of life and the creation of the universe in six literal days. Anything contrary to this perfect eyewitness testimony found in the Bible is purely conjecture.

The Creator God has described the origin of life in a logical and rational way (Genesis 1). In fact, the Bible tells us that creation itself is evidence of the Creator's existence and at least some of His attributes (Romans 1:20). In contrast, secular scientists promote evolutionary stories which have no real evidence that can stand up to scrutiny to support their claims of life evolving from a single-celled organism over millions of years. They *believe* microbe-to-microbiologist evolution happened, even though they have no fossil or experimental/observational evidence. As Hodge reiterates, "Evolution is a framework about the past that can never be repeated or tested and must be accepted by interpretation and authority. That is, by all measures, a belief."[17]

Both biblical creation and evolution require faith, so how can we know for sure the biblical account of creation is true and evolutionary hypotheses are false? Because God's perfect Word reveals to us the truth. It comes down to starting points: man's word or God's Word. Sadly, if a scientist does not begin with God's Word as their foundation, their results will not reflect God's glory but is ultimately an attempt to glorify themselves.

Science is not capable of discovering truth, verifying truth, and stating what is truth, but the Bible is inspired and without error and the only source of truth. So, the evidence is there, and science supports the Bible, but secular man chooses to ignore the evidence because they would have to acknowledge the existence of God and truth found only in God's Word.

How Does a Christian Answer the Question "What Is Science"?

As Christians, we should embrace science and the scientific method while recognizing its limitations. If something is not observable, repeatable, and testable, it is not science. Evolution is not science, but a secular model based on numerous assumptions in opposition to God's Word (e.g., naturalism, man is the supreme authority, etc.).

Biblical creation is also not testable using the scientific method, but a perfect eyewitness provided the exact details in His inerrant Word and this account is confirmed by science. Scientific research stems from our desire

---

17. B. Hodge, 2009, https://answersingenesis.org/what-is-science/the-limits-of-science/.

to discover. God created in us a mind that allows us to be curious and to hunger to solve the unknown and explore the unexplored.

Using science, we can feed this desire in the pursuit of knowledge about God's creation. Through observable, measurable, repeatable processes, Christian scientists have made significant advances in understanding the order and complexity evident in God's creation. At the same time, these scientists must not compromise the truth of God's Word. Misinterpreting or adding and subtracting words to the Bible (eisegesis) which are in direct opposition to the original "Scripture interprets Scripture" context (exegesis), opens the door to compromise, undermining God's authority in the Scriptures.

Though the Bible does not directly address science, when using God's Word as the foundation to study science, science aligns itself with the Bible every time. In his last narrative, famed creation scientist, Dr. Henry Morris, beautifully summarized how to study science:

> As a Christian, there are two valid assumptions upon which to study science: the universe is ordered and that order is comprehensible to the human mind. Both of these assumptions are guaranteed by God's Word.[18]

---

18. Henry M. Morris, *Some Call It Science: The Religion of Evolution* (Dallas, TX: Institute for Creation Research, 2008).

"

It is a religion. To call evolution science is a bait-and-switch tactic.

"

3 IS SCIENCE SECULAR?

As an active speaker, writer, and researcher for Answers in Genesis, **BODIE HODGE** has a master's degree in mechanical engineering from Southern Illinois University at Carbondale. After earning his master's degree, Bodie worked as a mechanical engineer for Grain Systems Incorporated, was a visiting instructor in mechanical engineering at SIUC, and worked as a test engineer through Aerotek Engineering for Caterpillar, Inc., in Peoria, Illinois, at the Peoria Proving Ground. While working at Caterpillar, Bodie continued to teach apologetics to junior high and high school students. He did this until accepting a position with Answers in Genesis in 2003.

Many people today insist that science can only be done by people who have a secular worldview — or at least by those who are willing to leave their religious views at the door as they enter the science lab. Several popular atheists and evolutionists have contended that people who reject the big bang and the evolution of living things are so backward that they cannot even be involved in developing new technologies.[1]

But is this really the case? Or are these opponents of a biblical worldview simply making assertions that cannot be supported with facts and substantial arguments, having an incorrect understanding of true science?

A friend of Answers in Genesis was recently challenged by the comment that science can only be done through a purely secular, evolutionary framework. Such statements are blatantly absurd and are a type of arbitrary fallacy called an "ignorant conjecture." In other words, these people simply do not know the past, nor are they familiar with what science really is.

Examples of Scientists Operating from a Christian Worldview

If science is a strictly secular endeavor without any need for a biblical worldview, then why were most fields of science developed by Bible-believing Christians? For example, consider Isaac Newton, Gregor Mendel, Louis Pasteur, Johann Kepler, Galileo Galilei, Robert Boyle, Blaise Pascal, Michael Faraday, James Joule, Joseph Lister, and James Clerk Maxwell. Were these "greats" of science not doing science? Francis Bacon developed the scientific method, and he was a young-earth creationist and devout Christian.

Even in modern times, the inventor of the MRI scanning machine, Dr. Raymond Damadian, is a Christian working with Christian principles. The founder of catastrophic plate tectonics, Dr. John Baumgardner, is also a devout Christian. And those who recently founded the scientific field of baraminology are also Christians. Also, I (Bodie Hodge) developed a new method for production of submicron titanium diboride for the materials science and ceramics industry. Professor Stuart Burgess developed a new mechanism for the two-billion-dollar European (ESA) satellite *Envisat*. Dr. John Sanford developed the gene gun. And let's not forget Werner von Braun, the young-earth Christian who was the founder of rocket science and led the United States to the moon. These are but a few examples of

---

1. As an example of this dismissive attitude, Eugenie Scott (formerly) of the National Center for Science Education (NCSE), a leading religious humanist, says, "Like other pseudosciences, 'creation science' seeks support and adherents by claiming the mantle of science." http://ncse.com/rncse/23/1/my-favorite-pseudoscience.

people who held to a biblical worldview and were quite capable as scientists and inventors of new technologies.

The Foundation for Science Is Biblical Christianity

Furthermore, science comes out of a *Christian* worldview. Only the God described in the Bible can account for a logical and orderly universe. God upholds the universe in a particular way, such that we can study it by observational and repeatable experimentation (see Genesis 8:22). Because God upholds the universe in a consistent manner, we have a valid reason to expect that we can study the world we live in and describe the laws that God uses to sustain the universe (Colossians 1:17).

In the secular view, where all matter originated by chance from nothing, there is no ultimate cause or reason for anything that happens, and explanations are constantly changing, so there is no *basis* for science. Though many non-Christians do science, like inventing new technologies or improving medical science, they are doing it in a manner that is inconsistent with their professed worldview. On what basis should we expect a universe that came from nothing and for no reason to act in a predictable and consistent manner? When non-Christians do real science by observable and repeatable experimentation, they are actually assuming a biblical worldview, even if they do not realize it.

It makes sense why "science" in the United States is losing out to other nations since our science education system now limits science in the classroom exclusively to the religion of secular humanism (and its subtle variations).

It Is Not "Science vs. Religion"

So, the debate is not "science versus religion." It is really "religion versus religion." Sadly, science is caught up in the middle.

The battle is between the religion of *secular humanism* (with its variant forms like agnosticism, atheism, and the like), which is usually called *secularism* or *humanism* for short, and *Christianity*. They both have religious documents (e.g., the Humanist Manifestos I, II, and III for humanists, and the Bible for Christians); both are recognized religions by the Supreme Court;[2] and both receive the same 501(c)(3) tax-exempt status. Both have different views of origins.

Humanism has astronomical evolution (big bang), geological evolution (millions of years of slow gradual changes), chemical evolution (life came

---

2.   US Supreme Court, *Torcaso v. Watkins*.

from non-life) and biological evolution (original, single-celled life evolved into all life forms we have today over billions of years) in its view of origins. In other words, evolution (as a whole) is a tenet of the dogma of the religion of humanism in the same way that biblical creation (as a whole, with six-day creation, the Fall, global Flood, and the Tower of Babel) is a tenet of the dogma of Christianity. It is a battle between two different religions.

In recent times, the state and federal governments kicked Christianity out of the classroom, thinking they kicked religion out; but instead, they just replaced Christianity with a godless religion of humanism. This was done as an attack designed by humanists.

An Evolutionary Worldview Equals Science?

There is a misconception that this evolutionary subset of humanism *is* science. Science means knowledge and scientific methodology that is based on the scientific method (observable and repeatable experimentation). However, evolution (whether chemical, biological, astronomical, or geological) is far from scientific. Consider the following facts:

1. No one has been able to observe or repeat the making of life from non-life (matter giving rise to life or chemical evolution).
2. No one has been able to observe or repeat the changing of a single-celled life form like an amoeba into a cow or goat over billions of years (biological evolution).
3. No one has been able to observe or repeat the big bang (astronomical evolution).
4. No one has observed millions of years of time progressing in geological layers (geological evolution).

The reason some people are confused about the religion of humanism — and specifically its subset of evolution — as being science is a bait-and-switch fallacy. Let me explain. One of the key components of humanism is naturalism. Basically, it assumes *a priori* there is nothing supernatural and no God. In other words, nature (i.e., matter) is all that exists in their religion (only the physical world).

As a clarifying note, Christians also believe in the natural realm; but unlike the naturalist or humanist, we believe in the supernatural realm, too (i.e., the spiritual, abstract, conceptual, and immaterial realm). Logic, truth, integrity, concepts, thought, God, etc., are not *material* and have no mass. So those holding to naturalism as a worldview *must* reject logic, truth, and all immaterial concepts if they wish to be consistent, since these are *not* material or physical parts of nature.

This is very important because naturalism or natural science has been added as one of the dictionary definitions of science. For example, it was not found in the 1828 Webster's dictionary, but it was added in one form in the 1913 edition. And, interestingly, they removed the definition that "the science of God must be perfect" in the 1913 edition.

So, although many appeal to observable and repeatable science through methodology to understand how the universe operates, another definition has been added to muddle this.[3] Science is now defined as "knowledge or a system of knowledge covering general truths or the operation of general laws especially as obtained and tested through scientific method."[4]

For example, evolutionists have continued to popularize Darwin's scientific observation of the changes in beaks of Galapagos finches as proof for the evolution of one animal kind into another. This is a great example of the bait-and-switch fallacy where scientists present real scientific evidence (the difference in finch beaks) but stretch the truth to say it gives validity to the mythology of microbes-to-man evolution (the "switch" part of the fallacy). This trick leads many to believe that evolution is real science. The only real science in this example is the observation of the difference in finch beaks.

People are baited with this good methodology of observational science (again developed by a Christian named Francis Bacon), and then they are told that evolution is science while subtly appealing to another added definition: that of "natural science" or "naturalism."

This is like saying another definition of science is "Nazism." Then Nazis could say they are "scientists" and get into a classroom! This is what has happened with humanism. The religion of humanism (with its founding principle of naturalism) has been disguised as *science* by adding another definition to the word *science*. But it is not the good science we think of that makes computers, space shuttles, and cars. It is a religion. To call evolution *science* is a bait-and-switch tactic.

Science and Processes That Supposedly Take Millions of Years

Many processes that evolutionists profess take millions of years do not. Using science in the present, we observe that processes that we have often

---

3. There is also the issue of operational science versus historical science. For more see: http://www.answersingenesis.org/articles/ee/what-is-science.
4. Merriam-Webster Online, s.v. "science," accessed March 8, 2013, http://www.merriam-webster.com/dictionary/science.

been indoctrinated to believe require millions of years really don't. Consider this list:

Evidence	Time to form (observed)	Scientific evidence for millions of years
Diamonds (vapor deposition)	A few days[1]	No
Diamonds (pressure and temperature method)	3–4 days[2]	No
Diamonds (from loved ones and pets' ashes)	Three months[3]	No
Coal	Months[4]	No
Oil from sewage	Days[5]	No
Oil from animal waste	Days[6]	No
Oil from brown coal	2–5 Days[7]	No
Oil from algae	30 minutes[8]–60 minutes[9]	No
Petrified wood (heat and chemical method)	Days[10]	No
Petrified wood (chemical method)	Hours[11]	No
Petrified wood (natural elements)	Less than 360 years[12]	No
Opals	Weeks[13]	No
Gemstones (volcanic origin)	Upon eruption[14]	No
Gemstones (lab origins, synthetic)	Days[15] with flame fusion, melt process, solution process	No
Fossils	Less than 24 hours[16]	No
Stalactites	Days,[17] less than 100 years[18]	No
Stalagmites	In one summer[19]	No

Rock	Less than 150 years, Bell encased in rock[20] Less than 125 years, Tarawera Items[21] Less than 50 years, Petrified Hat[22] 3 months, Yorkshire Bears[23] Hours, concrete (observed)	No
Rock layers (catastrophes)	Hours, Mt. St. Helens[24]	No
Rock layer lamina (lab; air + water)	Almost immediately[25]	No
Canyons	Days, Canyon Lake Gorge[26] Days, Little Grand Canyon[27] Six days, Burlingame Canyon[28] Georgia's Little Grand Canyon[29]	No

Footnotes for Table

1. Greg Hunter and Andrew Paparella, "Lab-Made Diamonds Just Like Natural Ones," September 9, 2015, *ABC News Internet Ventures*, produced for *Good Morning America*, http://abcnews.go.com/GMA/story?id=124787.
2. Ibid.
3. Rae Ellen Bichell, "From Ashes to Ashes to Diamonds: A Way to Treasure the Dead," NPR, January 19, 2014, http://www.npr.org/2014/01/19/263128098/swiss-company-compresses-cremation-ashes-into-diamonds.
4. R. Hayatsu, R.L. McBeth, R.G. Scott, R.E. Botto, R.E. Winans, *Organic Geochemistry*, vol. 6 (1984), p. 463–471.
5. Australian Stock Exchange Release, Environmental Solutions International Ltd, Osborne Park, Western Australia, Oct. 25, 1996. Media Statement, Minister for Water Resources, Western Australia, October 25, 1996.

6. Dr. Andrew Snelling, "The Origin of Oil," *Answers 2*, no. 1, p. 74–77, http://www.answersingenesis.org/articles/am/v2/n1/origin-of-oil.

7. Ibid.

8. Christopher Helman, "Green Oil: Scientists Turn Algae into Petroleum in 30 Minutes," Forbes.com, 12/23/2013, http://www.forbes.com/sites/christopherhelman/2013/12/23/green-oil-scientists-turn-algae-into-petroleum-in-30-minutes/.

9. B. Thomas, "One-Hour Oil Production," ICR, January 13, 2014, https://www.icr.org/article/7874/.

10. Editors, "Instant Petrified Wood," Physics.org, January 25, 2005, http://phys.org/news/2005-01-petrified-wood-days.html.

11. Hamilton Hicks, Sodium silicate composition, United States Patent Number 4,612,050, September 16,1986, http://www.google.com/patents/US4612050.

12. Andrew Snelling, " 'Instant' Petrified Wood," *Creation*, vol. 17, no. 4, September 1995, p. 38–40, online September 1, 1995, https://answersingenesis.org/fossils/how-are-fossils-formed/instant-petrified-wood/.

13. Dr. Andrew Snelling, "Creating Opals," *Creation ex nihilo* 17, no. 1, Dec. 1994: 14–17.

14. Editors, Mount St. Helens Gift Shop Website, http://www.mt-st-helens.com/obsidianite.html, downloaded April 7, 2014; Editors, "How Gemstones Are Formed," GemSelect, accessed August 18, 2015, http://www.gemselect.com/other-info/gemstone-formation.php.

15. Synthetic Ruby, http://www.madehow.com/Volume-4/Synthetic-Ruby.html.

16. Ben Coxworth, "Lab-made Fossils Cram 1000s of Years into 24 Hours," *New Atlas*, July 25, 2018, https://newatlas.com/lab-made-fossils/55619/.

17. Marilyn Taylor, "Descent," *Arizona Highways*, January, 1993, p. 11.

18. Emil Silvestru, *The Cave Book* (Green Forest, AR: Master Books, 2008), p. 46.

19. Ken Ham and Bodie Hodge, *A Flood of Evidence* (Green Forest, AR: Master Books, 2016), p. 125.

20. "Bell-ieve It: Rapid Rock Formation Rings True," *Creation*, vol. 20, no. 2, March 1998: 6, https://answersingenesis.org/geology/catastrophism/bell-ieve-it-rapid-rock-formation-rings-true/.

21. Renton Maclachlan, "Tarawera's Night of Terror," *Creation*, vol. 18, no. 1, December 1995: 16–19, https://answersingenesis.org/geology/catastrophism/taraweras-night-of-terror/.

22. John Mackay, "Fossil Bolts and Fossil Hats," *Creation Ex Nihilo*, vol. 8, Nov. 1986, p. 10.

23. M. White, "The Amazing Stone Bears of Yorkshire," Answers in Genesis, June 1, 2002, http://www.answersingenesis.org/articles/cm/v24/n3/stone-bears.

24. John Morris and Steve Austin, *Footprints in the Ash: The Explosive Story of Mount St. Helens* (Green Forest, AR: Master Books, 2003).

25. Guy Berthault, "Experiments on Lamination of Sediments," *Creation*, vol. 3, no. 1, April 1998, p. 25–29, https://answersingenesis.org/geology/sedimentation/experiments-on-lamination-of-sediments/.

26. Michael P. Lamb and Mark A. Fonstad, "Rapid Formation of a Modern Bedrock Canyon by a Single Flood Event," *Nature Geoscience*, June 20, 2010, p. 4, DOI: 10.1038/NGEO894.

27. John Morris and Steven A. Austin, *Footprints in the Ash* (Green Forest, AR: Master Books, 2003), p. 70–75.

28. John Morris, "A Canyon in Six Days," September 1, 2002, https://answersingenesis.org/geology/natural-features/a-canyon-in-six-days/.

29. Rebecca Gibson, "Canyon Creation," September, 1, 2000, https://answersingenesis.org/geology/natural-features/canyon-creation/.

So, Is Science Strictly Secular?

No. In summary, science can never be strictly secular for these reasons:

1. Real science is observable and repeatable experimentation that only makes sense in a biblical worldview where God's power keeps the laws of nature consistent. In other words, science proceeds from a biblical worldview.
2. Secular humanism, with its subset of evolution, is in reality a religion and not science.
3. Many of the greatest scientists were Bible-believing Christians whose biblical worldview motivated their scientific studies, showing that a strictly secular view is not necessary for performing science.

Where Humanism Leads

Christians will continue to conduct scientific inquiry and invent things, processes, and science fields as we always have. If the United States and other places neglect our accomplishments and inventions and continue to push the religion of humanism on unsuspecting kids in the classroom (usually unbeknown to most) by limiting its definition of science to the humanistic worldview, then my humble suggestion is that they will continue down the same road humanism travels. That is, people who are consistent in their naturalistic worldview shouldn't care about true science or the world, since ultimately, nothing matters in that worldview.

Now consider the 'goldilocks' nature of the earth and the impossibility of life spontaneously forming, let alone evolving into creatures of greater complexity. With all these 'lucky fortunes' lining up, how can they presuppose anything other than random chance to be their mantra?

4

SCIENCE FIELDS AND METHODOLOGY CAME FROM A CHRISTIAN WORLDVIEW

TROY LACEY earned his B.S. in Natural Sciences (biology/geology) degree from the University of Cincinnati. Troy currently serves with Answers in Genesis as correspondence representative (answering questions of science and faith sent to the ministry), science writer, and content support, as well as serving as chaplain services coordinator for Answers in Genesis–USA. He has studied Scripture for decades and contributes numerous articles to the Answers in Genesis website and publications.

If you look at any secular science book from the past few decades, you'll notice that there are no mentions of God or Providence or even allusions to Him. But this has not always been the case, and indeed used to be normative in science journals and letters from the scientists themselves.

The prevailing evolutionary paradigm has tried to pit science versus religion as being at best, two different realms whose studies do not overlap. At worst, it has denigrated religion (and especially Christianity) as being the opposite of science and labeled it superstition, magic, or a mental crutch.

Of course, not only are both of these views presenting a false dichotomy, but in reality ignore the development and history of science.

Did the Greeks Invent Science?

Now some may argue that the seeds of science began with the Greeks, and they certainly did not espouse a Christian worldview. However, one doesn't have to be a Christian to borrow from a biblical worldview. When the Apostle Paul was in Athens he told his audience that even their statues and poets pointed to the God of Scripture (Acts 17:22–31). Without knowing it, they were vainly groping for God.

Greek philosophers and scientists relied on the uniformity of nature, the ability of the human mind to reason, reliability of the senses, the existence of truth and knowledge, and so on in order to make their observations and conduct experiments.

Yet some (like the Epicureans) espoused basic evolutionary philosophies. Paul confronted them on their philosophical naturalism, and although his discourse recorded in Acts 17 was very brief, he went straight to the heart of the matter.

God was not some abstract entity, nor something made with human hands (or devised by human thoughts). God created everything, and this included the laws of nature. Paul was not just making a theological statement here; he was also making a scientific one. When Paul proclaimed "for in Him we live and move and have our being" (Acts 17:28),[1] he was including the concept that when we measure, observe, think, reason, and experiment, we are able to do so because God created us in His image (Genesis 1:27), has given us the ability to think and reason (Job 38:36), and upholds the universe (Colossians 1:16–17), allowing life on earth to proceed in an orderly way (Genesis 8:22).

Paul, though, was not inventing new arguments. He was resting in arguments rooted by God in the Old Testament Scriptures. These Scriptures

---

1. Scripture in this chapter is from the New King James Version (NKJV) of the Bible.

predate the Greek's alleged seeds of science — in some cases by more than a thousand years.

Consider the command that we are to observe ants and learn from their ways and be wise (Proverbs 6:6). We are commanded to use reason (Isaiah 1:18), given the ability to observe and map stars for seasons and timekeeping (Genesis 1:14), invent metallurgy (Genesis 4:22), invent musical instruments (Genesis 4:21), and so on. Observable and repeatable science is predicated on God upholding the world in a particular state to make observable and repeatable science possible (e.g., Genesis 8:22, see also Hebrews 1:3). Let's evaluate this further.

Laws of Nature

Any scientist must (and automatically does) assume that the laws of nature will be the same today as they were yesterday. They will trust that experiments performed under identical conditions will produce repeatable results. But do they ever stop to wonder *why* these things are true?

Consider the secular story. A "big bang" universe was created by a gravitational singularity, which itself came into being in an unknown fashion from nothing, creating time, space, and matter. This singularity then rapidly expanded outward (or perhaps a big bounce universe which eternally contracts and expands), and then was dependent upon supernova after supernova to provide heavier elements just to synthesize the basic ingredients of planetary formation. In this cosmic evolutionary paradigm, why should they expect uniformity of nature? One secular scientist, who believes in big bang, writes about the singularity:

> And before that, when the universe was a tiny, tiny, tiny fraction of a second old, everything in the entire universe was condensed into a ball the size of a piece of fruit. However, everything before the fruit-sized universe is unknown to us. When the universe is packed that closely together, things interact on a scale so small that normal physics just don't work. Our current knowledge of the laws of physics tell us little to nothing about what happens at that scale.[2]

In other words, the laws of physics no longer work when you go backward in time far enough. They must change. If secularists openly admit the laws of

---

2. Zeke Elkins, "Ask a Scientist: How Did the Big Bang Begin?" *Columbia Tribune*, November 6, 2018, http://www.columbiatribune.com/news/20181106/ask-scientist-how-did-big-bang-begin.

nature change, then why does science, which is based on the laws of science, not change? For all we know, the laws of science could change tomorrow in that view. And secularists *do* believe the laws of science will change again in the future — for sure at the big crunch — when the universe supposedly collapses on itself.

The Dumb Luck of Earth

Now consider the "goldilocks" nature of the earth and the impossibility of life spontaneously forming, let alone evolving into creatures of greater complexity. With all these "lucky fortunes" lining up, how can they presuppose anything other than random chance to be their mantra?

Then they have to strain credulity even further and believe this chance universe definitely has and exhibits order and natural laws. And then on top of that they have to believe that just by some cosmic accident, humanity has been granted the ability to think, reason, question, and amass knowledge down through history — all of which informs him that man alone has been able to conclude that he arrived here on this earth by chance acting through time via mutation and natural selection, and that there is no God.

Furthermore, the secularist believes that man alone can reason that there is no purpose for being on this orderly earth in a universe ruled by natural law, (other than propagating his genetic line — even that comes under question!). The Apostle Paul, guided by the Holy Spirit, rightly spoke of this as "suppression of the truth" that God has manifested to them (Romans 1:18–19).

Modern Science Comes Out of a Christian Worldview — the Early Years

But this has not always been the case for scientists. Many of the pioneers of scientific fields were Christians, and several of those were biblical creationists. They openly admitted that it was God who created the orderly universe and who gave them the reasoning skills they needed to accomplish or make the discoveries they did. Let's take a brief journey through the history of science over the past several hundred years and examine this more fully.

One of the men often credited with formulating the scientific method itself (boiled down to its essence — observe, question, hypothesize, experiment, confirm/reject hypothesis) was a creationist, Sir Francis Bacon (1561–1626). Ironically, it was another Bacon (Roger) who had 300 years earlier pushed for experimentation over argument alone as the basis for scientific progress. Roger Bacon (c. 1214–1292) was also a creationist.

Johannes Kepler (1571–1630), the astronomer who described planetary motions as ellipses, and who also in his study of optics, developed eyeglasses for both near and far-sightedness[3] often described his ability and motivation for his scientific studies.

> Those laws [of nature] are within the grasp of the human mind; God wanted us to recognize them by creating us after his own image so that we could share in his own thoughts.[4]

> It is a right, yes a duty, to search in cautious manner for the numbers, sizes, and weights, the norms for everything [God] has created. For He himself has let man take part in the knowledge of these things. . . . For these secrets are not of the kind whose research should be forbidden; rather they are set before our eyes like a mirror so that by examining them we observe to some extent the goodness and wisdom of the Creator.[5]

> I wanted to become a theologian. For a long time I was restless. Now, however, behold how through my effort God is being celebrated in astronomy.[6]

A Few of the Creationist Scientists in the 17th and Early 18th Century

Several prominent late 17th- and early 18th-century scientists were staunch creationists who proclaimed in their writings that their Christian religion was not incompatible with science. Robert Boyle (1627–1691) was a chemist and physicist, most famous for his formulation of Boyle's Law (relationship between pressure and volume for gases). Boyle made several statements about how Christianity influenced his scientific endeavors, and how the study of science made him glorify God for His creation.

> [W]hen with bold telescopes I survey the old and newly discovered stars and planets, when with excellent microscopes I discern in otherwise invisible objects, the unimitable subtility of

---

3. https://www.space.com/15787-johannes-kepler.html.
4. Letter (Apr. 1599) to the Bavarian chancellor Herwart von Hohenburg. Collected in Carola Baumgardt and Jamie Callan, *Johannes Kepler Life and Letters* (1953), p. 50.
5. "Epitome of Copernican Astronomy" in Michael B. Foster, *Mystery and Philosophy* (SCM Press, 1957), p. 61, https://todayinsci.com/K/Kepler_Johannes/KeplerJohannes-God-Quotations.htm.
6. Letter to Michael Maestlin (Oct. 3, 1595, https://todayinsci.com/K/Kepler_Johannes/KeplerJohannes-God-Quotations.htm.

nature's curious workmanship; and when, in a word, by the help of anatomical knives, and the light of chemical furnaces, I study the book of nature . . . I find myself oftentimes reduced to exclaim with the Psalmist, "How manifold are Thy works, O Lord! in wisdom hast Thou made them all!" [Psalm 104:24].[7]

The vastness, beauty, orderliness, of the heavenly bodies, the excellent structure of animals and plants; and the other phenomena of nature justly induce an intelligent and unprejudiced observer to conclude a supremely powerful, just, and good author.[8]

But neither the fundamental doctrine of Christianity nor that of the powers and effects of matter and motion seems to be more than epicycle . . . of the great and universal system of God's contrivances, and makes but a part of the more general theory of things, knowable by the light of nature, improved by the information of the scriptures so that both these doctrines . . . seem to be but members of the universal hypothesis, whose objects I conceive to be natural counsels, and works of God, so far as they are discoverable by us . . . in this life.[9]

A contemporary of Boyle was the physicist, astronomer, and mathematician Sir Isaac Newton (1642–1727). Newton is most famous for formulating the laws of gravity, motion, and the invention of calculus. Even so, he touched on most fields of science and biblical chronology in significant ways. He defended Archbishop James Ussher's chronology, as well. In perhaps his most famous written work *Principia*, Newton acknowledged God's central role in creation, and how science is merely the search for the truth of God's handiwork.

The most beautiful system of the Sun, Planets and Comets could only proceed from the counsel and dominion of an intelligent being.[10]

Blind metaphysical necessity, which is certainly the same always and everywhere, could produce no variety of things. All

7. Robert Boyle, *Seraphic Love* (Whitefish MT: Kessinger Publishing, LLC, 1992), p. 47.
8. Robert Boyle, *Works*, Vol. IV, p. 25, https://biblescienceguy.wordpress.com/2013/07/17/5-evidence-for-god-design-is-best-argument-for-god-simple/.
9. Robert Boyle, *The Excellency of Theology*, p. 20, https://www.earlymoderntexts.com/assets/pdfs/boyle1674b.pdf.
10. Isaac Newton, *Principia*, p. 35, https://archive.org/stream/newtonspmathema00newtrich?ref=ol#page/n7.

that diversity of natural things which we find suited to different times and places could arise from nothing but the ideas and will of a Being necessarily existing.

Thus, the diligent student of science, the earnest seeker of truth, led, as through the courts of a sacred Temple, wherein, at each step, new wonders meet the eye, till, as a crowning grace, they stand before a Holy of Holies, and learn that all science and all truth are one which hath its beginning and its end in the knowledge of Him whose glory the heavens declare, and whose handiwork the firmament showeth forth.[11]

In the 2nd edition of *Principia* (1713), Newton asked mathematician Roger Cotes to write the preface. Cotes, in the same vein as Newton, acknowledged:

Without all doubt, this world, so diversified with that variety of forms and motions we find in it, could arise from nothing but the perfectly free will of God directing and presiding over all. From this fountain . . . the laws of Nature have flowed, in which there appear many traces indeed of the most wise contrivance, but not the least shadow of necessity. These, therefore, we must not seek from uncertain conjectures, but learn them from observations and experiments.[12]

Several other notable scientists of the 18th century were creationists, including the famous botanist, zoologist, and founder of modern taxonomic classification, Carl Linnaeus (1707–1778), who was a contemporary of Newton. Born the same year, Leonhard Euler (1707–1783) was a mathematician (most famous for introducing several math symbols such as $f(x)$ and pi π), and he also wrote on hydrodynamics and astronomy.

A Few of the Creationist Scientists in the 18th and 19th Century

As you move from the 18th to the 19th century, several fields of science were developed or heavily influenced by Christian (and creationist) scientists. A trio of creation scientists and inventors were born in 1791 and contributed greatly to scientific advancement. Michael Faraday (1791–1867) was a chemist and a pioneer in the field of electricity and electromagnetism. Samuel Morse (1791–1872) helped improve the (nascent) photography

---

11. Ibid., p. 37.
12. Clifford Pickover, *Archimedes to Hawking: Laws of Science and the Great Minds Behind Them* (New York, NY: Oxford University Press, Inc.), p. 3.

field and is mostly known as the inventor of the telegraph. Charles Babbage[13] (1791–1871), mathematician and the father of modern computers, developed a working difference engine (calculator) that could calculate accurately out to 20 decimal places.

Babbage also invented the speedometer. Contrary to the common refrain of today that creationists cannot be scientists, not only was Babbage a brilliant scientist, but he was a founding member of the Royal Astronomical Society, the British Association for the Advancement of Science, and the Statistical Society. But perhaps Babbage's greatest invention and contribution to science was one which he never finished. His unpublished notes on his "analytical machine" (a larger and more powerful version of his difference engine) were found in 1937, and with newer technology then available, his work became the brainchild for the early 1940 and 1950s computers.

All three of these men (Faraday, Morse, and Babbage) attributed their impetus and success to God. Faraday summed up their separate thoughts by acknowledging that it was God's natural law that allowed reason and scientific knowledge.

> If you teach scientific knowledge without honouring scientific knowledge as it is applied, you do more harm than good. I do think that the study of natural science is so glorious a school for the mind, that with the laws impressed on all these things by the Creator, and the wonderful unity and stability of matter, and the forces of matter, there cannot be a better school for the education of the mind.[14]

Other great scientists of the 19th century included Joule (thermodynamics), Pasteur (microbiology/germ theory), Mendel (genetics), Lister (surgery, medical hygiene), Maxwell (electromagnetic theory/physics), and William Thompson, better known as Lord Kelvin (thermodynamics, absolute temperature scale). All of these scientists were Christians, and all were creationists. None were unable to "do science" because of their Christian faith; in fact, in every case each man remarked how his faith bolstered his scientific zeal.

James Joule summed this up quite well in a speech written (but not delivered, due to health problems) for the British Association for the Advancement of Science:

---

13. Babbage argued for the recent creation of man but appears to have been a Gap Theorist regarding the earth's age.
14. Giving Evidence to the Public Schools Commission (Nov. 18, 1862), as quoted in John L. Lewis, *125 Years: The Physical Society & The Institute of Physics* (1999), p. 168–169, https://todayinsci.com/F/Faraday_Michael/FaradayMichael-Knowledge-Quotations.htm.

After the knowledge of, and obedience to, the will of God, the next aim must be to know something of His attributes of wisdom, power, and goodness as evidenced by His handiwork. . . . It is evident that an acquaintance with natural laws means no less than an acquaintance with the mind of God therein expressed.[15]

A Few of the Creationist Scientists in the 20ᵗʰ and 21ˢᵗ Century

Moving into the 20ᵗʰ century, we continue to see several prominent creation scientists and inventors. John Ambrose Fleming (1849–1945) was a physicist most famous for working on the vacuum tube and radar (for the British military during WWII).

Douglas Dewar (1875–1957) was a prominent ornithologist. Charles Stine (1882–1954) was a chemist who was credited with creating a safer and more stable version of dynamite to be used in mining and as vice president of DuPont for assembling the team of scientists who developed nylon. Werner Von Braun (1912–1977) is mostly known for his rocket design contributions to the American space programs of Mercury, Gemini, and Apollo. All of these men were also creationists, and to some degree wrote or advocated against Darwinian evolution.

Moving into the 21ˢᵗ century, creation scientists are still studying God's handiwork and making great contributions to science. Whether it is designing life-saving diagnostic medical devices, like the MRI scanner by Dr. Raymond Damadian, or Dr. Stuart Burgess being responsible for designing mechanical parts for the European Space Agency or drive trains for bicycles which won six gold medals (for Great Britain in the 2016 summer Olympics) and set several world records, creationists are able to greatly contribute to science and technology despite being labeled as "unscientific" by some of their secular peers.

There are so many others like Dr. John Baumgartner (geophysicist, catastrophic plate tectonics), Dr. Alan White (chemist with a multitude of inventions), Dr. Georgia Purdom (genetics), Dr. Nathaniel Jeanson (genetics), Dr. Jason Lisle (astrophysics, discovered a planet), Dr. Andrew Snelling (geology), Dr. Danny Faulkner (astronomer and binary star expert), Dr. Tommy Mitchell (medical internist), and Dr. David Menton (anatomist famous for the Menton Collection). There are many more to name, some of whom have even contributed to this book.

---

15. Clifford Pickover, *Archimedes to Hawking: Laws of Science and the Great Minds Behind Them* (New York, NY: Oxford University Press, Inc.), p. 306.

It is obvious just from this cursory glance at Christian and creation scientists of the past 400 years that none were impeded in their scientific accomplishments because of their faith. On the contrary, most are on record saying that their Christian faith is what motivated them to study the world (and universe) around them.

There is no battle of faith versus science, there is only a battle over worldviews and presuppositions. Is it more logical for someone to be motivated to study nature when they believe it came about through random chaotic processes, or when they believe it came about through the purposeful design of the Creator God of the Bible?

Christianity is a reasoned faith, not a blind one. The Bible itself testifies that God expects mankind to seek after knowledge and wisdom and to study His creation and to understand as much as he can about it. Let us end this chapter with these words of Scripture, given to us by the Holy Spirit.

> When I consider Your heavens, the work of Your fingers, the moon and the stars, which You have ordained, what is man that You are mindful of him, and the son of man that You visit him? For You have made him a little lower than the angels, and You have crowned him with glory and honor. You have made him to have dominion over the works of Your hands; You have put all things under his feet (Psalm 8:3–6).

> The works of the LORD are great, studied by all who have pleasure in them (Psalm 111:2).

> A wise man will hear and increase learning, and a man of understanding will attain wise counsel, to understand a proverb and an enigma, the words of the wise and their riddles. The fear of the LORD is the beginning of knowledge, but fools despise wisdom and instruction (Proverbs 1:5–7).

> It is the glory of God to conceal a matter, but the glory of kings is to search out a matter (Proverbs 25:2).

> And I set my heart to seek and search out by wisdom concerning all that is done under heaven; this burdensome task God has given to the sons of man, by which they may be exercised (Ecclesiastes 1:13).

It is merely arbitrary and an appeal to man's opinions as supreme. Whether you realize it or not, man is seen as the absolute. More properly, man's ideas are seen as 'God.'

CREATION VS. EVOLUTION — IS IT AN AUTHORITY ISSUE?

In addition to his work with the ministry of Answers in Genesis, **BODIE HODGE** is a published author, general editor of and contributor to numerous DVDs and books including *World Religions and Cults Vols. 1–3, The Fall of Satan, Confound the Critics, Dragons, Dinosaurs, & the Bible, The War on Christmas, The New Answers Book series, Answer Books for Kids, Tower of Babel, Demolishing Supposed Bible Contradictions Vols. 1–2, The Flood of Noah, Dragons: Legends and Lore of Dinosaurs*, and more. Bodie attended Southern Illinois University at Carbondale (SIUC) and received a BS and MS (in 1996 and 1998, respectively) in mechanical engineering. His specialty was a subset of mechanical engineering based in advanced materials processing, particularly starting powders.

The creation vs. evolution debate is not entirely about creation vs. evolution. Creation and evolution are just part of the debate. Creation and evolution are like two different castles standing in opposition to each other.

Authority

Even castles have foundations. But when you look at the foundations, it's actually about authority. Consider these diagrams Answers in Genesis has used in the past:

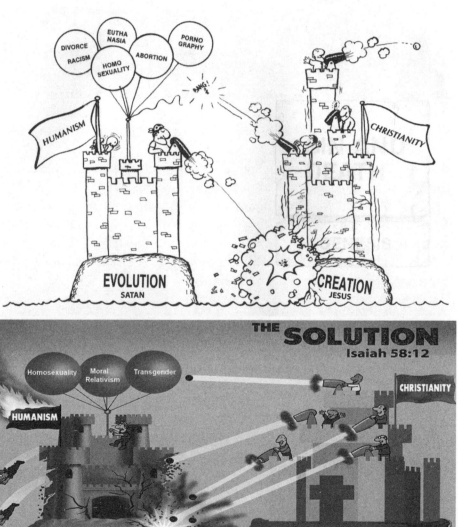

Are these in contradiction? Not at all when you understand the progression of the foundation of belief. Evolution requires "millions of years" — you don't hear evolutionists saying that all life evolved from a single-celled organism beginning about 6,000 years ago!

So, millions of years *is* the foundation to evolution. But what *is* the foundation of millions of years (geological evolution and cosmological evolution [big bang])? Millions of years (long ages) and big bang is predicated on man's ideas and opinions (even if it was Satan influenced) being the supreme authority about the past including:

- Naturalism — nature is all that there is.
- Materialism — all that exists is matter and energy — no God or Creator, no immaterial realm, no spiritual realm exists; thus, no creation event by Christ or other supposed lesser "gods."
- Uniformitarianism — rates in the past have always been the same as today; no major catastrophes so that rock layers are presumed to be laid down slowly and uniformly over long ages (not by the Flood of Noah for example) and uniformitarian dating methods (e.g., radiometric dating methods) can be applied.

Popular evolutionist Professor Richard Lewontin admitted that God should be kicked out of science when he said:

> We take the side of science *in spite* of the patent absurdity of some of its constructs, *in spite* of its failure to fulfill many of its

extravagant promises of health and life, *in spite* of the tolerance of the scientific community for unsubstantiated just-so stories, because we have a prior commitment, a commitment to materialism. It is not that the methods and institutions of science somehow compel us to accept a material explanation of the phenomenal world, but, on the contrary, that we are forced by our *a priori* adherence to material causes to create an apparatus of investigation and a set of concepts that produce material explanations, no matter how counter-intuitive, no matter how mystifying to the uninitiated. Moreover, that materialism is an absolute, for we cannot allow a Divine Foot in the door.[1]

But notice that *materialism, naturalism,* and *uniformitarianism* is predicated on man's ideas as the ultimate authority. In other words, man's opinions about the past and the nature of reality are considered the absolute truth in an effort to arrive at *materialism, naturalism, uniformitarianism,* and subsequently building on those for *long ages* and *evolution.* This method, however, is begging the question, a fallacy. Put it like this:

> "How do you know materialism, naturalism, and uniformitarianism are true?"
>
> "Because materialism, naturalism, and uniformitarianism are true."

This is a mere restatement of what is being asked and, therefore, fallacious. It is merely arbitrary and an appeal to man's opinions as supreme. Whether you realize it or not, man is seen as the absolute. More properly, man's ideas are seen as "God." But these opinions about the past, are simply that — opinions. Mere opinions carry no weight in an argument, but are arbitrary and without reason.

If man's reason is deemed as "God," then God is not deemed as God. So, man's ideas are elevated to a godlike status and God is demoted to be less than God. Even Charles Darwin, the father of modern evolutionary ideas, recognized this and went so far as to say that man, then, even invented God:

> The same high mental faculties which first led man to believe in unseen spiritual agencies, then in fetishism, polytheism, and ultimately in monotheism, would infallibly lead him, as long

---

1.   Richard Lewontin, "Billions and Billions of Demons," *The New York Review*, p. 31, January 9, 1997.

as his reasoning powers remained poorly developed, to various strange superstitions and customs.[2]

> The idea of a universal and beneficent Creator does not seem to arise in the mind of man, until he has been elevated by long-continued culture.[3]

You need to understand that God disagrees with Darwin and with anyone who presumes that He should be demoted. And God will judge them properly on judgment day, for falsely judging Him. There is no greater authority than God (Hebrew 6:13). God is omnipresent, omniscience, and omnipotent. Man isn't. God says:

> Stop regarding man in whose nostrils is breath, for of what account is he? (Isaiah 2:22).[4]

The issue is authority. God is the infallible authority, and not man. When man's fallible reason is elevated to the position of supreme authority, then it is the religion of *humanism* in its broadest sense. It is also called "man's religion."

It's a Religious Debate, Not a Science Debate

Regarding the authority of man vs. the authority of God debate, it is a *religious* debate — humanism vs. Christianity. It is not a science debate. Good operational science is observable and repeatable. Big bang, millions of years, and evolution are not observable and repeatable. Such alleged events as big bang, millions of years, and evolution supposedly reside in the past. It is more of a history question than a science question.

This now dives into the issue of "historical" or "origins" science (using science in the present to help us understand history). This is different from "operational" science (also called "observable" or "repeatable" science) that we observe and repeat today. Operational science is utilized by both creationists and evolutionists working side by side today in chemistry labs, to build computers, cell phones, mining equipment, and space shuttles.

Some evolutionists often recognize that it is a religious debate and are quite open about it — usually. Evolutionary organizations get religious tax-

---

2. Charles Darwin, *The Descent of Man, and Selection in Relation to Sex*, chapter 3, "Mental Powers of Man and the Lower Animals," in Great Books of the Western World, Volume 49, Mortimer Adler, editor (Chicago, IL.: William Benton Publisher, 1952, original publication date 1871), p. 303.
3. Darwin, *The Descent of Man, and Selection in Relation to Sex*, chapter 21, "General Summary and Conclusion," p. 593.
4. Scripture in this chapter is from the English Standard Version (ESV) of the Bible.

exempt status in the USA and UK and other countries. The U.S. Supreme Court recognized secular humanism as a religion.[5]

Humanistic biologist George Klein admits atheism is based in faith in his book *The Atheist in the Holy City*,

> I am an atheist. My attitude is not based on science, but rather on faith. . . . The absence of a Creator, the non-existence of God is my childhood faith, my adult belief, unshakable and holy.[6]

Philosopher and atheist Michael Ruse said,

> . . . if you want a concession, I've always said that naturalism is an act of faith.[7]

Interestingly, when it comes to state schools where religion is to be kept out of the classroom, we suddenly see an intense switch. With a dogmatic stance, evolutionists cry in loud voices that evolution, naturalism, humanism, materialism, and the like are not religious, so that they can remain in the classroom. It is a double standard fallacy. Atheist John Dunphy was open about imposing humanistic religion on school children. He said,

> I am convinced that the battle for humankind's future must be waged and won in the public school classroom by teachers who correctly perceive their role as the proselytizers of a new faith: a religion of humanity that recognizes and respects the spark of what theologians call divinity in every human being. These teachers must embody the same selfless dedication as the most rabid fundamentalist preachers, for they will be ministers of another sort, utilizing a classroom instead of a pulpit to convey humanist values in whatever subject they teach, regardless of the educational level — preschool day care or large state university. The classroom must and will become an arena of conflict between the old and the new — the rotting corpse of Christianity, together with all its adjacent evils and misery, and the new faith of humanism.[8]

---

5. The U.S. Supreme Court, in Torcaso v. Watkins, 81 S.Ct. 1681 (1961), stated the following: "Among religions in this country which do not teach what would generally be considered a belief in the existence of God, are Buddhism, Taoism, Ethical Culture, Secular Humanism, and others."

6. George Klein, *The Atheist in the Holy City* (Cambridge, MA: MIT Press, 1990), p. 203.

7. Michael Ruse (quoted by Robert Stewart) in *Intelligent Design: William A. Dembski & Michael Ruse in Dialogue* (Minneapolis, MN: Fortress Press, 2007). p. 37.

8. John Dunphy, "A Religion for a New Age," *Humanist*, Jan–Feb 1983, p. 26.

God Is the Authority vs. Man Is the Authority

The battles over creation vs. evolution are part of a larger war. It is a war over the hearts and mind of the next generation. This war has been fought since Genesis 3, when humanism first reared its ugly head as Adam and Eve held their own views about the fruit of the Tree of the Knowledge of Good and Evil as supreme over the absolute Word of God.

God was right. Adam and Eve died and their entire dominion fell, and down through the ages, mankind, including ourselves, are in that fallen dominion in need of a Savior. That Savior, God Himself in the person of Jesus Christ, became a man (John 1; Colossians 1; Hebrews 1) and died the death we deserve to satisfy God's wrath upon sin and make salvation possible (e.g., Romans 6:10; 2 Corinthians 5:21). Thus, Jesus is the Last Adam (1 Corinthians 15:45) who now will have final and eternal dominion (e.g., 1 Peter 4:11, 5:12; Revelation 1:6).

Ever since that first sin, the sinful heart of man has elevated a sinful concept of humanism in defiance of God. The creation and evolution debate today is being fought on one branch of the tree of humanism. So long as the secular forms of humanism permeate our culture, many will be deceived and follow this false religion into the grave and hell.

When someone objects to God's Word, be it Adam and Eve or you and me, by what authority can they do it? It would only be by our *own* authority. Consider the words of the Holy Spirit:

> But each person is tempted when he is lured and enticed by his own desire. Then desire when it has conceived gives birth to sin, and sin when it is fully grown brings forth death (James 1:14–15).

It is via our *own desires* that we leave God and His Word and cling to sin in disobedience. This happened in the Garden (Genesis 3) and it happens today. When we appeal to our own opinions as an authority to oppose God and His Word, we are effectively claiming to be God, as we are appealing to ourselves as an authority *above* God. But we are not God. We are fallen beings, imperfect, broken, fallible, with nothing to compete with God's true authority. As such, this is a fallacious appeal to a false authority (i.e., false authority fallacy or faulty appeal to authority).

But at the most basic foundational point — it is God vs. man. It is a battle over the authority of God's Word (Scripture) versus the fallacious, fallible, and imperfect whims and opinions of man (consider Isaiah 2:22 or Psalm 118:8).

There Are Only Two Religions in the World

In light of this, there are only two religions in the world — God's and not God's. If it doesn't come from God, it comes from man (even demonic or satanic ideas are still presented through the mind of man, e.g., 2 Timothy 2:26). This is humanism or man's religion. Man's religion can be broken into a variety of beliefs. Four major ones emerge. They are:

1. Spiritualistic (e.g., Eastern Mysticism like Taoism, Hinduism, New Age, etc.) where all things that exist are spirit and all is one. No material things exist, you are merely deceived into thinking they are.[9]
2. Materialistic (e.g., atheism, agnosticism, naturalism, Epicureanism, materialism, evolutionism, etc.) where all things are material and subsequently immaterial and spiritual things do not exist.[10]
3. Moralistic (e.g., classic paganism, witchcraft, Confucianism, Buddhism, mythologies, Spiritism, etc.) where some sort of arbitrary moral code — not necessarily biblical morals — is imposed and you can have gods or not, but no adherent really knows for certain since they are arbitrary!).[11]
4. Counterfeits of Christianity (e.g., Judaism, Islam, Mormonism, Jehovah's Witnesses, Zoroastrianism, other cults, etc.) where groups deviate from Scripture and elevate an authority to take you away from Scripture (even while affirming that the Bible is true usually) whether the Talmud, Koran, Book of Mormon, etc.[12]

In each case, these religions deviate from God and His Word because of man's humanistic beliefs and ideas that deviate from Scripture, whether Muhammad, Buddha, Confucius, ancient sages, Joseph Smith, Charles Taze Russell, Charles Darwin, Talmudic Rabbis, or many others.

Secular forms of humanism (i.e., leave God out of it) have begun to dominate the Western World. This is why we use the castle diagrams to illustrate the battle in our secularized culture. But bear in mind that creation vs. evolution is but one of many battles in the larger war against God and His Word.

Cultures around the world deal with humanism in other ways. For example, isolated areas may deal with Eastern mysticism, pagan (moralistic), or

---

9. If all is one, then being logical and being illogical are one and the same — which means knowledge, logic, and truth cannot exist within these worldviews — thus, they are refuted.
10. If everything is material, then logic, knowledge, and truth cannot exist, so these religions are self-refuting.
11. Each of these religions are openly opinions of man, which are arbitrary; thus refuted.
12. Each of these counterfeits contradict God's Word and cannot be true, thus they are refuted.

counterfeits more than secular. But we must be honest, the secular religions are now permeating cultures around the globe. From Buddhists to adherents of Judaism, evolutionary and humanistic ideas are mixing with their religions.

Sadly, many Christians are not immune. Far too often we see believers compromise God's Word and give up Scripture to adopt evolutionary ideas, too. Some Christians mix their religion with secular humanism by taking big bang, millions of years, and evolution and inserting it into Genesis 1, for instance. They reinterpret the Bible (demote what God says) to accommodate big bang, millions of years, and evolution (man's opinions about the past that disagree with God's Word). They do this in several way:

1. Gap Theory
   a. Precreation chaos
   b. Ruin reconstruction
   c. Pre-time gap
   d. Late gap
   e. Soft gap
2. Day Age
   a. Classic Day Age
   b. Progressive creation
3. Theistic Evolution
   a. Evolutionary creation
   b. Framework Hypothesis
   c. Cosmic Temple

What Are These in More Detail?

Virtually all Christians who have bought into an old earth (that is millions and billions of years of long ages) place the millions of years *prior* to Adam.

We have genealogical lists that connect Adam to Christ (e.g., Luke 3). For the *old-earth Christians*, it would be blatantly absurd to try to insert millions and billions of years into these genealogies and say that Adam and Eve were made at the beginning of creation.[13]

Instead, old-earth creationists (as they are often denoted[14]) take these long ages and insert them somewhere prior to Adam; hence, creation week

---

13. In Mark 10:6, Jesus says: "But from the beginning of creation, 'God made them male and female.' "
14. In many other cases, those Christians who adhere to long ages are called "compromised Christians" since they are compromising by mixing these two religions' origins accounts (humanism and Christianity). Properly, this is syncretism, where they merge the religions of Christianity and humanism into one blended religion.

has been a divisive point in Christianity ever since the idea of long ages such as millions of years became popular in the 1800s. Here are some of the differing positions within the Church — but all have one common factor — endeavoring to somehow fit millions of years into the Bible:

Gap Theories (incorporating geological and astronomical evolution)

1. **Pre-time gap.** This view adds long ages prior to God creating in Genesis 1:1.[15] The pre-time gap falls short for a number of reasons, such as having death before sin, allowance of man's ideas about millions of years to supersede God's Word, having *time* before time existed, and the like. As another example, how can one have millions of years of time prior to the creation of time? It is quite illogical.

2. **Ruin-reconstruction gap.** This is the most popular gap idea — it adds long ages between Genesis 1:1[16] and Genesis 1:2.[17] Scottish pastor Thomas Chalmers popularized it in the early 1800s as a response to long ages, which was becoming popular. This idea is promoted in the Scofield and Dake Study Bibles and is often associated with a Luciferian fall and flood — but that would make Lucifer (Satan) in his sinful state very good and perfect. After God created Adam, God said everything He made was "very good" (Deuteronomy 32:4[18]; Genesis 1:31).[19]

3. **Modified gap/precreation chaos gap.** This view adds long ages between Genesis 1:2[20] and 1:3,[21] and it is primarily addressed in the International Conference on Creation.[22] It has many of the same problems already mentioned in the first two gaps already discussed.

---

15. In the beginning, God created the heavens and the earth.
16. Ibid.
17. The earth was without form and void, and darkness was over the face of the deep. And the Spirit of God was hovering over the face of the waters.
18. The Rock, his work is perfect, for all His ways are justice. A God of faithfulness and without iniquity, just and upright is he.
19. Ken Ham, "What About the Gap & Ruin-Reconstruction Theories?" in *The New Answers Book 1*, Ken Ham, gen. ed. (Green Forest, AR: Master Books, 2006); for a technical response see also, W. Fields, *Unformed and Unfilled* (Collinsville, IL: Burgener Enterprises, 1997).
20. The earth was without form and void; and darkness was over the face of the deep. And the Spirit of God was hovering over the face of the waters.
21. And God said, "Let there be light," and there was light.
22. One refutation of this view is in Andrew Snelling, ed., *Proceedings of the Sixth International Conference on Creationism* (Dallas, TX: Institute for Creation Research, 2008), "A Critique of the Precreation Chaos Gap Theory," by John Zoschke.

4. **Soft gap.** This also includes a gap between Genesis 1:2[23] and 1:3,[24] but unlike previous views, it has no catastrophic events or destruction of a previous state. Furthermore, it merely proposes that God created the world this way and left it for long periods of time in an effort to get starlight here. In essence, this view has a young earth and an old universe. The problem is that stars were created after the proposed gap (day 4), and it is unnecessary to make accommodations for long ages to solve the so-called starlight problem. Getting distant starlight to earth is not a problem for an all-powerful God. It is only a problem in a strict naturalistic view.

5. **Late gap.** This view has a gap between chapters 2 and 3 of Genesis. In other words, some believe that Adam and Eve lived in the Garden for long ages before sin. This view has problems too. For example, Adam and Eve were told by God to be "fruitful and multiply" in Genesis 1:28,[25] and waiting long ages to do so would have been disobeying God's Word. This doesn't make sense. In addition, there is the problem of Adam only living 930 years as recorded in Genesis (Genesis 5:5[26]).[27]

When someone tries to put a large gap of time in the Scriptures when it is not warranted by the text, this should throw up a red flag to any Christian. In many gap theory models, Satan allegedly rebels between Genesis 1:1 and 1:2[28] (or otherwise in the first three verses of Scripture).

Consider the theological problem of Satan, in his sinful state being called "very good" in Genesis 1:31.[29] This would make an evil Satan very good. In fact, this would make *sin* very good too. Satan could not have fallen into sin until after this declaration in Genesis 1:31.[30]

---

23. The earth was without form, and void; and darkness was over the face of the deep. And the Spirit of God was hovering over the face of the waters.
24. And God said, "Let there be light," and there was light.
25. And God blessed them. And God said to them, "Be fruitful and multiply and fill the earth and subdue it, and have dominion over the fish of the sea and over the birds of the heavens and over every living thing that moves on the earth."
26. Thus all the days that Adam lived were 930 years, and he died.
27. Bodie Hodge, *The Fall of Satan* (Green Forest, AR: Master Books, 2011), p. 23–26, https://answersingenesis.org/bible-characters/adam-and-eve/when-did-adam-and-eve-rebel/.
28. In the beginning, God created the heavens and the earth. The earth was without form and void, and darkness was over the face of the deep. And the Spirit of God was hovering over the face of the waters.
29. And God saw everything that he had made, and behold, it was very good. And there was evening and there was morning, the sixth day.
30. Ibid.

Day Age Models (each model adheres to geological and astronomical evolution)

1. **Day-Age.** This idea was popularized by Hugh Miller in the early 1800s after walking away from Thomas Chalmers' idea of the gap theory, and prior to his suicide. This model basically stretched the days of creation out to be millions of years long. Of course, lengthening the days in Genesis to accommodate the secular evolutionist view of history simply doesn't match up with what is stated in Genesis 1.[31]

2. **Progressive Creation.** This is a modified form of the Day-Age idea (really, in many ways it's similar to Theistic Evolution) led by Dr. Hugh Ross, head of an organization called *Reasons to Believe*. He appeals to nature (actually the secular interpretations of nature) as the supposed 67th book of the Bible, and then uses these interpretations to supersede what the Bible says. Recall that nature is cursed according to Genesis 3 and Romans 8. Dr. John Ankerberg is also a leading supporter of this viewpoint.[32] This view proposes that living creatures go extinct repeatedly over millions of years, but God, from time to time, makes new kinds and new species all fitting with a geologically and cosmological/astronomically evolutionary view of history.[33] Things are out of order in creation week in the progressive creation view, and death before sin is devastating to this position.

Theistic Evolutionary Models (each variant basically adheres to geological, astronomical, and biological evolution)

1. **Theistic Evolution (Evolutionary Creation).** Basically, the idea of Genesis 1–11 is thrown out or heavily reinterpreted to allow for evolutionary ideas to supersede the Scriptures. Harvard botany professor Asa Gray was a contemporary of Darwin and promoted this idea, but Darwin opposed Gray's mixing of Christianity with

---

31. T. Mortenson, "Evolution vs. Creation: The Order of Events Matters!" *Answers in Genesis*, April 4, 2006, https://answersingenesis.org/why-does-creation-matter/evolution-vs-creation-the-order-of-events-matters/.

32. J. Seegert, "Responding to the Compromise Views of John Ankerberg," *Answers in Genesis*, March 2, 2005, https://answersingenesis.org/reviews/tv/responding-to-the-compromise-views-of-john-ankerberg/.

33. K. Ham and T. Mortenson, "What's Wrong with Progressive Creation?" in Ken Ham, gen. ed., *The New Answers Book 2* (Green Forest, AR: Master Book, 2008), p. 123–134.

evolution since they were two opposing views. They wrote several letters to one another. Charles Hodge and Benjamin B. Warfield (who were great in many respects) of Princeton Theological Seminary in the mid-to-late 1800s also advocated the mixing of Christianity with evolution. Today, this view is heavily promoted by a group called BioLogos. Basically, they accept the prevailing evolutionist (false) history, including the big bang, and then add a demoted form of God to it. BioLogos writers have different ways of wildly reinterpreting Genesis to accommodate evolution into Scripture.

2. **Framework Hypothesis.** Dr. Meredith Kline (1922–2007), who accepted many evolutionary ideas, popularized this view in America.[34] It is very common in many seminaries today. Those who hold to Framework treat Genesis 1 as a literary device (think poetic or semi-poetic), with the first three days paralleling and equating to the last three days of creation. These days are not seen as 24-hour days but are taken as metaphorical or allegorical to allow for ideas like evolution/millions of years to be entertained. Hence, Genesis 1 is treated as merely being a literary device to teach that God created everything (essentially in 3 days[35]).[36] However, Genesis 1 is not written as poetry but as literal history.[37]

3. **Cosmic Temple.** Dr. John Walton agrees the language of Genesis 1 means ordinary days, but since he believes in evolution, he had to do something about it. Walton proposes that Genesis 1 has nothing

---

34. It was originally developed in 1924 by Professor Arnie Noordtzij in Europe, which was a couple of decades before Dr. Kline jumped on board with Framework Hypothesis.

35. "For in six days the LORD made heaven and earth, the sea, and all that is in them, and rested on the seventh day. Therefore the LORD blessed the Sabbath day and made it holy (Exodus 20:11). "It is a sign forever between me and the people of Israel that in six days the LORD made heaven and earth, and on the seventh day he rested and was refreshed" (Exodus 31:17).

36. T. Chaffey and B. McCabe, "What Is Wrong with the Framework Hypothesis?" *Answers in Genesis*, June 11, 2011, https://answersingenesis.org/creationism/old-earth/whats-wrong-with-the-framework-hypothesis/.

37. Hebrew expert Dr. Steven Boyd writes: "For Genesis 1:1–2:3, this probability is between 0.999942 and 0.999987 at a 99.5% confidence level. Thus, we conclude with statistical certainty that this text is narrative, not poetry. It is therefore statistically indefensible to argue that it is poetry. The hermeneutical implication of this finding is that this text should be read as other historical narratives." Dr. Steven Boyd, Associate Professor of Bible, The Master's College, *Radioisotopes and the Age of the Earth*, Volume II, Editors Larry Vardiman, Andrew Snelling, and Eugene Chaffin (Dallas, TX: Institute for Creation Research, 2005), p. 632.

to do with material origins but instead is referring to "God's Cosmic Temple" — which is purely arbitrary. By relegating Genesis 1 to be disconnected from material origins of earth, then he is free to believe in evolution and millions of years.

In each of these views, Christians (many of whom I respect) take the ideas of man as superior to Scripture and reinterpret (demote) Scripture in light of man's opinions to have a fossil record of death existing prior to its formation during the Flood, appeal to a local Flood, etc. Christians can fall short by mixing their religion with millions of years, big bang, and evolution, which are tenets of the religion of humanism. This introduces problems like having death before sin (which undermines the gospel), neglects a global Flood, proposes God not being involved in creation since the big bang is a model that has "no God required," and so on.

We need to be honest with ourselves and repent if we have done this. Even I have struggled with this in my past. I needed to get back to God's Word as the authority, particularly in Genesis. It was tough, but don't let pride get the better of you.

Conclusion

There is no greater authority than God (e.g., Hebrews 6:13). When we elevate our own thoughts and beliefs to supersede God, we are the ones in error. God is always right. Always.

When man's ideas, our own or someone else's, are used as an authority above God, that is the religion of humanism and leads you down a false path. This is called autonomous human reason. When we follow autonomous human reason (reason apart from God), we are being a law unto ourselves by demoting God and biblical authority.

This is a primary foundation to the creation-evolution debate — it is a matter of trust. Will you trust in the opinions of man with its eternal consequences or will you surrender to a perfect God and receive His mercy?

We would go one step further than Dr. Boyd, who left open the slim possibility of Genesis not being historical narrative, and say it is historical narrative and all doctrines of theology, directly or indirectly, are founded in the early pages of Genesis — though we appreciated Dr. Boyd's research.

> *The assumption that nature is all that exists is the key assumption of atheism. Not all scientists are atheists, but most scientists for the past 150–200 years have done their scientific work as if nature is all that exists.*

6 MILLIONS OF YEARS: WHERE DID THE IDEA COME FROM?

DR. TERRY MORTENSON is a historian of geology, a theologian, and a speaker, writer, and researcher for Answers in Genesis. Prior to joining AiG, he served for 26 years with Campus Crusade for Christ in the U.S. and in Eastern Europe. He holds an MDiv from Trinity Evangelical Divinity School and a PhD in the history of geology from Coventry University in England, and he is an active member of the Evangelical Theological Society. Since the late 1970s he has lectured on creation and evolution in 28 countries. He has written, edited, and contributed to many books and articles.

Today, most people, including most professing Christians in the world, believe that the earth and the universe are billions of years old.[1] Billions of years are an incomprehensible amount of time. But where did the idea come from? It's a relatively recent idea that developed slowly over the last 200 years. What led scientists to this conclusion? How did the rest of the world, including most seminary and Christian college professors, become convinced of this?

The idea developed in the late 18th and early 19th centuries in Christian Europe. For the first 1,800 years of church history, the almost universal belief of the church was that God created the whole universe about 4,000 years before Jesus Christ.[2] But in the late 1700s, deistic and atheistic scientists began to develop naturalistic theories of earth history.[3] They rejected the biblical account of history and instead assumed that the origin and history of the earth could be explained by time and chance and the laws of nature working on matter, which either God created in a simple state or was eternal. Initially, those who believed in a supernatural beginning were thinking of a few million years. So, in the early 19th century, three views of earth history were in competition to explain the rock layers, fossils, and topography of earth.[4]

One view became known as "catastrophism." Proponents of this view believed that God created the world and the first forms of life but every so often there was a flood of continental or global extent that destroyed most or all of the creatures living at the time. Many of them were buried in sediments and became fossils. These major floods were separated by long periods of time, and after each flood God either created new forms of life to replace what had perished or survivors repopulated the earth. This long series of major floods produced the many sedimentary rock layers.

A second view was called "uniformitarianism." Advocates rejected the idea of global or continental-size floods and insisted that all the processes of geological change (erosion, sedimentation, earthquakes, volcanoes, etc.) have always gone on in the past at the same rate, frequency, and power as we observe on

---

1. Evolutionists say that earth is about 4.5 billion years old and the universe is about 13.8 billion years old.
2. See chapters 1–2 in Terry Mortenson and Thane H. Ury, eds., *Coming to Grips with Genesis* (Green Forest, AR: Master Books, 2008).
3. For an explanation of the religion of naturalism, see Terry Mortenson, "The Religion of Naturalism," https://answersingenesis.org/world-religions/religion-of-naturalism/.
4. See chapter 3 of *Coming to Grips with Genesis* or Terry Mortenson, *The Great Turning Point: the Church's Catastrophic Mistake on Geology — Before Darwin* (Green Forest, AR: Master Books, 2004).

average per year today. It's been a relatively uniform, slow and gradual process that has produced the rock layers and geological features of the earth.

In response to these two old-earth views, some scientists and non-scientists, who collectively became known as "scriptural geologists," defended the biblical, traditional view. They argued for a supernatural creation week of six literal days followed about 1,600 years later by Noah's Flood, which they believed produced most of the geological record of rock layers and fossils, and then the earth recovered from that event. They raised biblical, philosophical, and geological arguments against these old-earth views.

Early 19th Century Views of Earth History

Catastrophist view (e.g., Georges Cuvier, William Smith)
SB-------C---------C---------C----------C---------C----------C-------C--------P
("untold ages" = millions of years)

Uniformitarian view (e.g. James Hutton, Charles Lyell)
SB?--P
("untold ages" = millions of years)
Biblical/traditional view ("scriptural geologists")
SCW----NF-----------------P
(ca. 6000 years)

Code: SCW = Supernatural Creation Week, NF = Noah's Flood, P = Present
SB = Supernatural Beginning, C = Catastrophic flood

Old-earth Christian Compromise

But many other Christians quickly accepted the millions of years, even while the uniformitarians and catastrophists were debating. These Christians reinterpreted Genesis to accommodate all this "deep time." Some advocated the "gap theory," putting the millions of years between Genesis 1:1 and 1:3. Others argued that the days of creation were not literal but figurative of long periods of time (the "day-age" view). Noah's Flood was reduced to geological insignificance by viewing it as a peaceful flood or a localized flood in the Middle East. Theological liberals insisted that Genesis 1–11 was mythology.

By about 1840, the uniformitarian view became the ruling view in geology. Catastrophism was rejected and belief in a global Flood at the time of Noah was largely abandoned in the church. By the time of Charles Darwin's *Origin of Species* in 1859, virtually the whole church had rejected the biblical chronology and embraced the idea of millions of years. Around 1840 was also the time when geology became a paid profession. Prior to this it was a hobby practiced largely by independently wealthy people. Also, universities began to offer degrees in geology. All this meant that everyone who studied to become a professional geologist was trained to think like a uniformitarian.

Two Key Men and Three Key Assumptions

Two men were extremely important in the triumph of uniformitarianism in geology: James Hutton (1726–1797) in Scotland and Charles Lyell in England (1797–1875). Hutton published his *Theory of the Earth* in 1795, and building on that work Lyell's three-volume *Principles of Geology* appeared in 1830 to 1833. The uniformitarianism that they promoted was not derived from scientific experiments or observations of rock layers and fossils. Rather, it grew out of an anti-biblical, philosophical, and religious worldview. In subtle and not-so-subtle ways they advocated three key assumptions that took control of geology and have now taken control of all fields of science.

The first assumption they advocated indirectly was that nature is all that exists — or if there is a God, He only created the initial matter in a relatively simple form, endowed it with the laws of nature, and let the creation unfold or develop according to those laws. Hence, He is a distant, hands-off, never-intervening-in-creation kind of God. The assumption that nature is all that exists is the key assumption of atheism. Not all scientists are atheists, but most scientists for the past 150–200 years have done their scientific work *as if* nature is all that exists.

The second assumption that took control of geology (and now controls all of the sciences) is that in working out the past history of the earth (and of life and the universe), we must explain everything by time + chance + the laws of nature working on matter. James Hutton put it this way: "The past history of our globe must be explained by what can be seen to be happening now. . . . No powers are to be employed that are not natural to the globe, no action to be admitted except those of which we know the principle."[5] In other words, in reconstructing earth history, we must limit our explanations to *present, natural* processes. So, before he ever looked at the geological evidence, he ruled out creation and Noah's Flood. Neither creation nor the Flood were happening when he made this statement. Furthermore, creation (as described in Genesis 1) was supernatural, not the result of natural processes, and Noah's Flood was initiated and governed by

---

5. James Hutton, "Theory of the Earth," *Transactions of the Royal Society of Edinburgh*, 1785, quoted in A. Holmes, *Principles of Physical Geology* (UK: Thomas Nelson and Sons Ltd., 1965), p. 43–44.

God's supernatural intervention in the normal course of nature. The Flood was not just a fluke of nature.

Hutton wrote, "But, surely, general deluges form no part of the theory of the earth; for, the purpose of this earth is evidently to maintain vegetable and animal life, and not to destroy them."[6] In other words, look at the world. It is obviously designed to support plant and animal life. So, says Hutton, we can't allow a global flood in our reconstruction of earth history because that would destroy all plant and animal life. He was erroneously reasoning that "the present is the key to the past." Actually, God's biblical revelation is the key to understanding the present and the past. We need God's inerrant eyewitness testimony about the key events in the past so that we can correctly interpret the observable evidence in the present (e.g., rock layers, fossils, living creatures, DNA, sun, moon, stars, etc.) that is a result of unrepeatable and unobservable events in the past.

The third key assumption that Hutton, Lyell, and many other early geologists made (and is now embraced by the vast majority of scientists) is that the Bible is irrelevant to geology and that the Flood could not produce the rock layers and fossils. These geologists didn't prove these things scientifically or biblically. They simply assumed this. As an application of this assumption Lyell insisted,

> I have always been strongly impressed with the weight of an observation of an excellent writer and skillful geologist who said that "for the sake of revelation as well as of science—of truth in every form—the physical part of Geological inquiry ought to be conducted as if the Scriptures were not in existence."[7]

This is like trying to reconstruct Roman history by looking at ancient Roman artifacts but insisting that we ignore the eyewitness testimony of ancient Roman historians. Lyell was insisting on a very anti-biblical approach to the interpretation of the geological record. In fact, in a letter to another uniformitarian geologist, Lyell said he wanted to "free the science [of geology] from Moses."[8] In other words, he wanted to silence God's eyewitness testimony about creation, the Flood, and the age of the earth.

---

6. James Hutton, *Theory of the Earth* (Edinburgh: William Creech, 1795), vol. 1, p. 273.
7. Charles Lyell, Lecture II at King's College London on May 4, 1832, quoted in Martin J.S. Rudwick, "Charles Lyell Speaks in the Lecture Theatre," *The British Journal for the History of Science*, Vol. IX, Pt. 2, No. 32 (July 1976), p. 150.
8. Charles Lyell's letter to George P. Scrope on June 14, 1830, in Katharine Lyell (Lyell's sister-in-law), *Life, Letters and Journals of Sir Charles Lyell, Bart* (London: John Murray, 1881), I:268.

Naturalistic Uniformitarianism Spreads to Other Sciences

The idea that the history of the rocks of the earth could be and must be worked out by considering only *present, natural* processes operating at *present rates* (resulting in slow gradual change) over untold ages of time was absorbed and applied by Darwin in his "theory" about the origin and history of living creatures. He wrote,

> I always feel as if my books came half out of Lyell's brains and that I never acknowledge this sufficiently, nor do I know how I can, without saying so in so many words — for I have always thought that the great merit of the *Principles* [*of Geology*], was that it altered the whole tone of one's mind & therefore that when seeing a thing never seen by Lyell, one yet saw it partially through his eyes.[9]

Note carefully, neither Hutton nor Lyell nor Darwin was an unbiased objective pursuer of truth, just "letting the facts" (rocks, fossils, living creatures) "speak for themselves." There is no such person. Every scientist has a worldview, a set of assumptions about God (He exists or doesn't), God's involvement in the world (He's distant and inactive or ever-present and intervenes), and the Bible (it's God's inerrant Word or it's just the words of ancient pres-cientific fallible people). And that worldview affects what the scientist sees in the world and how he interprets what he sees. Hutton, Lyell, and Darwin were biased against God and His Word, just as creation scientists in the early 19th century or today are biased for God and His Word.

By the end of the 19th century, the consensus view of geologists was that the earth was at least 300 million years old. Radioactive isotopes were not discovered until 1896 and radiometric dating methods were not developed until 1906.[10] So geologists were locked into millions of years for a century before these dating methods were developed. And these dating methods are based on the same naturalistic, uniformitarian assumptions. On that

---

9.   Charles Darwin, *The Correspondence of Charles Darwin, Vol. 3* (Cambridge, UK: Cambridge Univ. Press, 1987), p. 55.

10.   Radioactive isotopes were discovered in 1896 by the French physicist Henri Becquerel (1852–1908). Heat from their decay negated Kelvin's conclusion, supporting the geologists' calls for hundreds of millions of years. Between 1903 and 1906, the famous New Zealand physicist Ernest Rutherford (1871–1937) determined that isotopes could be used to date rocks. See Terry Mortenson, "The Historical Development of the Old-Earth Geological Time-Scale," https://answersingenesis.org/age-of-the-earth/the-historical-development-of-the-old-earth-geological-time-scale/, August 8, 2007.

presuppositional basis, and with improved techniques for measuring isotopes in rocks, the age of the earth steadily expanded by about 1940 to today's age of about 4.6 billion years. The big bang theory for the origin of the universe over 13.8 billion years ago is based on the same naturalistic uniformitarian assumptions. Slow gradual processes of nature that we observe today can, given enough time, explain the origin of everything: stars and galaxies, planets and solar systems, the earth and its geological features, all living creatures, and man himself. Time is the hero of the plot. So we are told.

So, we really need to grasp the fact that evolution is a three-part story about the past to explain all of reality: cosmological, geological, and biological (including human) evolution. All of it is based on the worldview assumptions of naturalistic uniformitarianism.

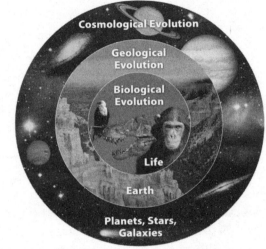

From Darwin to the Present

As I indicated above, by the time of Darwin's *Origin of Species* (1859) virtually the whole church had accepted the millions of years. Many great, godly, well-meaning Christian leaders and scholars, who helped the church in so many ways, continued to promote the acceptance of this old-earth idea over the next 150 years. I want to quote from a few of them to explain how the acceptance of millions of years became so widespread in the church over the past 150 years.

In an 1855 sermon as a young pastor, the great Baptist preacher Charles Spurgeon (1834–1892), spoke about "many millions of years before the time of Adam." He said, "Our planet has passed through various stages of existence, and different kinds of creatures have lived on its surface, all of which have been fashioned by God."[11] Trusting the claims of geologists, he apparently held to the gap theory. But in all his writings and sermons he never gave any significant attention to the Bible's teaching on the Flood or the age of the earth, though he did clearly reject biological evolution.

11. Charles H. Spurgeon, "The Power of the Holy Ghost" (sermon preached on June 17, 1855), *The New Park Street Pulpit* (Pasadena, TX: Pilgrim Publ. 1990), vol. 1, p. 230.

C.I. Scofield, whose 1909 reference Bible has gone into millions of Christian homes, had this statement in his marginal note of Gen. 1:2, which remained until the 1967 edition: "The first creative act refers to the dateless past, and gives scope for all the geologic ages. . . . Relegate fossils to the primitive creation, and no conflict of science with the Genesis cosmogony remains."[12] But it's not "science" versus Genesis: it's rather naturalistic interpretations of geological evidence that are contrary to Genesis.

R.A. Torrey (1856–1928), second president of Moody Bible Institute, was an old-earth, day-age proponent and one of the editors of *The Fundamentals*. This collection of 90 articles was published in 1910–1915 and sent free to English-speaking church leaders all over the world. Most of the articles are still helpful. Six of the 90 articles dealt with Genesis and science. While two articles opposed evolution, three clearly accepted the millions of years, and none of the others took a stand for the biblical chronology or globality of Noah's Flood.[13]

More recently, Gleason Archer (1916–2004), a great Old Testament scholar who held to the day-age view but rejected biological evolution, wrote,

> From a superficial reading of Genesis 1, the impression would seem to be that the entire creative process took place in six twenty-four-hour days. If this was the true intent of the Hebrew author . . . this seems to run counter to modern scientific research, which indicates that the planet Earth was created several billion years ago.[14]

But it is not the "scientific research" that indicated billions of years. Rather, it is naturalistic *interpretations* of some of the scientific evidence obtained from the research.

Denver seminary theologians Gordon Lewis and Bruce Demarest argue in their generally very helpful theology text for the day-age view, concluding that "ultimately, responsible geology must determine the length of the

---

12. C.I. Scofield, *The Holy Bible* (Lake Wylie, SC: Christian Heritage, 1917), p. 3-4. This *Scofield Reference Bible* was first published in 1909. This comment remained in the notes of subsequent editions for many decades. The notes of the 1967 edition are modified in several places in Genesis 1, but still are worded in such a way that leaves the door open to the acceptance of millions of years.

13. Terry Mortenson, "Exposing a Fundamental Compromise," https://answersingenesis.org/theistic-evolution/exposing-a-fundamental-compromise/, July 1, 2010.

14. Gleason Archer (1916–2004), *A Survey of Old Testament Introduction* (Chicago: Moody, 1985), p. 187.

Genesis days."[15] By "responsible geology" they clearly meant the consensus view in geology today. But why doesn't historical, grammatical, contextual exegesis determine the length of the creation days? Should responsible biology (i.e., the consensus view of evolutionary biologists) determine whether the virgin birth or Resurrection of Jesus were literal physical miracles or not?

Wayne Grudem, one of the most influential evangelical theologians today, says in his *Systematic Theology* (translated into 12 major languages with six more in progress),[16] "Although our conclusions are tentative, at this point in our understanding, Scripture seems to be more easily understood to *suggest* (but not to require) a young-earth view, while the observable facts of creation seem increasingly to favor an old-earth view."[17] But it is not the "observable facts of creation" that favor the old-earth view; it's the anti-biblical *assumptions* used to *interpret* the facts that leads to this view. I've tried many times since Dr. Grudem was my supervisor in seminary (1989–1992) to get him to reconsider this statement, but without success.[18]

C. John Collins, prominent Old Testament professor at Covenant Seminary and editor of the OT notes in the ESV Study Bible, said in defense of his old-earth, "analogical days" view of Genesis 1,

> I conclude, then that I have no reason to disbelieve the standard theories of the geologists, including their estimate for the age of the earth. They may be wrong, for all I know; but if they are wrong, it's not because they have improperly smuggled philosophical assumptions into their work.[19]

But as I have shown, this is *precisely* what the secular (and most Christian) geologists have done, knowingly or unknowingly: they have smuggled *anti-biblical* philosophical assumptions into their work. I've also tried many times to show Dr. Collins his error here. But he persists in it.

---

15. Gordon R. Lewis and Bruce A. Demarest, *Integrative Theology* (Grand Rapids: Zondervan, 1996), vol. 2, p. 29.

16. As of April 24, 2016; http://www.waynegrudem.com/how-can-i-find-your-book-systematic-theology-in-other-languages/.

17. Wayne Grudem, *Systematic Theology* (Downers Grove, IL: IVPress, 1994), p. 307 (italics in the original).

18. One of my many attempts was this paper, which he read but was unwilling to discuss with me: Terry Mortenson, "Systematic Theology Texts and the Age of the Earth: A Response to the Views of Erickson, Grudem, and Lewis and Demarest," https://answersingenesis.org/age-of-the-earth/systematic-theology-texts-and-the-age-of-the-earth/, Dec. 16, 2009.

19. C. John Collins, *Science and Faith: Friends or Foes?* (Wheaton, IL: Crossway, 2003), p. 250.

I could quote many other deceased and contemporary evangelical theologians, Bible scholars, philosophers, and apologists who have reasoned the same way and taught the church to accept millions of years. In fact, most Christian college and seminary professors don't believe Genesis regarding Noah's Flood and age of the earth. But as I have read many of their writings or interacted with them, I see no evidence that they recognized or understood the role of anti-biblical *presuppositions* used in the *interpretations* of the geological evidence that supposedly proves millions of years. They also fail to see the serious gospel problem of having millions of years of death, disease, violence, and extinction in the non-human creation before Adam's Fall.[20]

The Surprising Challenge to Uniformitarianism

This is unfortunate because had they lived to see or if they became aware of what has been happening in geology over the last 40 years, I think many of these Christian leaders would have thought differently about Genesis and the age of the earth. Lyell's uniformitarianism ruled geology for 130 years, but something every unexpected happened in the mid-20th century.

First, in 1961, Henry Morris and John Whitcomb published their epic book *The Genesis Flood*, which launched the modern young-earth creationist movement. Since then a number of Ph.D. creation geologists and paleontologists have marshaled abundant geological evidence confirming the truth of Genesis.[21]

Secondly, in the 1970s, some influential evolutionary, old-earth geologists began to reject uniformitarianism and return to the idea of catastrophism. One prominent evolutionist was Derek Ager (1923–1993), who was professor and head of the Geology Department at University College Swansea (in Wales) for 19 years and one-time president of the British Geological Association (1988–1990). He visited 57 countries to study the rocks, and he wrote 200 papers and five books on geology. In his last book, *The New Catastrophism*, published posthumously, Ager tells us,

20. For a short article on this, see Ken Ham, "Millions of Years — Are Souls at Stake?" https://answersingenesis.org/theory-of-evolution/millions-of-years/are-souls-at-stake/, Jan. 1, 2014. For a fuller discussion, see Terry Mortenson, "The Fall and the Problem of Millions of Years of Natural Evil," https://answersingenesis.org/theory-of-evolution/millions-of-years/the-fall-and-the-problem-of-millions-of-years-of-natural-evil/, July 18, 2012.

21. For an introduction to that geological evidence, see John Morris, *The Young Earth* (Green Forest, AR: Master Books, 2007). For more depth, see Andrew Snelling, *Earth's Catastrophic Past* (Green Forest, AR: Master Books, 2010).

Just as politicians rewrite human history, so geologists rewrite earth history. For a century and a half, the geological world has been dominated, one might even say brainwashed, by the gradualistic uniformitarianism of Charles Lyell. Any suggestion of "catastrophic" events has been rejected as old-fashioned, unscientific, and even laughable.[22]

He added, "Perhaps I am becoming a cynic in my old age, but I cannot help thinking that people find things that they expect to find. As Sir Edward Bailey (1953) said, 'to find a thing you have to believe it to be possible.' "[23] Ager had come to believe that major catastrophes were possible and in fact were responsible for much of the geological record. But to his death, and due to his expressed hostility to the Bible as a pantheist,[24] he never allowed the global Flood of Noah as a possibility in his thinking. So, he never found the evidence that was staring him in the face on every continent. Most geologists before and after Ager (including most Christian geologists) have missed the evidence for the Flood for the very same reason.

The famous professor of geology and paleontology at Harvard University, Stephen J. Gould, informs us,

Charles Lyell was a lawyer by profession, and his book is one of the most brilliant briefs published by an advocate. . . . Lyell relied upon true bits of cunning to establish his uniformitarian views as the only true geology. First, he set up a straw man to demolish. In fact, the catastrophists were much more empirically minded than Lyell. The geologic record does seem to require catastrophes: rocks are fractured and contorted; whole faunas are wiped out. To circumvent this literal appearance, Lyell imposed his imagination upon the evidence. The geologic record, he argued, is extremely imperfect and we must interpolate into it what we can reasonably infer but cannot see. The catastrophists were the hard-nosed empiricists of their day, not the blinded theological apologists.[25]

22. Derek Ager, *The New Catastrophism* (Cambridge, UK: Cambridge Univ. Press, 1993), p. xi.
23. Ibid., p. 190–191.
24. Ibid., p. xi, xix, and 196.
25. Stephen J. Gould, *Natural History*, (Feb. 1975), p. 16.

Actually, it was the "scriptural geologists" that I studied in my PhD research[26] who were really the hard-nosed empiricists of their day — paying close attention to God's eyewitness testimony of Scripture as well as the data of geology, and using the biblical testimony as the key to correctly interpret the geological evidence.

So, again, the rocks don't "speak for themselves." They must be interpreted. And a person's worldview (or religious/philosophical) assumptions will greatly affect what a person observes and how he interprets what he observes. For the past 200 years, most geologists have used anti-biblical naturalistic presuppositions to interpret the rocks.

Those same naturalistic assumptions also took control of astronomy and biology and all other fields of science. Many Christians reject biological evolution (including human evolution), but they accept the big bang and the geological ages. However, it is important to realize that evolution is really a three-layered theory to explain all of reality simply by time and chance and the laws of nature. All are driven by naturalism and the denial of God's Word, including what it says about Adam, the Fall, and the gospel.

The Apostle Paul warned in 2 Corinthians 10:3–5 that we are involved in a great spiritual battle.

> For though we walk in the flesh, we do not war according to the flesh, for the weapons of our warfare are not of the flesh, but divinely powerful for the destruction of fortresses. We are destroying speculations and every lofty thing raised up against the knowledge of God, and we are taking every thought captive to the obedience of Christ.[27]

We are either taking every thought captive to the obedience of Christ (which means captive to His Word) or we will fall prey to high and lofty speculations (masquerading as "science") that are raised up against the knowledge of God and therefore against His Word. Paul also warned in Colossians 2:8, "See to it that no one takes you captive through philosophy and empty deception, according to the tradition of men, according to the elementary principles of the world, rather than according to Christ." Either we are captive to the Word of Christ or we are captive to the traditions and philosophies of men.

And let's remember, the whole Bible (including Genesis) is the Word of Christ, not just the red words in the Gospels.

---

26. See Terry Mortenson, *The Great Turning Point*, and my DVD lecture by the same title as this chapter, https://answersingenesis.org/store/product/millions-of-years/?sku=30-9-500.
27. Scripture in this chapter is from the New American Standard Bible (NASB).

Conclusion

Today in the Western world the evolutionists are getting more and more aggressive in pushing biological, geological, astronomical, and anthropological evolution as a weapon against Christianity. At the same time, an increasing number of evangelical scholars are encouraging the church to accept evolution and are questioning or even denying that there was a literal Adam and literal Fall.[28] How did we get to this state of affairs? In 1 Corinthians 5:6 Paul said, "a little leaven leavens the whole lump of dough." The idea of millions of years was the leaven.

For the first 1,800 years of church history, the almost universal belief of faithful Christians was a literal six-day creation about 6,000 years ago, and a global Noachian Flood. Since the early 1800s we have witnessed the slippery slide in the church away from biblical truth. The teaching of evolution and millions of years has been a major cause of that slide, and without the widespread acceptance of millions of years in the early 19th century, Darwin's theory of evolution would have been dead in the womb. Once the church compromised with the lie of millions of years, it had no sustainable defense against the lie of evolution. As a result, most of the church today has been taken captive by speculations and philosophy masquerading as "science."

Scripture is right: a little leaven leavens the whole lump. Small error that doesn't seem to hurt anything grows into big error that becomes a massive assault on the gospel. The church's compromise 200 years ago with the idea of millions of years has been the foundation of the growing spiritual confusion and moral anarchy in America, the UK, Western Europe, Australia, and many other countries. The battle over the age of the earth is one of the most important issues facing the church today.

The dogma of millions of years is one of the greatest attacks on the clarity, reliability, and authority of Scripture, and therefore on the truth of the gospel. The church needs to repent of its compromise with the traditions and philosophies of sinful man. Our final authority must be the Word of God.

---

28. See Terry Mortenson, ed., *Searching for Adam: Genesis and the Truth about Man's Origin* (Green Forest, AR: Master Books, 2016).

> *How many church planters in cities in the UK and the USA have trained their missionaries to refute secular humanism, Darwinism, atheism, etc.? ...Tax dollars are spent on the secular religions through schools, state-funded museums, science journals, and so on. All the while, there is a false claim that 'secularists aren't religious.'*

7 SECULAR, EVOLUTIONARY, AND ATHEISTIC RELIGIONS

Since 2003, **BODIE HODGE** has worked with Answers in Genesis, serving currently as a writer, speaker, and researcher. He also served in the ministry's Outreach Department and has overseen the Correspondence Department, and been part of the Creation Museum Speaker series. The various roles he has served in have allowed him to correspond with countless believers, as well as seekers, skeptics, and hardened nonbelievers.

With a BSEd degree in biology from Montana State University, **ROGER PATTERSON** is a steady contributor to the Answers in Genesis website, featuring numerous articles that engage newsworthy and cultural issues and questions of faith, science, and theological truth.

Secular religions (atheism, evolutionism, agnosticism, secular humanism, naturalism, etc.) possess a unique status in our Western world. Having a past that has typically been uneventful, the 1800s saw an explosion of these religious variants.

Fueled by the likes of Charles Lyell in the 1830s (geological evolution or "millions of years") and Charles Darwin beginning in 1859 (biological evolution from a common ancestor), the secular takeover of the West continued. We still see the fruit of these religious views in our day and age.

Secular religions now dominate areas like the media, education, law, museums, sexual expression, and, sadly, the minds of the next generation according to recent statistics.[1] This makes sense, since secular religious views flow freely in the education system due to secular laws imposed upon state schools. Young minds are molded into secular form, and few realize it until it is too late.

In the Western world (United States, United Kingdom, Germany, etc.), these secular religions are the biggest stumbling block for the next generation of Christians and Christian missionaries seeking to proclaim the gospel. The once great West, whose churches sent missionaries out to the whole world, is now crumbling at a foundational level due in part to the influence of secularism. Secular religious doctrines are even infiltrating the church!

Essentially, the West needs missionaries to rise up and "rebuild the wall," so to speak, of the church in the West. But to do so, we need to deal decisively with the religion of the day — the secularism that stands like Goliath in our culture. So how do we, as a church, deal with it?

Immunizing the New Missionaries

Consider this hypothetical situation with which missionaries have to deal. Missionaries are sent to minister with the gospel to a place that has deadly diseases. The missionaries contract a disease and the missionaries die. You send more missionaries; they contract the same disease and die.

Now, if you were a sending church, what would you do? Do you simply send more missionaries to their potential doom? Or do you take the time to prepare your missionaries with the proper protection for what they are about to encounter — medicine or inoculation from the disease? Obviously, you want to protect your missionaries and give them what they need to be effective for the gospel work for which they are sent.

---

1. See Ken Ham and Britt Beemer with Todd Hillard, *Already Gone* (Green Forest, AR: Master Books, 2009); Ken Ham with Jeff Kinsley, *Ready to Return* (Green Forest, AR: Master Books, 2015).

Now consider this same problem, but from a spiritual angle, in our Western world. The United States and the United Kingdom were once nations greatly influenced by Christians, and churches could be found in abundance, particularly in cities. But now, churches have closed their doors *en masse* in many places in England. The same trend is happening to the United States, albeit at a delayed pace.

Today, cities have precious few churches, and those that are there are typically shallow with little doctrine (there are exceptions) and compromise the authority of God's Word. In other words, they are struggling and dying themselves. Many Christians recognize that there is a need for churches in cities. The cities like Cincinnati, New York, Salt Lake City, Los Angeles, Chicago, London, and Bristol are ripe for church plants.

Interestingly, few of these church plants are as effective as they hoped. Some church plants grow slowly, others plateau, some merely take people from other churches, and others struggle and die. A lot of excuses are given — wrong church model, not enough funding, wrong music, too traditional, etc. But the main problem is that they were not dealing with the false religion that has entwined the people of the mission field.

When a missionary goes to Africa or the Amazon or Papua New Guinea, they train themselves to know what religions are in the area (e.g., Animism, Islam, Spiritism, etc.), and they learn how to refute those false beliefs so they can be an effective witness in presenting the truth of the Bible and the gospel. They don't go with the intent of just telling people to be moral and to add Jesus to what they believe.

How many church planters in cities in the UK and the USA have trained their missionaries to refute secular humanism, Darwinism, atheism, etc.? How many pastors in church plants in New York are trained to refute secular attacks on Christianity like radiometric dating, alleged missing links, big bang, and so on?

The even bigger problem is that many of the church planters may have *agreed* with the secularists and believe big bang is true, embrace millions of years, or even prefer evolution over the Bible's origins account. Imagine if we sent a missionary to Muslims who had bought into many tenets of Islam!

While we must certainly affirm that the message of the gospel is the power of God to salvation, apologetics is an important aspect of evangelism. While we proclaim the truth of Jesus as Lord and Savior, we must also help others see how their own religious views are insufficient to deal with their sin. We might also need to answer questions that explain the foundational elements of how sin entered the world and why they need a Savior.

If a missionary is not refuting the false religion prevalent in their mission field (i.e., secularism in much of the Western world), then why would we expect that missionary to be effective? Dealing with secularism and refuting it is a key to mission work in the "new" Western world. But refuting it is only part of the step. Secular refutations should not be divorced from the preaching of the gospel and teaching disciples to obey all Jesus commanded, embracing the authority of the Bible in all areas — starting in Genesis.

What Are Secular Religions?

There are a lot of forms of secularism. They are religions that are humanistic (i.e., man is the supreme authority). Here is a list of some of the forms or aspects of secular/humanistic religions:

- Atheism and New Atheism
- Agnosticism
- Existentialism
- Extra-terrestrial Humanism
- "Nonreligious" Religious Humanism
- Naturalism
- Stoicism
- Materialism
- Relativism
- Nazism
- Hedonism (including perverted sexual expression)
- Communism
- Nature Worship
- Idealism/Dualism
- Satanism (Church of Satan)
- Epicureanism (Evolutionism)
- Modernism
- Scientism
- Post-modernism
- Secular Humanism

As you can see, there is a wide variety of secular/humanistic religious views. Those who profess a humanistic religion often blend these aspects in various ways. For example, a person might identify generally as an atheist and hold to a materialistic view of the universe and a relativistic understanding of morality. Professor Richard Dawkins is a new atheist but also believes in aliens/extra-terrestrial life as a possible explanation for the origin of life on earth. Bill Nye professes to be an agnostic (he can't know for certain if God exists), but then proceeds to argue from an atheistic perspective (no God exists, cf. Psalm 14:1).

Sometimes these religions have great variations even while sharing many commonalities. For example, Hedonism promotes sexual perversions like homosexuality (e.g., LGBT) when Nazism absolutely opposed it. Yet both share the same view that man is the supreme authority, and both share an evolutionary view of origins, opposing the Bible, looking to bring human prosperity, etc.

Some of these are philosophical aspects that are utilized by each variant — like naturalism, materialism, and relativism. Even *within* the various flavors of humanistic religions you can have variations. For example, within hedonism (cf., Ecclesiastes 9:7–10) there are two very different forms:

> Quantitative Hedonism (get as much as you can for your enjoyment before you die)

> Qualitative Hedonism (enjoy the highest quality of things in life before you die)

There are even variations within atheism. One view presents itself from *classical atheism* (says there is no God(s) but refrains from caring what others believe, also known as soft atheism) and then there is *new atheism* (which doesn't believe God(s) exists but tries to force this view on others, also known as hard atheism).

Consider what the Bible says:

> In those days there was no king in Israel. Everyone did what was right in his own eyes (Judges 17:6).[2]

> That we may no longer be children, tossed to and fro by the waves and carried about by every wind of doctrine, by human cunning, by craftiness in deceitful schemes (Ephesians 4:14).

It should not surprise us that a religious view that sets man as the authority has as many variations as there are people — since all people consider themselves to be the captain of their own soul. Man can invent all sorts of evil (Romans 1:30) and diversity of evil and deceptive doctrine (2 Timothy 3:12–13). These things should be tested against the absolute standard of God's Word (1 Thessalonians 5:21).

---

2.   Scripture in this chapter is from the English Standard Version (ESV) of the Bible.

How Secular Religions Took over the West — and the Failure of the Church to Properly Respond

About 200 years ago, the United States and England were strongly influenced by Christianity. England, at least in a legal sense, is a Protestant nation headed by a Protestant monarch. The queen or king is the Supreme Governor of the Anglican Church. They cannot take the throne without being of the Protestant faith — there is a long history to this establishment. This influence extended to the British colonies and the nations that developed from those colonies.

But when we see the culture today, the USA, UK, and many other Western nations are highly secular. The ubiquity and brazen display of lies, immorality, murder, greed, hatred of Christians, child sacrifice, idolatry, the love of money, and many other evils are a daily reminder that our culture has changed. So how did it get this way? One part of the answer is the failure of the church to seriously engage these issues. And, *Deo volente* (God willing), they will be in a better position to address the trend. But the church has failed in two areas:

1. Instead of combatting the slow secularization that began to unfold in the West in the early 1800s, many in the church and their leaders embraced various aspects of secularization.
2. The church gave most teaching of children over to a third party (that became secular), so subsequent generations within the church were not equipped and fell to the secular onslaught.

In America in the 1800s for example, Christians began giving their children over to state schools to educate them. At the time, it seemed like a good idea, as state schools used the Bible in the classroom. They used it to teach history, logic, philosophy, literature, science, and so forth.

So the church, by and large, didn't have to focus on those subjects. Instead, they began concentrating on teaching the gospel, theology, and morality. As man's ideas about long ages, millions of years, astronomical evolution, and biological evolution began taking over school systems, most Christians either didn't notice or fell victim themselves.

By 1925, geological evolution (millions of years) and animal evolution were being taught in schools with full backing by the state. As human evolution began to be taught, the battle lines finally erupted with the famous Scopes Trial.

Even so, as the humanistic religion began to permeate the state schools under the influence of men like John Dewey, the Bible was removed, creation was taken out, prayer was silenced, the 10 Commandments banished, and so on. Now entire generations of kids have been raised up being taught the religion of secular humanism.

But what did the church do to specifically counter this false religious teaching? By and large — nothing! Many churches still teach morality, the gospel, and theology (not that these are bad things) but then most parents (90% by the latest stats)[3] still send their children to state schools to be taught a different religion.

So for about 40 hours a week, kids from Christian homes are taught the religious tenets of secular humanism, and the church (who scarcely teaches the kids 2–3 hours per week) wonders why the kids are walking away from the faith and following after humanistic religions. Those that remain in the church have often brought secular baggage with them. They often hold to evolution and millions of years, secular morality, secular views of sexuality, marriage, race, and so on.

What does this do to a local church? It causes it to be stagnant, impotent, or die as members are actually mixing secular religions with their Christianity. It is no different from the former godly Israelites in the Old Testament mixing true worship of God with worship of Baal. The mere difference is with *which religion* the modern Christians mix their Christianity — secularism rather than Baal.

With this in mind, we as Christians have to "pull the plank out of our own eye" in the Church before we "reach for the speck of sawdust" in the culture's eye. The church needs to get back on the right track first. Thus, the church has a big job to reeducate their congregations in the truth of the Bible in all areas like history, science, logic, and so forth. See chapter 5 for a discussion on how Christians mix or syncretize long ages with Genesis.

Secularists: "But We Don't Have a Religion!"

The secularists are the first to cry, "We are not part of a religion!" "We are irreligious" or "nones" or "non-religious." Why is this the case? There are a couple of reasons.

First, they don't want to be kicked out of the place of influence in the government school classrooms. Second, the secularist can more easily deceive kids into thinking that it is okay to believe what they teach and that it should have no conflicts with their respective religious beliefs.

---

3.   Ken Ham, "Yes, We Are Losing the Millennials," Answers in Genesis, May 13, 2015, https://answersingenesis.org/christianity/church/yes-we-are-losing-millennials.

Secular and humanistic religions like evolution, atheism, and agnosticism are part and parcel of the same pie. They have free reign under tax-supported dollars in the UK, USA, Australia, Germany, and so many others. It is strange that Christianity was kicked out of the classroom and yet another religion is taught in its place.

Tax dollars are spent on the secular religions through schools, state-funded museums, science journals, and so on. All the while, there is a false claim that "secularists aren't religious."

There is a simple way to test this claim. If something isn't religious, then it cannot oppose religious claims. Does the secular origins view (big bang, millions of years, and evolution) oppose the religious claim of special creation by God in 6 days and subsequently a young earth? Yes. Thus, secular views are religious. Anyone who claims that they are not religious and then makes judgments about religious topics (e.g., the deity of Christ, the existence of God, the morality of adultery, the truthfulness of the Bible, etc.) has made a religious statement. Though they may claim to be irreligious, they show that they are religious by attempting to oppose and refute another religious view.

Does atheism, which says "there is no God," oppose the religious claim that God exists (as found in the pages of the Bible)? Again, yes. Thus, atheism is religious. It is easy to prove that humanistic religions are religious.

But even many secularists openly admit to their faith. One instance is John Dunphy while writing for a secular magazine:

> I am convinced that the battle for humankind's future must be waged and won in the public school classroom by teachers who correctly perceive their role as the proselytizers of a new faith: a religion of humanity that recognizes and respects the spark of what theologians call divinity in every human being. These teachers must embody the same selfless dedication as the most rabid fundamentalist preachers, for they will be ministers of another sort, utilizing a classroom instead of a pulpit to convey humanist values in whatever subject they teach, regardless of the educational level — preschool day care or large state university. The classroom must and will become an arena of conflict between the old and the new — the rotting corpse of Christianity, together with all its adjacent evils and misery, and the new faith of humanism.[4]

---

4.   J. Dunphy, "A Religion for a New Age," *The Humanist*, Jan.–Feb. 1983, p. 23.

The US Supreme Court in *Torcaso v. Watkins*, 81 S.Ct. 1681 (1961), stated the following: "Among religions in this country which do not teach what would generally be considered a belief in the existence of God, are Buddhism, Taoism, Ethical Culture, Secular Humanism, and others." Additionally, these groups are eligible for the same tax benefits as other religious groups, and secular and atheist chaplains even function within the military. You can't have your cake and eat it too. Humanists are religious, and they act in religious ways.

Refutations

Secular worldviews like atheism and the like have serious problems. When refuting false worldviews, there are three ways that are typically used to prove them false. They are:

1. Arbitrariness
2. Inconsistency
3. Borrowing from the Bible (preconditions of intelligibility)

Arbitrariness includes things like mere opinions, relativism, conjectures (prejudicial), and unargued biases.

Inconsistencies include logical fallacies, "actions speak louder than words" in behavior and attitudes, presupposition issues that are irrational, and views that are *reduced to absurdity* based on where the argument is heading.

Borrowing from the Bible is couched in philosophical terminology like preconditions of intelligibility. In brief, it is when a worldview cannot account for something that is foundational. For example, in a materialistic worldview, why would love exist? Love is not material. You don't drink some love to increase your daily dose of love.

So, when a secular materialist claims they love something or someone, then it is highlighting a problem with their preconditions. In other words, the materialist in this case believes love exists, but his religious convictions say otherwise. Some of the problems with secular viewpoints will be analyzed using these criteria (arbitrariness, inconsistencies, etc.) without being exhaustive, of course.

Arbitrariness

In the case of God and His Word, they are not arbitrary. This is because there is no greater authority than God (cf., Hebrews 6:13). There is no greater authority that can be appealed to than God — and, by extension, His Word.

However, all secular views fail to appeal to God as their final authority, instead appealing to man. Man is a lesser authority and not absolute. Thus, any authority of man is a mere opinion to the absolute and supreme authority of God and His Word. All secular religions are based on the ideas of fallible man and thus arbitrary next to God.

The fact that many secular religions deviate from one another in their belief systems shows how relative they are regarding man's opinions. Thus, relativism reigns supreme among them. But relativism is fallacious, being arbitrary. So, from two fronts, secular religions fail to pass the test.

In response, some secularists have touted that there is variation among Christians and the outworkings of the Bible, thus the Bible is arbitrary, too. However, this misses the point — it is not about what Christians believe, but about what God says. Christian outworkings (e.g., denominations, church splits, doctrinal misinterpretations) are based on man's (less than perfect) understanding of the Scripture. But this has nothing to do with God being the absolute authority. Just because an authority is misinterpreted or misunderstood does not undermine its authority.

Inconsistent

Have you noticed that many secularists want to be good and want to do the moral thing? Herein lies the problem. If there is no God who sets what is right and wrong or defines good and bad, then why be moral and how can "good" be defined? It is utterly inconsistent to try to do good or be moral when your religion, *at its very base*, says there is no need or compulsion to do so.

We've seen atheists, agnostics, hedonists, and others get upset with brutality, people lying and deceiving, and terrorist activities, and yet, they hold to positions that encourage abortion (murdering babies in the womb). Note the inconsistency.

Christians are commonly attacked for believing God's authority regarding the truth of the Bible, but they turn around and hold to a position based on trusting man's authority! Think of it like this:

> Secular claim: You Christians blindly take the Bible as an authority because the Bible tells you to.
> Christian response: By what authority do you reject God's Word?
> Secular response: I read a book (or heard someone) that told me to believe the Bible is wrong, and I trust them.

Again, note the inconsistency. The difference is that man's authority is mean-ingless when compared to the absolute authority that is God's Word. If God *is* God, then what authority would supersede God's? There is none. God must reveal Himself as the final and superior authority.

Another secular claim, particularly from empiricists, is that "seeing is believing." They argue that truth claims can only be known through the senses. But there is an inconsistency here. How does the secularist know that alleged truth claim is true? Their senses are not involved in that alleged truth claim (that all truth claims can only be known through the senses). To fur-ther elaborate, they claim that all truth claims are known by senses, but how do they know that? Did they see or sense that truth? Sadly, they usually hold such a position because someone told them to — like a book or teacher.

Secular religions are largely materialistic and naturalistic. Matter (including energy and space-time) is all that exists — nature is all that exists . . . thus, the term naturalism. This stands in direct opposition to the Chris-tian worldview based on the Bible where the supernatural also exists. God is God of both the natural and supernatural (i.e., spiritual realm). This is why Christians are not as limited as secularists on many issues.

But a materialistic/naturalistic worldview causes undeniable problems for secular views. If matter is all that exists, then nonmaterial (immaterial) things cannot exist. There are many things that cannot exist if materialism is correct. They include:

- Logic
- Truth
- Abstractions
- Propositions
- Concepts
- Rights
- Shame
- Reason
- Knowledge
- Dignity
- Honor
- Love
- Sadness

It would be inconsistent (i.e., a behavioral inconsistency) for a secularist to appeal to logic, reason, truth, etc., to argue for a secular worldview that says immaterial things cannot exist!

Another absurd inconsistency reveals itself during discussions of God's Word being the authority. Some secularists go so far as to proclaim that they don't believe the Bible, as though that settles the debate. But it doesn't. When a secularist (or anyone else) professes that they disagree with the Bible, then they are claiming to be God. To disagree with God is to view oneself as God. This is fallacious reasoning.

Allow me to explain this further. When one claims to disagree with God, then they are elevating their own thoughts to be greater than an omniscience, omnipotent, and omnipresent God. Therefore, one is (usually inadvertently) elevating themselves to *be that* God! This is clearly absurd.

Borrow from the Bible

Many secularists live their lives borrowing from God's Word, though they fail to realize it. If people are merely evolved animals and there is no God, then who sets right and wrong, and why wear clothes? Why get married? Why get an education? Squirrels don't set up universities to discuss philosophical methodology.

Why celebrate the popular Christian holidays called weekends, which is based on the Sabbath Day and the Lord's Day? Why have holidays anyway? A holiday is a holy day, yet there exists nothing holy in a secular worldview.

Why heal sick people (medicine) when survival of the fittest should take its course as it has in the past without our interference. Why have laws? God may set laws, but if we are our own authority, then law is meaningless.

Why waste time on science? In fact, how can the secularist know the laws of nature won't change tomorrow? From a Christian perspective, God has promised to uphold nature as it is in the future. From a secular viewpoint, they can't know the future will be uniform. If they argue that it has always been like that, then it begs the very question at hand! Thus, it is a fallacious circular argument. Yes, even the possibility of observable and repeatable science is based on God's Word being true.

Conclusion

When it comes down to it, secular views fail on a number of aspects. Sadly, many have been deceived into believing that secular worldviews are the truth, when in fact truth cannot exist if secular worldviews are correct (as truth is not material).

Our hope is that those caught up in secular religions, whether they knew it or not, will repent. Our hope is to see them realize the truth of the

Scripture by the power of the Holy Spirit. Secular religions ultimately say things came from nothing, are going to nothing, and nothing matters. But with Christianity, there is the power of hope based on a truthful God who made a way to save us for all eternity.

> *Even Darwin was willing to admit that there may be evidence that would invalidate his hypothesis. That is no longer the view held by the vast majority of evolutionists today — evolution has become a 'fact,' even a 'scientific law' (on par with the law of gravity), in the minds of many.*

8

ARE THERE DIFFERENT MODELS OF EVOLUTION?

DR. TERRY MORTENSON is a historian of geology, a theologian, and a speaker, writer, and researcher for Answers in Genesis. Prior to joining AiG, he served for 26 years with Campus Crusade for Christ in the U.S. and in Eastern Europe. He holds an MDiv from Trinity Evangelical Divinity School and a PhD in the history of geology from Coventry University in England, and he is an active member of the Evangelical Theological Society. Since the late 1970s he has lectured on creation and evolution in 28 countries. He has written, edited, and contributed to many books and articles.

With a BS Ed degree in biology from Montana State University, **ROGER PATTERSON** has been featured in DVDs and ministry materials of Answers in Genesis. He was also a speaker at the World Religions Conference in 2017 and author of *Evolution Exposed: Biology*, which has sold over 100,000 copies. He has numerous articles on the Answers in Genesis website regarding cultural issues and faith questions.

C harles Darwin first published his ideas on evolution in 1859. Since then, we have come to understand the complexity of life, and many new scientific fields have shed light on the question of the validity of Darwin's evolutionary hypothesis.

Few people have actually read the works of Darwin and if they did, they might be shocked to read some of Darwin's ideas. In this chapter, we are going to take a look at what Darwin and other early evolutionists believed and how those ideas have changed over time ("evolved," if you will).

Darwin was wrong on many points, and there would be few who would disagree with this claim. But, if Darwin was wrong on some points, does that mean that the entire hypothesis of evolution is proven wrong?

What Is Evolution?

Like many words, *evolution* has many different uses, depending on its context. The general concept of the word is "change over time." In that sense, one might say that a butterfly evolves from an egg to a caterpillar to a winged butterfly, and a child evolves into an adult. There is no disputing that individual organisms change over time. However, using the word in this way is quite misleading for the origins debate. Darwin's hypothesis involves a very different concept.

As evolution is used in this chapter and in all science textbooks, natural history museums, and science programs on TV, it refers to the biological idea that all life on earth has descended from a single common ancestor. There are many different variations on this theme as well as several explanations of how the first organism came into existence from non-living matter.

Examining some of the historical evolutionary positions and comparing them to the ideas that are popular in scientific circles today shows how much those concepts have changed. In general, evolution will be used to refer to the concept of molecules turning into men over time. This concept of evolution is in direct opposition to the biblical account of creation presented in the Book of Genesis.[1]

Evolution — an Ancient Idea

The concept of organisms changing over time is certainly not a new idea. Several Greek philosophers before the time of Christ wrote on the topic. For example, Lucretius and Empedocles promoted a form of natural selection

---

1. For an explanation of some of the contradictions between the biblical creation account and the widely held evolution story, see the article "Evolution vs. Creation: The Order of Events Matters!" at www.answersingenesis.org/docs2006/0404order.asp.

that did not rely on any type of purpose. In *De Rerum Natura (On the Nature of Things)* Lucretius writes:

> And many species of animals must have perished at that time, unable by procreation to forge out the chain of posterity: for whatever you see feeding on the breath of life, either cunning or courage or at least quickness must have guarded and kept that kind from its earliest existence. . . . But those to which nature gave no such qualities, so that they could neither live by themselves at their own will, nor give us some usefulness for which we might suffer to feed them under our protection and be safe, these certainly lay at the mercy of others for prey and profit, being all hampered by their own fateful chains, until nature brought that race to destruction.[2]

This stands in opposition to the thinking of Aristotle who promoted the idea of purpose in nature. Aristotle also saw forms of life advancing through history, but he believed nature had the aim of producing beauty.[3] This idea of purpose in nature, or teleology, is later seen in the works of Thomas Aquinas and other Christian philosophers.

The concept of evolution was not lost from Western thinking until Darwin and his immediate precursors rediscovered it — it was always present in various forms. Because much of the scientific thinking was dominated by Aristotelian ideas, the idea of a purposeless evolutionary process was not popular. Most saw a purpose in nature and the interactions between living things.

The dominance of the Roman Catholic Church in Europe (Europe is where modern science was born) and its adherence to Aristotelian philosophies also played a role in limiting the promotion of evolution and other contrary ideas, as these would have been seen as heresy. As the Enlightenment took hold in Europe in the 17th and 18th centuries, explanations that looked beyond a directed cause became more popular.

Erasmus Darwin

Coming to the mid-to-late 18th century, Kant, Liebnitz, Buffon, and others begin to talk openly of a natural force that has driven the change of organisms from simple to complex over time. The idea of evolution

2.   Sharon Kaye, "Was There No Evolutionary Thought in the Middle Ages? The Case of William of Ockham," *British Journal for the History of Philosophy* 14 no. 2 (2006): 225–244.

3.   Henry Fairfield Osborn, *From the Greeks to Darwin* (London: Macmillan, 1913), p. 43–56.

was well-established in the literature, but there seemed to be no legitimate mechanism to adequately explain this idea in scientific terms.

Following the spirit of the Greek poets Lucretius and Empedocles, Erasmus Darwin, the atheist grandfather of Charles, wrote some of his ideas in poetic verse. Brushing up against the idea of survival of the fittest, Erasmus speaks of the struggle for existence between different animals and even plants. This struggle is a part of the evolutionary process he outlines in his *Temple of Nature* in the section titled "Production of Life":

> Hence without parent by spontaneous birth
> Rise the first specks of animated earth;
> From Nature's womb the plant or insect swims,
> And buds or breathes, with microscopic limbs.[4]

And he continues:

> Organic Life beneath the shoreless waves
> Was born and nursed in Ocean's pearly caves;
> First forms minute, unseen by spheric glass,
> Move on the mud, or pierce the watery mass;
> These, as successive generations bloom,
> New powers acquire, and larger limbs assume;
> Whence countless groups of vegetation spring,
> And breathing realms of fin, and feet, and wing.[5]

Starting with spontaneous generation from inanimate matter, Erasmus imagined life evolving into more complex forms over time. He did not identify any mechanisms that may have caused the change, other than general references to nature and a vague driving force.

In the introduction to this work, Erasmus Darwin states that it is not intended to instruct but, rather, to amuse, and he then includes many notes describing his ideas. Despite his claimed-to-be innocent intentions, this poem lays out the gradual progression of matter to living creature — simple to complex, a view very consciously different from the biblical account of creation with which the vast majority of his contemporaries were quite familiar.

He traces the development of life in the seas to life on land, with the four-footed creatures eventually culminating in humans and the creation of

---

4. Erasmus Darwin, *The Temple of Nature* (London: Jones & Company, 1825), p. 13.
5. Ibid., p. 14–15.

society.[6] There is no doubt that when Charles began his studies, the idea of evolution apart from the supernatural was present in Western thought (even in his own extended family). The arguments in support of special creation were certainly prominent, but evolutionary ideas were being pressed into mainstream thinking in the era of modernism.[7]

To underscore the early acceptance of evolution, the following passage from *Zoonomia* illustrates his belief that all life had come from a common "filament" of life.

> From thus meditating on the great similarity of the structure of the warm-blooded animals . . . would it be too bold to imagine that, in the great length of time since the earth began to exist, perhaps millions of ages before the commencement of the history of mankind would it be too bold to imagine that all warm-blooded animals have arisen from one living filament?[8]

Lamarckian Evolution or Use and Disuse

In France, and at the same time as Erasmus, Jean Baptiste Lamarck developed his beliefs of the origin and evolution of life. Initially, he had argued for the immutability of species, but in his later works he lays out a clear alternative to the special creation of plants and animals.

Lamarck believed that the geology of the earth was the result of gradual processes acting slowly over vast periods of time — a view later to be known

---

6. Compare this to Romans 1:20-24 which says, "For since the creation of the world His invisible attributes are clearly seen, being understood by the things that are made, even His eternal power and Godhead, so that they are without excuse, because, although they knew God, they did not glorify Him as God, nor were thankful, but became futile in their thoughts, and their foolish hearts were darkened. Professing to be wise, they became fools, and changed the glory of the incorruptible God into an image made like corruptible man — and birds and four-footed animals and creeping things" (NKJV).

7. Modernism was the dominant philosophy in Western culture from the late 18th to the late 20th centuries. This philosophy placed science as the supreme authority for determining truth. Science was viewed as the "savior" of mankind — finding cures for all diseases, ending war, famine, etc. Though it has been largely replaced by post-modernism, this modernist thinking is still very prominent among scientists and many others in our culture. Post-modernism, on the other hand, is a radical skepticism about anyone's ability to know truth. Post-modernists argue that truth and morality are relative — there are no absolutes. (Post modernists hold to this with *absolute* adherence which proves to be self-refuting!) It also reflects disenchantment with the promises made by modernist philosophers and scientists. Both philosophies reject Scripture as authoritative truth and are based on evolutionary thinking.

8. Erasmus Darwin, *Zoonomia* (Philadelphia: Edward Earle, 1818), 1:397.

as uniformitarianism. Lamarck developed four laws of evolution and put them forward in his *Philosophie Zoologique* published in 1809.

Lamarck proposed that an internal force and the need for new organs caused creatures to develop new characteristics. Once developed, the use or disuse of the organs would determine how they would be passed on to a creature's offspring. This idea of the transmission of acquired characteristics is the hallmark of this model of evolution.

Lamarck's mechanism of use and disuse of characters was widely rejected in his lifetime, especially by the prominent French naturalist Georges Cuvier, and was never supported by observations. Lamarck did attempt to explain how the characters were inherited, but there was still no clear biological mechanism of inheritance that would support his claims.

Lamarck also proposed a tree of life with various branching structures that showed how life evolved from simple to complex forms. Much of what Lamarck proposed seems unreasonable to us today with a modern understanding of genetics. A husband and wife who are both bodybuilders will not have an extraordinarily muscular child — that acquired trait does not have any effect on the genetic information in the germ cells of the parents' bodies. But there are many good reasons to expect that this would provide no support for the idea of molecules-to-man evolution.[9]

Darwinian Evolution

Charles Darwin was at least familiar with all of these different views, and their influence can be found throughout Darwin's writings. Darwin referred often to the effects of natural selection along with the use or disuse of the parts. The legs and wings of the ostrich, the absence of feet and wings in beetles, and the absence of eyes in moles and cave-dwelling animals are all mentioned by Darwin as a result of use or disuse alongside natural selection.[10]

Exactly how this process happened was a mystery to Darwin. He proposed the idea of "pangenesis" as the mechanism of passing traits from parent to offspring. This idea is not significantly different from Lamarck's,

9.   Even if Lamarckian mechanisms are uncovered, the fossil record would not support the evolution story. See Duane Gish, *Evolution: the Fossils Still Say No*, and Carl Werner, *Evolution: The Grand Experiment vol. 1* and *Living Fossils, vol. 2*. Natural selection can only "select" from existing genetic information (it cannot create new information) and mutations cause a loss of genetic information or reshuffling of existing information. See the DVD *Origin of the Species: Was Darwin Right?* and John Sanford, *Genetic Entropy and the Mystery of the Genome*. Also, what bacteria can do should not be directly applied to other forms of life because bacteria are categorically and significantly different.

10.   Charles Darwin, *The Origin of Species* (New York: The Modern Library, 1993), p. 175–181.

for it relies on the use and disuse of organs and structures that are passed on to offspring through pangenes over vast ages.

In his work *The Variation of Animals and Plants under Domestication,* Darwin suggested that gemmules are shed by body cells and that the combination of these gemmules would determine the appearance and constitution of the offspring. If the parent had a long neck, then more gemmules for a long neck would be passed to the offspring. In Darwin's defense, he was not aware of the work of his contemporary, Gregor Mendel. In his garden in the Czech lands, Mendel was studying the heredity of pea plants.

Neither man knew of the existence of genes or the DNA that genes are composed of, but both of them understood there was a factor involved in transmitting characteristics from one generation to the next. Despite evidence from experiments conducted by his cousin Francis Galton, Darwin clung to his pangenesis hypothesis and defended it in his later work, *Descent of Man.*

Darwin believed that all organisms had evolved by natural processes over vast expanses of time. In the introduction to *Origin of Species* he wrote:

> As many more individuals of each species are born than can possibly survive; and as, consequently, there is a frequently recurring struggle for existence, it follows that any being, if it vary however slightly in any manner profitable to itself, under the complex and sometimes varying conditions of life, will have a better chance of surviving, and thus be *naturally selected.* From the strong principle of inheritance, any selected variety will tend to propagate its new and modified form.[11]

Darwin's belief that slight modifications were selected to produce big changes in organisms over the course of millions of years was the foundation of his model for the evolution of life on earth. We know today that Darwin's notion of gemmules and pangenes leading to new features or the development of enhanced characteristics is a false notion. However, that does not mean, by itself, that Darwin's conclusion is wrong — just that his reasoning was faulty.

Neo-Darwinian Evolution and the Modern Synthesis

The discovery of DNA and the rediscovering of Mendel's work on heredity in pea plants have shown that Darwin's hereditary mechanism does not

---

11. Ibid., p. 21.

work, but his conclusion of molecule-to-man transformation over millions of years is still held as true by proponents of evolution. In the early 20th century, Mendelian genetics was rediscovered and it came to be understood that DNA was responsible for the transmission and storage of hereditary information. The scientific majority was still fixed on a naturalistic explanation for the evolution of organisms. That evolution happened was never a question — finding the mechanism was the goal of these naturalistic scientists.

Mutation of genetic information came to be viewed as the likely mechanism for providing the rare material for natural selection to act on. Combining genetic studies of creatures in the lab and in the wild, models of speciation and change over time were developed and used to explain what was seen in the present. These small changes that resulted from mutations were believed to provide the genetic diversity that would lead to new forms over eons of time.

This small change was referred to as "microevolution" since it involved small changes over a short amount of time. The evolutionists claim that the small changes add up to big changes over millions of years, leading to new kinds of life. Thus, microevolution leads to "macroevolution" in the evolutionary view. However, the acceptance of these terms just leads to confusion, and they should be avoided.

This is not fundamentally different from what Charles Darwin taught; it simply uses a different mechanism to explain the process. The problem is that the change in speciation and adaptation is heading in the *opposite* direction needed for macroevolution. The small changes seen in species as they adapt to their environments and form new species through mutation are the result of losses of information.

Darwinian evolution requires the addition of traits (such as forelimbs changing into wings and scales turning into feathers in dinosaur-to-bird evolution), which requires the addition of new information. Selecting from information that is already present in the genome and that was damaged through copying mistakes in the genes cannot be the process that adds new information to the genome.

Today, evolution has been combined with the study of embryology, genetics, the fossil record, molecular structures, plate tectonics, radiometric dating, anthropology, forensics, population studies, psychology, brain chemistry, etc. This leads to the intertwining of so many different ideas that the modern view of evolution can explain anything. It has become so plastic that it can be molded to explain any evidence, no matter how inconsistent the explanations may become.

Even Darwin was willing to admit that there may be evidence that would invalidate his hypothesis. That is no longer the view held by the vast majority of evolutionists today — evolution has become a "fact," even a "scientific law" (on par with the law of gravity), in the minds of many — even though molecules-to-man evolution has not been observed or repeated.

To help us see this more clearly, let us take a look at the idea of different "races." Darwin published his views on the different races in *Descent of Man*. Though Darwin spoke against slavery, he clearly believed that the different people groups around the world were the result of various levels of evolutionary development.

> At some future period, not very distant as measured by centuries, the civilized races of man will almost certainly exterminate and replace the savage races throughout the world. At the same time the anthropomorphous apes . . . will no doubt be exterminated. The break between man and his nearest allies will then be wider, for it will intervene between man in a more civilized state, as we may hope, even than the Caucasian, and some ape as low as a baboon, instead of as now between the negro or Australian [Aborigine] and the gorilla.[12]

It seems quite reasonable that different rates of evolution would lead to different classes of humans — this is the conclusion Darwin came to. He often refers to the distinction between the civilized Europeans and the savages of various areas of the world. He concludes that some of these savages are so closely related to apes that there is no clear dividing line in human history "where the term 'man' ought to be used."[13] Consistent with his naturalistic view of the world, Darwin saw various groups of humans, whether they are distinct species or not, as less advanced than others.

This naturally leads to racist attitudes and, as popular evolutionist Dr. Stephen J. Gould noted, biological arguments for racism "increased by orders of magnitude following the acceptance of evolutionary theory," though this was likely only an excuse to act on underlying social prejudices.[14]

Dr. James Watson (co-discoverer of the double-helix structure of the DNA molecule and a leading atheistic evolutionist) was caught in a

---

12. Charles Darwin, *The Origin of Species and The Descent of Man* (New York: The Modern Library, 1936), p. 521.

13. Ibid., p. 541.

14. Stephen Jay Gould, *Ontogeny and Phylogeny* (Cambridge, MA: Belknap Press of Harvard University Press, 1977), p. 127.

storm of evolutionary racism in 2007. *The Times* of London reported in an interview:

> He says that he is "inherently gloomy about the prospect of Africa" because "all our social policies are based on the fact that their intelligence is the same as ours — whereas all the testing says not really," and I know that this "hot potato" is going to be difficult to address. His hope is that everyone is equal, but he counters that "people who have to deal with black employees find this not true." He says that you should not discriminate on the basis of colour, because "there are many people of colour who are very talented, but don't promote them when they haven't succeeded at the lower level." He writes that "there is no firm reason to anticipate that the intellectual capacities of peoples geographically separated in their evolution should prove to have evolved identically. Our wanting to reserve equal powers of reason as some universal heritage of humanity will not be enough to make it so."[15]

Though he later stated that he did not intend to imply that black Africans are genetically inferior, he is being consistent with his evolutionary beliefs. His remarks were considered offensive, even by those who endorse evolution. This exposes an inconsistency in the thinking of many evolutionists today — if we evolved by random chance, we are nothing special. If humans evolved, it is only reasonable to conclude that different groups have evolved at different rates and with different abilities and mental ability could be higher in one group than another. If the data supported this claim, in the evolutionary framework, then it should be embraced. Those who would suggest that evolution can explain why all humans have value must battle against those evolutionists who would disagree.

This exposes the inconsistent and plastic nature of evolution as an overarching framework — who gets to decide what evolution should mean? Darwin and Watson are applying the concepts in a consistent way and setting emotion and political correctness aside, when it is deemed necessary. Darwin noted that "it is only our natural prejudice and . . . arrogance" that lead us to believe we are special in the animal world.[16]

---

15. Charlotte Hunt-Grubbe, "The Elementary DNA of Dr Watson," Times Online [London], October14, 2007, http://entertainment.timesonline.co.uk/tol/arts_and_entertainment/books/article2630748.ece.
16. Darwin, *The Origin of Species and The Descent of Man*, p. 411–412.

Without an objective standard, such as that provided by the Bible, the value and dignity of human beings are left up to the opinions of people and their biased interpretations of the world around us. God tells us through His Word that each human has dignity and is a special part of the creation because each one is made in the image of God. We are all of "one blood" in a line descended from Adam, the first man, who was made distinct from all animals and was *not* made by modifying any previously existing animal (Genesis 2:7).

Saltation and Punctuated Equilibrium

Contrasted with Darwin's view of a gradual process of change acting over vast ages of time, others have seen the history of life on earth as one of giant leaps of rapid evolutionary change sprinkled through the millions of years. Darwin noted that the fossil record seemed to be missing the transitions from one kind of organism to the next that would confirm his gradualistic notion of evolution.

Shortly after Darwin there were proponents of evolutionary *saltation*; the notion that evolution happens in great leaps. The almost complete absence of transitional forms in the fossil record seemed to support this saltation concept and this was later coupled with genetics to provide a mechanism where "hopeful monsters" would appear and instantaneously produce a new kind of creature (e.g., changing a reptile into a bird). These monsters would be the foundation for new kinds of animals.

Saltation fell out of favor, but the inconsistency between the fossil record and the gradualism promoted by Darwin and others was still a problem. The work of Ernst Mayr, Stephen J. Gould, and Niles Eldredge was the foundation for the model of "punctuated equilibrium." This model explained great periods of stasis in the fossil record punctuated with occasional periods of rapid change in small populations of a certain kind of creature.

This rapid change is relative to the geologic timescale; acting over tens of thousands of years rather than millions. This idea is not inconsistent with Darwin's grand evolutionary scheme. However, it seems that Darwin did not anticipate such a mechanism, though he commented that different organisms would have evolved at different rates. Whether evolution has occurred by gradual steps or rapid leaps (or some combination) is still a topic of debate among those who hold to the neo-Darwinian synthesis of mutations and natural selection as the driving forces of evolutionary change.

Myth

Conclusion

Newton provided us with a general theory of gravity (and described laws in support of that theory) based on observational science and, even in light of modern understandings, those laws still apply today. Einstein did expand the concepts, but the functionality of Newtonian physics still applies today as much as ever.

The same cannot be said for Darwin's ideas. Darwin's hypothesized mechanism of natural selection (even with the added understanding of mutations) has failed to provide an explanation for the diversity of life we see on earth today. His confident expectation that the fossil record would confirm his hypothesis has utterly failed, and the mind-boggling irreducible complexity seen in biological systems today defies the explanations of Darwin or his disciples. To say that evolutionary thinking today is Darwinian in nature can only mean that evolutionists believe that life has evolved from simpler to complex over time. Beyond that, what is called Darwinism today bears little resemblance to what Darwin actually wrote.

All of these ideas of the evolution of organisms from simple to complex are contrary to the clear teaching of Scripture that God made separate kinds of plants and animals and one man-kind to each reproduce after its own kind. As such, these evolutionary ideas are bound to fail when attempting to describe the history of life and to predict the future changes to kinds of life in this universe where we live.

When we start our thinking with the Bible, we can know we are starting on solid ground. Both the fossil record and the study of how plants, animals, and people change in the present fit perfectly with what the Bible says about creation and the Flood and the Tower of Babel in Genesis 1–11. The Bible makes sense of the world around us.

> *Interestingly, evolutionists will often tout stasis as evidence for evolution. However, it is really the exact opposite of evolution, since the creature didn't change.*

9 LIVING FOSSILS

BODIE HODGE frequently speaks on topics such as dinosaurs and the Bible, how we can know God's Word is true, and the Tower of Babel. He has teamed up with apologetics powerhouse Ken Ham on numerous projects, including *Inside the Nye Ham Debate: Revealing Truths from the Worldview Clash of the Century*.

Actively answering questions related to evolution, science, creationism, and more, **TROY LACEY** also contributes articles for Answers in Genesis' varied publications and website features. With a B.S. in Natural Sciences from the University of Cincinnati, he continues to be an avid student of Scripture, and works to provide essential answers to people's questions of faith, culture, and the Bible.

The coelacanth ("see luh canth") fish is probably the most popular living fossil. It was named by Louis Agassiz in 1839 and was known from fossils in rock layers that evolutionists ultimately placed at about 409 million years ago in the early Devonian sediments.[1] From a biblical viewpoint, the Devonian rock layers are merely Flood sediment in the earlier stages of the deluge about 4,350 years ago.

Evolutionists also made the pronouncement that the coelacanth fish (*coelacanth granulatus*) went extinct about 65–70 million years ago, since its fossils were no longer seen in any sediment above the Cretaceous. Evolutionists made the assumption that if something wasn't buried in a layer anymore, then it had gone extinct and therefore no longer existed.

Even so, the coelacanth was hailed as a missing link that connected fish to amphibians in the evolutionary scenario. The evolutionary story is that fish evolved into amphibians by crawling out on land more and more.

The coelacanth, which has some awkward-looking pectoral fins at the bottom of it, was seen as the prime candidate for stepping out on land in the early days of evolution; while some remained in the sea others crawled out on land. Thus, evolutionists used this evidence as the next great step in evolution. This fish was hailed as a missing link on the road to evolution.

But then it happened. In 1938, this evolutionary story shattered when living coelacanths were found thriving off the coast of Madagascar. And so, the coelacanth fish passed from being a missing link to a "living fossil."

What Is a Living Fossil?

A living fossil is a creature — an animal or a plant — that was thought to be extinct but is found living or growing today. The coelacanth was one great example.

Another excellent example is the Huntsman spider. Its fossil which was found in amber, in the evolutionary tale, goes back an alleged 35–50 million years ago and then disappears.[2] And yet, there they are, alive and well today.

What Are Some Other Living Fossils?

Living fossils are more extensive than you might realize. Here is a *short* list of living fossils.

---

1. https://www.nature.com/articles/ncomms1764.
2. Elizabeth Mitchell, *Answers in Genesis*, May 28, 2011, https://answersingenesis.org/fossils/living-fossils/tropical-huntsman/.

Living Fossil	Alleged Secular Age (MYA)	Reference
Ginko Biloba	190 MYA	http://www.ucmp.berkeley.edu/seed-plants/ginkgoales/ginkgofr.html
Alligators	83 MYA	http://museum.wa.gov.au/explore/dino-saur-discovery/deinosuchus
Crocodiles	95 MYA	https://journals.plos.org/plosone/article?id=10.1371/journal.pone.0030471
Cockroaches	130 MYA	https://entomologytoday.org/2017/10/10/old-but-not-that-old-debunking-the-myth-of-ancient-cockroaches/
Karaurus/ Hellbender Salamander	208–144 MYA	Carl Werner, *Evolution the Grand Experiment: Living Fossils* (Green Forest, AR: New Leaf Press, 2008), p. 132–133.
Army Ants	100 MYA	https://www.sciencedaily.com/releases/2003/05/030507081357.htm
Sea Lilly/ Crinoids	485 MYA	http://geokansas.ku.edu/crinoids
Dragonflies	325 MYA	http://www.ucmp.berkeley.edu/arthropoda/uniramia/odonatoida.html
Hedgehog	144–65 MYA	Carl Werner, *Evolution the Grand Experiment: Living Fossils* (Green Forest, AR: New Leaf Press, 2008), p. 176–177.
Horseshoe Crab	445 MYA	https://www.sciencedaily.com/releases/2008/02/080207135801.htm
Nautiloids	500 MYA	http://www.oum.ox.ac.uk/thezone/fossils/inverts/nautilo.htm
Neopilina Mollusks	550 MYA	http://nopr.niscair.res.in/bitstream/123456789/10594/1/SR%20 47%2811%29%20%28Living%20Fossile%29.pdf
Gulf Sturgeon	225 MYA	https://www.floridamuseum.ufl.edu/discover-fish/species-profiles/acipenser-oxyrinchus-desotoi/
Gar	153 MYA	https://www.nature.com/articles/s41598-017-17984-w
Wollemi Pine	110 MYA	http://www.wollemipine.com/fast_facts.php
Velvet Worm	500 MYA	

Parrot	65 MYA	Thomas Stidham, "A Lower Jaw from a Cretaceous Parrot," *Nature*, Vol. 396 (November 5, 1998): 29, doi:10.1038/23841.
Loons	66 MYA	Sankar Chatterjee, "A New Fossil Loon from the Late Cretaceous of Antarctica and Early Radiation of Foot-Propelled Diving Birds," *Journal of Vertebrate Paleontology* (2006): 151, https://www.researchgate.net/profile/Sankar_Chatterjee/publication/295288636_A_new_fossil_loon_from_the_late_cretaceous_of_antarcticaand_early_radiation_of_foot-propelled_diving_birds/links/570ebfd308aee76b9dadfe09/A-new-fossil-loon-from-the-late-cretaceous-of-antarcticaand-early-radiation-of-foot-propelled-diving-birds.pdf.

What Do Living Fossils Prove?

Living fossils prove that just because a creature isn't found buried in a rock layer, doesn't mean it didn't exist when that layer was deposited and turned to rock. Prior to its "rediscovery," when coelacanth fossils were being analyzed there was the assumption that if a creature wasn't found buried in a rock layer, then it didn't exist. As we continue to see with living fossils, this assumption is not a good one to make.

Living fossils also prove that just because two things aren't found buried together doesn't mean they didn't live contemporaneously. Coelacanths and humans are not found buried together, but they live at the same time.

Furthermore, living fossils are powerful evidence against evolution. They show that many plants and animals underwent very little change. Not that this is a big deal for the biblical creationist. Although we expect creatures to have variation within their kinds, we also predict that very little change would be the norm for some kinds since the Flood of Noah's day — which was a matter of thousands of years ago. This would be especially true of marine creatures, plants, and possibly insects, which would not have experienced the severe bottleneck that land-dwelling air-breathing creatures did at the Flood.

Stasis

Because a living fossil often shows very little change compared to its modern counterpart, it doesn't easily mesh with the evolutionary story. So evolutionists have come up with a rescuing device — a term called "stasis" which means the creature remained "static" or without change for long periods of time.

Interestingly, evolutionists will often tout stasis as evidence for evolution. However, it is really the exact opposite of evolution, since the creature didn't change. Stasis is predicted by creationists as one of the possible outcomes of variation within the created kinds as time progresses. After all, it's much easier to conceive of an organism facing fewer environmental or other selection stressors in a few thousand years than over 400 million years.

Living Fossils and Their Survival

Living Fossils also have implications for actual or presumed extinct organisms the fossil record. In fact, the journal *Science News* published an article in September 2018 which had this warning sentence in the abstract:

> Using the fossil record to accurately estimate the timing and pace of past mass extinctions is no easy task, and a new study highlights how fossil evidence can produce a misleading picture if not interpreted with care.[3]

In this study, a team of researchers from the Florida Museum of Natural History decided to perform a thought experiment. It went something like this — if we go to a present coastal location and imagine that a mass extinction has wiped out all marine life, could we reconstruct the extinction of mollusks using 130-ft. core samples? Quite surprisingly, the researchers found that only 6 of the 119 modern species at their chosen location in Italy were found near the tops of the cores. The other 113 were scattered throughout deeper parts of the core sample. If this had happened with an actual core of extinct fossils, it would be interpreted as suggesting small bursts of extinctions over a long timeline, not a single massive extinction (which is what they thought they would find). Again, according to the journal paper, the "faux fossil core" showed some disturbing patterns:

> The cores also depicted a false pattern of extinction, with the majority of offshore species disappearing in a single large "pulse" in the lower part of the cores and shallow-water and brackish species fading out in several smaller pulses. This is because species followed their preferred habitats as they shifted with changing sea levels. Deeper-water dwellers vanished first, as the local river delta

---

3.   https://www.sciencedaily.com/releases/2018/09/180914100341.htm.

started to expand into the Adriatic Sea, replacing open sea with coastal conditions. When shorelines advanced even farther, shallow-water species disappeared as well.[4]

"If you apply methods based on the assumption of random fossilization, you get a precise estimate, but it may be wrong by millions of years," Nawrot said. "Not only the pattern of extinction but also the timing of extinction would be wrongly interpreted, so this is quite important."[5] While the above example was only a thought experiment, it highlights the inherent bias in the system. Finding fossils in a particular location and then attempting to reconstruct a complete history and ecosystem for the extinct organisms even in a local setting may not work.

Some living fossils may be living precisely because they *did* move out of their previously preferred habitats during an ecological disaster (or even an ecological shift). Others may be *living* fossils because they were providentially spared from radical environmental changes and/or selection pressures.

The Gingko tree most likely only survived extinction due to its remote location in southwestern China.[6] Likewise, the Wollemi Pine likely survived because it was in a remote region,[7] and subsequently was not located in areas where human demand for timber might have spelled its doom.

Living fossils are often considered unique and "primitive" looking. But they are not primitive, some are highly specialized while others (like cockroaches) have adapted to virtually every habitat. While it is true that many living fossils represent (at present) the only genera (or even species) left of their original created kind, this itself may also be a premature characterization.

Conclusion

Living Fossils demonstrate that there are problems with interpreting the fossil record as a completely ordered progression of organisms, over millions of years. The Coelacanth was considered extinct for tens of millions of years, then a lone species (*Latimeria chalumnae*) was discovered in 1938 off the coast of South Africa. Then 61 years later, in 1999, another species (*Latimeria menadoensis*) was discovered off the coast of Indonesia. Who is to say that more species might not be discovered in the future.

---

4.   Ibid.
5.   Ibid.
6.   https://kwanten.home.xs4all.nl/fossils.htm.
7.   https://blogs.scientificamerican.com/artful-amoeba/the-lost-valley-of-the-wollemi-pine/.

The same holds true for many living fossils, and some at present considered extinct. Contrary to evolutionary dogma, the "hero of the plot" for living fossils is the fact that there haven't been hundreds of millions of years or Darwinian evolution, there have been only a little over 6,000 years since creation, and approximately 4,350 years since the Flood. Some of these creatures have only managed to dodge our discovery of them for the past few thousand years, but with increasing technology and robotic devices, we may find many more "living fossils" in the near future.

We are only scratching the surface of living fossils in this chapter. If you would like to learn more, we recommend that you invest in a copy of Dr. Carl Werner's book, *Evolution the Grand Experiment: Living Fossils*.[8]

---

8.   Dr. Carl Werner, *Evolution the Grand Experiment: Living Fossils* (Green Forest, AR: New Leaf Press, 2008).

> *Neither DNA evidence nor observations of animals has ever shown that one kind of animal can make the drastic genetic informational changes necessary to evolve into a new kind of creature.*

10 ARE SIMILARITIES IN LIFE FORMS EVIDENCE OF COMMON DESIGN OR COMMON ANCESTRY?

DR. TOMMY MITCHELL graduated with a BA with highest honors from the University of Tennessee-Knoxville in 1980 with a major in cell biology. For his superior scholarship during his undergraduate study, he was elected to Phi Beta Kappa Society, Dr. Mitchell subsequently attended Vanderbilt University School of Medicine, where he received his medical degree in 1984. He completed his residency at Vanderbilt University Affiliated Hospitals in 1987. He is Board Certified in Internal Medicine. In 1991, he was elected a Fellow of the American College of Physicians and had a thriving medical practice in Tennessee for 20 years. In 2006, he chose to pursue creation ministry full time. Dr. Mitchell speaks to thousands of adults, youth, and children in a variety of settings, clearly communicating reasons to trust the Bible, and has written articles for AiG's website and other publications.

When we see artwork or architectural marvels with distinctive, unique features, we suspect they were designed by the same person — a common designer. On the other hand, when we see three children who look like they were cast in the same mold, we assume they share a common ancestor, likely the same parent.

But what about the designs we see in nature? Features like a bilaterally symmetrical body plan (i.e., animals look the same on their left side as they do on their right side) with a vertebral column and four limbs. Or limbs with bones arranged in a common pattern. Or a four-chambered heart. Or blood that uses some form of hemoglobin to carry oxygen. Or a camera-type eye. Do living things sharing such characteristics share a common ancestor or a common designer? How can we know?

Homology — The Study of Similarities

Patterns of similarities and differences help us make sense of our world. Even the youngest child must learn that round toys fit through round holes and square toys through square ones. Scientists throughout history have grouped the plants and animals they observed according to their similarities and then studied their differences to learn more about them. Similar structures — whether a skeletal limb pattern or the molecular structure of a protein — are said to be *homologous*.

As in biology, in the history of inanimate objects we find similar structures. Sometimes we can follow their history and understand how they developed differences through descent with modification from a common ancestor.

For example, today's baseball can be traced back to similar balls cobbled together from scrap rubber cores, wrapped in yarn and tightly stitched leather covers. Baseballs from the 19th century are clearly recognizable as baseballs despite many easily seen differences. Somewhere along the way, figure eight shapes in the leather covering became popular, thanks to the resilience they gave to the ball. Today's official standard ball with red stitching is a product of descent with modification from common ancestors — the earliest baseballs of the 19th century.

Within a family, a study of portraits across generations may reveal that today's children have a distinctive appearance traceable to descent with modification from a common ancestor. The portraits provide observable evidence of this process and the children's common ancestry, revealing the changes and similarities across generations.

A prime place to find an example of "ancestral" homology is in embryology. Some of the reproductive organs in male and female human babies are embryologically related. The ovaries and testicles, for example, are formed from homologous structures, which about 40 days after conception differentiate into their distinctive male and female forms under the direction of the embryo's DNA.

Such ancestral homology is observable for several structures that ultimately differentiate along different paths in the male and female forms during embryonic development. This has nothing to do with evolution. The organs do not evolve from the "ancestral" organs in the embryo. They simply differentiate from homologous structures in accord with the information already present in their DNA.

Highly Versatile Homologous Designs

When we compare similar structures in different kinds of organisms, we also observe homologies — similarities in basic structure. For example, the vertebrate forelimb follows a common pattern. The forelimbs — arms, legs, wings, or flippers — of bears, bats, dogs, dolphins, people, and penguins have the same skeletal pattern. Nearest the body is one bone. Below (distal to) this is a pair of long bones. Then, after a cluster of wrist-type bones, there are bones associated with one or more digits, even if these digits are enclosed within a wing or flipper.

Rather than comparing the way this pattern plays out in different kinds of creatures, though, let's look at two uses of this bone pattern that should be familiar to everyone reading this book. Within your own human body, you can readily see how this one-bone/two-bone arrangement is versatile and useful. Our "hindlimbs" — our legs — share the same bone pattern as that found in our arms.

In both our arms and legs, the "one bone" is attached to the body's main axis by a ball and socket joint, providing a great range of motion. Similar joints in the arm and leg — the shoulder and the hip — differ in ways that maximize range of motion in the shoulder while sacrificing some range of motion for stability and strength in the hip.

The "two bone" portion of our arm and leg is attached with a hinge joint to the "one bone," keeping the joint — elbow or knee — stable. The "two bone" section of our arm is designed to twist below this joint much more than in the leg. The two bones differ greatly in size in the leg, and in some animals one of the "two bones" is so short it doesn't reach the ankle. The two bones — whether in our arms or legs or the limbs of animals —

are nevertheless bound tightly together for strength and provide stable attachment points for many muscles.

The one-bone/two-bone limb plan is a highly versatile design. The differing proportions and nuances of shapes among these bones, as well as the varying mobility of the joints connecting them, when compared in many kinds of vertebrates, demonstrates the wide range of functional adaptations possible within this basic bone pattern. Variations in the one-bone/two-bone pattern equip a bird to fly, a cheetah to run, and a baseball player to throw a ball.

Vertebrate limb homologies are the footprints of a wise common Designer. Our Creator God created a highly versatile, strong, stable design and used it in many kinds of creatures to fit them for a variety of lifestyles (e.g., God, in His infinite power, made man from dust and a woman from the man's rib and flesh — Genesis 2:7, 21–23). This should not surprise us. Wouldn't a good human engineer re-use a good design, varying it to fit as many applications as possible? We should expect no less of God!

Non-Ancestral Homologies

The question we want to address here is how homologous structures in different kinds of creatures came to be. Is a shared common Designer the only explanation? Could vertebrate limb bones be homologous because vertebrates evolved from a common ancestor?

In addressing this question, let's consider what is observable and what is not. While scientists have observed that animals reproduce after their kinds — dogs producing more dogs, penguins producing more penguins, and so forth — no scientist has ever observed animals reproducing to make completely different kinds of animals. In fact, much as evolutionists would like to have us believe that dinosaurs once upon a time evolved into birds, no scientist has ever observed a bird hatch from anything except eggs laid by birds. Just as the first chapter of Genesis mentions that God designed animals to reproduce. They did so within their created kinds, so scientists — even today — observe this occurring in nature.

Horses, for instance, may produce horse descendants with a wide variety of sizes and even hoof variations, but horses never produce offspring that are not horses. Why is this? Animals reproduce and vary only within their created kinds because each kind of creature carries within its cells a genome — a set of genes dictating how it is designed. Genes are the coded informational subunits of DNA.

Creation scientists were not at all surprised, therefore, when DNA recovered from a fossilized horse bone preserved at Thistle Creek in the Canadian permafrost was found to be quite similar to the DNA from modern domestic horses, donkeys, and the wild Przewalski horse. Before finding that DNA sample, this question was controversial in the evolutionary community. It seems that a horse is a horse, of course.

Neither DNA evidence nor observations of animals has ever shown that one kind of animal can make the drastic genetic informational changes necessary to evolve into a new kind of creature. That being the case, we cannot reasonably believe that the homologies we observe in different kinds of creatures are the result of processes that scientists have never observed.

Homologies can only honestly be seen as evidence for Darwinian evolution if one already believes in Darwinian evolution. No matter how much evolutionary scientists and evolutionary educational materials tout homologies as evidence of common evolutionary ancestry, such an interpretation is the result of an evolutionary worldview, not support for it.

Homologies are evidence of common design. To claim them as evolutionary evidence is to stretch them beyond the limits of observational science.

Homologous Embryonic Development

If we want to see — to actually *observe* — how an anatomical structure forms, what better place to look than in the embryo? Could evolutionists find, in the embryo, evidence justifying their claim that homologous structures result from evolutionary descent with modification from common ancestors? Let's consider that carefully.

Only by studying the sequential formation of the embryonic structures to mature forms can we appreciate how cells multiply and differentiate. Cells may, for instance, multiply to form a sheet of cells that rolls into a tube and then twists and segments itself into distinctive sections. Within those sections, cells further differentiate to become more and more like the mature cells the embryo's DNA has decreed they shall be.

Or cells may multiply to form a rod that acts as a scaffold around which other structures form. Many embryonic cells signal other cells to form particular structures, putting out molecules that activate or inactivate certain genes. And sometimes an embryonic structure, after finishing its job, disappears.

Everything that happens during a normal embryo's development follows the blueprint laid out in its DNA. Each kind of living thing has its own genome. And while dramatic variations can occur within a particular genome, those variations are never the sort that could add up to produce a different kind of animal. How do we know? Because scientific observation has confirmed that genetic variations occur only within the confines of an organism's genome, without exception.

Not surprisingly, the pattern of embryonic development that produces homologous anatomical structures is typically similar. After all, if a great bit of biological engineering works well in many different species, we would expect the process that develops those structures in the embryo to likewise be similar. Much has been learned about the embryology of limb development from studying the similarities and differences of limb growth in mice and chicks.

Many of the molecules that cells use to signal other cells, activating certain genes for particular periods of time to grow and differentiate into the target structures, are similar in various species. Again, it is not surprising that the wise Designer who designed the biochemistry and genetic code by which all living things on earth operate would use similar biochemical signals and similar genes to accomplish similar purposes.

It is tempting for evolutionary scientists to extrapolate the embryonic development of particular kinds of creatures to create mechanisms by which one kind of creature might have evolved into another. After all, the embryonic path to something like a forelimb demonstrates an observable way that a forelimb forms. And the paths to form the forelimbs of different kinds of creatures are similar. So why not suggest that evolutionary change from one kind of creature into another would follow a similar sort of path? After all, such claims would *appear* to be based on scientific *observations*!

But wait! They are not! Observations of embryonic development only occur *within* a particular species. There is *no* observational science supporting the notion that one kind of creature can evolve into a new, completely different kind of creature.

The study of comparative embryology is not new. Scientists were doing it back in the 19th century. In fact, the scientific world's most famous fraud, Ernst Haeckel, doctored his illustrations of vertebrate embryos to "prove" that embryos re-played Darwinian evolutionary history as they developed.

Some modern apologists for Haeckel have claimed that though he made up the sketches to prove a point, he only meant that particular traits, or structures, followed an evolutionary path of development. In other words, they assert that while evolutionary scientists now admit that embryos do not really replay their evolutionary history, the development of the forelimb or other structures does.

The Creator God, our wise Designer, designed embryonic development of homologous structures to follow similar paths in different kinds of creatures. Based on the Bible's assertions — that creatures were created "after their kinds" and told to reproduce — and scientific observations, we can only use embryological evidence to support the shared common Designer of homologies, not a common ancestry.

Claiming that the evolution only occurs in individual structures does not get around this barrier. After all, the anatomical structures do not exist independently of the organism they are in. There is no observational scientific evidence to support such compartmentalized evolution.

Homologous Embryonic Structures with Diverse Destinies

What starts out as something similar (combined DNA strand) in the embryos of various organisms can end up forming very different things. A typical example is Meckel's cartilage. Meckel's cartilage, found in the region of the so-called embryonic "gill slits," has different destinies in different creatures. (Mammalian "gill slits" are neither gills nor slits, by the way. They are just tiny folds in the embryo's neck.) Meckel's cartilage supports the gills in cartilaginous fish. It ossifies to form the jaws of bony fish and reptiles. In mammalian embryos, Meckel's cartilage helps shape the middle ear bones and lower jaw; then it pretty much disappears.

The different structures formed from Meckel's cartilage in perch, pythons, and people can be thought of as homologous. But does this mean they developed through common evolutionary ancestry? No, not at all! Just as observational science has never shown any mechanism by which the genetic information to produce new and different kind of organisms can be acquired, so there is no known mechanism by which the information to produce pieces of new and different kinds of organisms can be acquired. Such is magical thinking. It has no place in science.

Meckel's cartilage develops into different structures in different kinds of embryos because those embryos have different genomes directing their development, not because "evolution" somehow discovered how to make Meckel's cartilage do new tricks.

Common Design, Common Designer

To paraphrase what Solomon said in Ecclesiastes 12:13, "what's the conclusion of the issue?" No matter what sort of homologies we compare in different kinds of living things — bones and organs, embryonic development, or even the genes that direct their development — we find no plausible scientific way that one kind of living thing can evolve into another.

What we do find are a lot of fantastic designs. And these fantastic designs appear with variations over and over again, in different kinds of organisms throughout the biological world. Living things share such common designs because they share a common Designer, the Creator God of the Bible.

> *Admissions like this make it clear that these scientists are being driven by an ideology (a belief) rather than scientific evidence and that there is currently no convincing natural explanation for the origin of life.*

THE ORIGIN OF LIFE

DR. ALAN WHITE earned his BS in Chemistry from the University of Tennessee and his PhD in Organic Chemistry from Harvard University in 1981. He worked for 30 years at Eastman Chemical Company and reached the rank of Research Fellow. Alan spent his career at Eastman working in Research and Development in the fields of organic and polymer chemistry. His achievements include the development of a commercial biodegradable polymer and the improvement of many commercial polymer processes. Dr. White has been granted 45 U.S. patents and is an author on 18 scientific publications. He has recently retired to spend more time in research, writing, and speaking in the area of creation science, discussing current issues such as climate change. Over the last 15 years, he has lectured on three continents emphasizing the consistency of scientific data with God's Word.

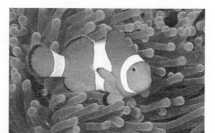

O ur blue planet is full of water[1] and full of *life*.[2] We see wondrous creatures every day — creatures in the water, in the air, and on the land. Yet, most days, we do not appreciate how extraordinary life is.

How long has it been since you thought about how easily a fish swims and breathes underwater, or how skillfully a tiny hummingbird hovers in the wind and drinks nectar, or even how we are able to see all these things in such fine detail?

Against the backdrop of the emptiness of deep space, our world is exploding with diverse, complex life. Why is there life here at all? How did it begin? Our answers to these important questions will profoundly affect how we view this world and, consequently, how we live our lives.

Two Explanations for the Origin of Life

While many theories for the origin of life have been proposed, they all fit into one of two categories — either random, natural processes are responsible for life, or God created life.

Despite the efforts of many scientists, the natural explanations for the origin of life are not convincing. The commonly accepted belief asserts that life began around 3.8 billion years ago. Supposedly, chemicals available on

---

1. The oceans contain about 320,000,000 cubic miles of water or about 352,670,000,000,000,000,000 gallons. The estimate was provided by the National Oceanic and Atmospheric Administration, US Dept. of Commerce, https://oceanservice.noaa.gov/facts/oceanwater.html.

2. There are about 8.7 million plant and animal species known on earth ± 1.3 million. Camilo Mora, Derek P. Tittensor, Sina Adl, Alastair G. B. Simpson, Boris Worm, "How Many Species Are There on Earth and in the Ocean?" *PLoS Biology*, 2011; 9 (8): e1001127 DOI: 10.1371/journal.pbio.1001127.

the early earth became more complicated, randomly organized themselves into a "simple" cell, and that simple cell "learned" to reproduce.[3]

Scientists call this transition from non-living chemicals to "simple" life *abiogenesis* (or chemical evolution). This question of the origin of life is an incredibly difficult one from a naturalistic perspective. It might have *seemed* easy decades ago when scientists knew almost nothing about the inner workings of the cell.

But now scientists are more fully aware of the complexity of the parts inside even the simplest cells, and they are beginning to understand how well all these intricate parts work together. While most secular scientists still contend that simple life began by chemical evolution, some now candidly admit how unlikely chemical evolution is. George Whitesides, a famous organic chemist and professor at Harvard, put it this way.

> **The Origin of Life.** This problem is one of the big ones in science. It begins to place life, and us, in the universe. Most chemists believe, as do I, that life emerged spontaneously from mixtures of molecules in the prebiotic Earth.
>
> How? I have no idea. . . . On the basis of all the chemistry that I know, it seems to me *astonishingly improbable* (emphasis mine).[4]

Admissions like this make it clear that these scientists are being driven by an ideology (a belief) rather than scientific evidence *and* that there is currently no convincing natural explanation for the origin of life. Scientific investigations can give us insight into what might have happened years ago, but cannot give us certain answers.

Scientific experiments are done in the present, not the past. We are not able to see into the distant past nor are we able to create things *ex nihilo* ("out of nothing").

The biblical account of how living things were created is given in Genesis 1–2. God, who has always been, spoke all the different kinds of plants and animals into existence on days 3, 5, and 6 of creation week and proclaimed His creation to be very good (Genesis 1:31). These different kinds

---

3. Some have proposed that the first life was a self-replicating molecule. For example, Jerry Coyne, *Why Evolution is True* (New York: Penguin, 2009), p. 3. No known molecule is complicated enough to do that. The mechanism for replication even in a simple cell is astoundingly complicated, requiring many complex molecules working together (see below).

4. George M. Whitesides, *Revolutions in Chemistry, Chemical and Engineering News*, Volume 85, Issue 13, March 26, 2007, p. 12–17, https://cen.acs.org/articles/85/i13/Revolutions-Chemistry.html.

have a designed-in capability to vary within the limits of their kind thus giving a beautiful diversity to life.

Clearly, the plants and animals have the type of specified complexity, beauty, and adaptability that would be expected of creatures that were designed and created by a being much more knowledgeable and powerful than we can imagine. Even the "simplest" organisms contain complex machines whose operation is mind-boggling.

But one of the strongest pieces of scientific evidence for the creation of life is DNA, which is an ingenious information system that is common to all life. Nevertheless, secular scientists claim that the presence of DNA in all life is strong evidence for a common ancestor and evolution. The opposite is true. Random processes cannot explain the origin of the information in DNA nor the origin of life.

All of God's Word is true, including the truth about the origin of life. Sadly, the situation with life on this planet is no longer "very good." In Genesis 3 we see that Adam and Eve disobeyed God's instruction and brought sin and death into God's creation. We see disintegrations, mutations, and detrimental effects on creatures. Despite that, we see the remnant evidence of the original brilliant design in life today. How marvelous life must have been before sin, and how marvelous it will be again when all is made new![5]

What Is Life?

In order to more fully address this issue of the origin of life, we must first be clear about what "life" means. Surprisingly, secular scientists have had great difficulty agreeing on a definition for life. Most people probably think that they can recognize life when they see it; but, when scientists put words to paper, it became obvious that they don't truly understand it.

Take the NASA[6] definition, for example: "Life is a self-sustaining chemical system capable of Darwinian evolution."[7] This sounds more like the evidence that scientists *hope* to find rather than a statement of what life is. Is life strictly chemicals, or is it more? Must life be the result of evolution?

Having given up on a definition for life, secular scientists have chosen to describe life by listing the characteristics of living things, such as the ability to respond to stimuli; the ability to grow, develop, and reproduce;

---

5. Revelation 21.
6. National Aeronautics and Space Administration.
7. NASA Astrobiology Department, https://astrobiology.nasa.gov/research/life-detection/about/.

the ability to control internal conditions (homeostasis); and the ability to utilize energy (metabolism).[8] What an impressive list!

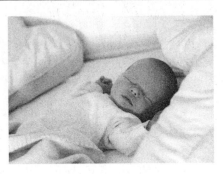

Every one of these capabilities requires different, highly complex molecular systems working together. These characteristics do help us understand how dramatically different life is from a random mixture of chemicals.

While biologists consider all plants, animals, fungi, protists,[9] archaea,[10] and bacteria to be alive, the Bible speaks only of animals and mankind as being alive.[11] Despite that, these other organisms are still miraculous creations of God — designed to do what they do.[12]

The Bible makes two other distinctions about life that are completely opposite of the naturalistic view. First, the Bible makes it clear that life comes from life (biogenesis) in Genesis 1.[13] Later, the Bible asserts that God the Father has life (John 5:26); and, through His wisdom and power, He gave that life and other marvelous gifts to all people (Acts 17:25).

Second, the Bible declares that human life consists of a physical body *and* a spirit.[14] In the naturalistic view there is only a physical body. Zechariah 12:1 tells us of three miraculous things that God did.

> Thus declares the LORD, who stretched out the heavens and founded the earth and formed the spirit of man within him.[15]

8. For example, see K.A. Mason, J.B. Losos, and S.R. Singer, *Biology* (New York: McGraw-Hill, 2014), p 2–3.

9. Protists are microscopic organisms and are not considered plants or animals.

10. Archaea are microscopic organisms that include many extremophiles.

11. Michael Todhunter, "Do Plants and Leaves Die?" *New Answers Book 4*, Ken Ham, Gen. Ed. (Green Forest, AR: Master Books, 2013), p. 23–26.

12. To try to avoid confusion, when referring to different organisms, the word "life" for the remainder of this chapter will be used, as it is currently understood in the world today, to include all things that are based on DNA and are independent of other organisms.

13. This is essentially the biological *Law of Biogenesis* which states that life comes from life, not non-life.

14. There is a debate over the soul and the spirit being one and the same (*dichotomous*) or the body, spirit, and the soul being distinct (*trichotomous*). This debate is not for discussion here. In either case, there is a non-physical aspect to life for man, and we know this since life also exists in non-material being such as angels, Satan, God, and so on.

15. All Scripture in this chapter is from the English Standard Version (ESV) of the Bible.

How could God form an invisible, living spirit inside of us? "With man this is impossible, but with God all things are possible" (Matthew 19:26). We are ultimately all made with a physical body and in the likeness of our Creator — who is Spirit[16] — thus *we* are both body and spirit.[17] Followers of Christ, for instance, are not "dancing to their DNA," but led by the Spirit.

The Molecules of Life

All forms of life function because specific, complicated molecules are present and working together properly. Water, a small molecule, is the medium for all the chemical reactions that take place in the body.

While numerous types of molecules are critical to human life, the two most relevant to the question of the origin of life are proteins and DNA. Naturally, their existence alone still wouldn't constitute life, but is vital to life's beginning.

Proteins

Besides water, the most abundant molecules in your body are proteins. Proteins are also critical to the functioning of less complicated life forms like bacteria.

Proteins are very long chains of molecules. Each protein chain takes on a specific shape and performs a specific function. The "links" that make up these long chains are relatively small molecules called amino acids (e.g., alanine).

Each functional protein has a specific sequence of amino acids made from up to 20 different ones.[18] The median number of amino acids in a chain is about 300–400.[19] This diversity in structure among proteins allows them to accomplish an astonishingly wide

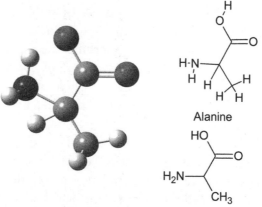

Alanine

---

16. Genesis 1:26, John 4:24.
17. James 2:26: "For as the body apart from the spirit is dead, so also faith apart from works is dead." 2 Timothy 1:7: "For God gave us a spirit not of fear but of power and love and self-control."
18. This doesn't count the two rare ones, Selenocysteine and pyrrolysine.
19. L. Brocchieri and S. Karlin, *Nucleic Acids Res.*, 33(10): 3390–3400 (2005).

HEMOGLOBIN

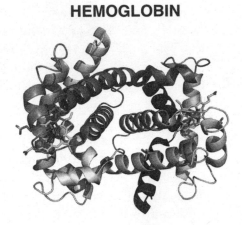

variety of different tasks, such as being structural components, being enzymes that make chemical reactions go faster, being hormones like insulin that help control blood sugar, or being transporter molecules like hemoglobin which carry oxygen to all our cells. Hemoglobin, for example, has four protein subunits with a total of about 575 amino acids and can bind four oxygen molecules.

An almost endless number of protein sequences are possible because each "link" in the chain could be any one of 20 different amino acids; however, only a tiny percent of those possible proteins are useful. The chance of producing any particular protein by a random process is infinitesimally small (approximately 1 in 20^{300}, or 1 in 20 multiplied by itself 300 times). A number that large is hard to even comprehend. The chance of getting just the first 20 amino acids of a protein in a particular order is approximately 1 in 105,000,000,000,000,000,000,000,0 00,000 (1.05×10^{26}). It is unreasonable to think that a random process could have produced even a single functional protein, much less all those needed for life.

But it isn't just the sequence of amino acids that determines a protein's function — it is the shape into which the protein is folded. Just as the sequence of amino acids is specific, the shape is also specific. Molecules named *chaperonins* generally aid in that folding.[20] These chaperonins are themselves proteins, and they have a beautiful structure.

To the right is a complex of 14 chaperonin proteins in the shape of two donuts stacked on each other with a cap on top. Newly formed proteins fold inside this structure. But which came first — the functional proteins or the chaperonin proteins that helped to make them functional? This is hard to explain from a naturalistic worldview.

Chaperonin GroEL/ES
(top view)

20. Fumihiro Motojima, *Biophysics (Nagoya-shi)*, 11, p. 93–102 (2015).

In the early 1950s, Stanley Miller with Harold Urey did some famous experiments in an attempt to shed light on the origin of life. He reacted some of the chemicals that he thought were present on the early earth in water under conditions that he thought were like those on

Stanley Miller

the early earth. He did so hoping to produce chemicals related to life.

In fact, he did produce a few amino acids in his experiments along with a myriad of other products not related to life. The scientific world considered those results and the results of similar experiments to be earth shattering, and they are still being discussed today. But those results should not give us confidence that life began by a natural process. Many daunting questions remain.

Some scientists today think that different chemicals than those that Miller used were present on the early earth.[21] Amino acids might well not be produced using those different chemicals.

Even if amino acids were formed on the early earth as Miller suggests, proteins would not form naturally in water. Water would preferentially break down those proteins into amino acids.

Scientists have proposed other environments for the origin of life, such as near hydrothermal vents, on ice at the poles of the earth, or even in outer space. All of these have chemistry-related issues.

Proteins are formed in your body with a very complex machine (ribosome) driven by the energy from the oxygen we breathe and the food we eat. DNA provides the necessary information to get the sequence of amino acids exactly right. Brilliant designers, not random processes, make complex machines that make specific, useful products.

If all these issues were not enough, there is another critical problem with the amino acids produced by Miller. Each amino acid actually occurs in two

21. J. Kasting, "Earth's Early Atmosphere," *Science*, 259, 920–926 (Feb. 12, 1993).

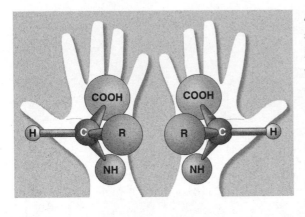

almost identical forms[22] — a right-handed and a left-handed form. Molecules with this property are said to be chiral (like a mirror image).

In Miller's experiments and in any laboratory experiment today, equal amounts of both forms are produced. The easiest way to understand the difference in the two forms of amino acids is to think about the difference between your two hands. Both of your hands have four fingers and a thumb, but your right hand is not exactly the same as your left. Your right hand will not fit in your left glove. Both forms contain the same atoms, but they bonded together differently.

While a random process always produces both forms in equal amounts, your body produces *exclusively* the left-handed form of *every* amino acid. Life essentially exists using left handed amino acids (also called *levorotatory* or simply abbreviated as "L")!

Right-handed amino acids (also call *dextrorotatory* or abbreviated "D") are unnatural to our bodies. If enough of them were included in our proteins, we would not survive.

This specificity is completely unexpected from a natural worldview, but not at all surprising if our bodies were created. In order to make a functional protein, it must be formed into a specific shape. That shape is only obtained when *only* one specific form of each amino acid is used. This specificity is seen in many structures in your body, including the sugar part of DNA, which is also chiral.

DNA (Deoxyribonucleic Acid)

An incredible amount of information is required to construct any form of life. From what is known today, the majority of that information is contained in DNA. Each cell contains two strands (or chains) of DNA that are wound around each other into a double helix. The chains are complimentary to each other but run in opposite directions.

---

22. The simplest amino acid, glycine, only comes in one form. The other 19 come in two forms.

The "links" in each chain are called "nucleotides," and the number of nucleotides in the chains varies widely depending on the life form. In humans, each chain has about *three billion* nucleotides. Each nucleotide is weakly bonded to its complementary nucleotide on the other chain.

The nucleotides in DNA consist of a nitrogenous base, a sugar and a phosphate group bonded together. These nucleotides are much less stable than the amino acids in proteins. Therefore, the DNA chains, which are critical to life, require frequent repair by sophisticated molecular machines. How could the first organism have survived long enough to evolve sophisticated repair machines?

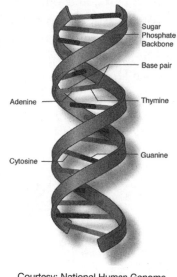

Courtesy: National Human Genome Research Institute

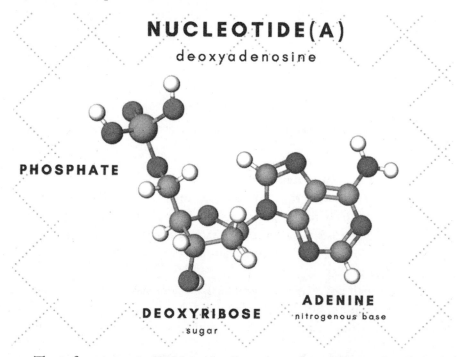

The information in DNA is stored as a specific sequence of nucleotides in the chains. It is like a language. For DNA, the language consists of four letters (A, T, C, and G), which represent the four different nucleotides. So each of us has his or her own unique sequence of about three billion pairs of nucleotides, and your sequence is approximately 99.8% the same as all other human beings.[23]

Each DNA sequence is analogous to an instruction book, although it is much more complex.[24] It tells your body how to make itself. Each form of life has a different sequence of nucleotides in its DNA, just like each type of instruction book has a different sequence of letters and spaces.

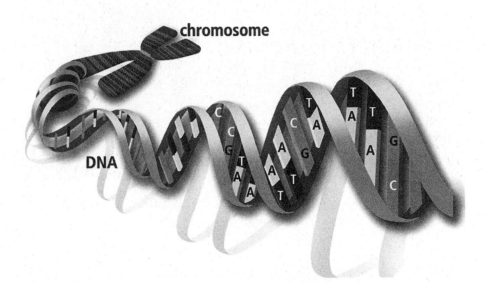

Photo from Biological and Environmental Research Information Systems (Dept. of Energy)

In order to make a protein, the information in DNA is first transferred to messenger RNA (transcription). The messenger RNA is then decoded to build protein chains with the correct sequence of amino acids (translation). When secular scientists began to understand translation, they realized that only about 1.5% of the DNA information was needed to code for all the proteins in our bodies.

Based on their belief in evolution, secular scientists assumed that the rest of the DNA was junk. On the other hand, if DNA were more like an instruction book, one would expect that all the sequence would have some utility.

---

23. This number keeps getting refined with new data. Yes, identical twins have identical DNA sequences, with the possible exception of mutations and epigenetic changes.
24. See this concept in John Sanford's book, *Genetic Entropy*.

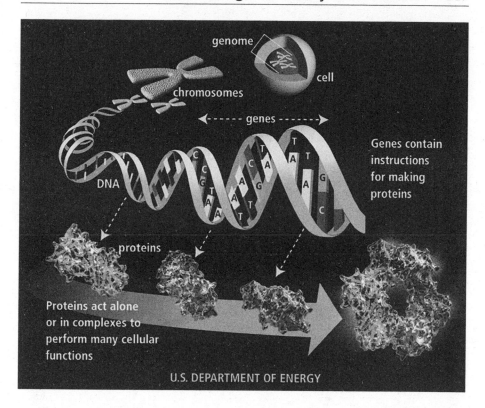

Genes contain instructions for making proteins

Proteins act alone or in complexes to perform many cellular functions

U.S. DEPARTMENT OF ENERGY

Recent experiments by secular scientists on the ENCODE project have indicated that a much, much greater percentage of the DNA than 1.5% has a function,[25] but many of those scientists continue to vehemently argue this point, presumably due to their belief in evolution. We are just beginning to understand the functions of DNA.

If almost all the information for our bodies is stored in our DNA, then it makes sense that we need much more information than just how to make the proteins. Most processes in our bodies are tightly controlled. The information required for those control systems must be immense. Surprisingly, the same DNA molecule is in every one of your 200+ different kinds of cells, and it instructs each kind of cell how to function. Life is not an accident.

Finally, the property that unmistakably separates life from other molecular processes is its ability to reproduce. Even the first life form had to be able to reproduce. The critical step in reproduction is copying DNA (replication). Every new cell requires DNA, whether it replaces an old cell or initiates a new life. Even the simplest organisms use a fantastically complex

25. ENCODE = **En**cyclo**p**edia of **D**NA **E**lements; M. Kellis et al., Proceedings of the National Academy of Sciences, April 29, 2014. 111 (17) 6131–6138.

system made of many elaborate enzymes working together to copy DNA.[26] The design of this system is beyond brilliant.

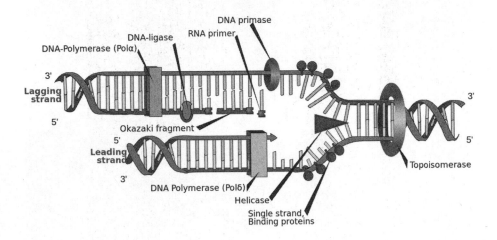

Leading Naturalistic Explanations for the Origin of Life

Much scientific work has been focused on this area of research. Despite that, no convincing explanation has resulted. The following are some of the ideas that have been proposed:

1. **The RNA World** — The paradigm of an RNA World has become very popular among secular scientists as an explanation of how life originated from non-life. That's because even committed naturalists understand how unlikely it is that two highly complex molecules like DNAs and proteins would emerge simultaneously.[27] RNA was chosen as the type of molecule that could potentially function in both roles. But, while RNAs could carry information and act as a mediocre catalyst, they could not be structural parts of the body like a protein. There are three other major problems with life beginning from one complex molecule like RNA. First, it is inconceivable that there is any type of molecule that is both simple enough to be formed on the early earth by random processes yet complicated enough to reproduce. Second, there is no credible explanation as to how all the information needed to produce even the simplest life could be selected before there was life. Third, there is no reasonable

---

26. No one picture can fully and clearly portray the complexity of DNA replication, but this picture by Mariana Ruiz is a good start to understanding how many enzymes are involved.

27. L.E. Orgel, *Critical Reviews in Biochemistry and Molecular Biology*, 39, p. 99 (2004).

description of how chiral (right- or left-handed) molecules could have resulted from randomness. The idea of the RNA World is popular, but not supported by the scientific evidence.

2. **Deep-sea vents** — The relatively recent discovery of hydrothermal vents on the ocean floor has provided the naturalists another possible venue for the origin of life. These vents do provide great heat and many simple molecules, but that does not explain the formation of highly specific, information-containing molecules required for life. The same argument can be made against the theories involving *lightning strikes*.

3. **Clay or mineral surfaces** — This proposal was made more than 50 years ago. It was expected that these materials could themselves have been the precursor to biological life or that they could have played a role in the process by being a catalyst or a substrate. There is still no solid experimental evidence of how these materials might be involved.

4. **Ice crystals** — It was hoped that the polar icecaps would provide an environment that would protect molecules like RNA that are unstable outside the cell. However, it seems highly unlikely that all the biochemical reactions needed for the origin of life would occur under these cold conditions.

5. **Directed Panspermia** — A number of scientists have actually favored the idea that life on earth resulted from aliens bringing living organisms here. This is probably more an indication of how weak the scientific evidence is for chemical evolution on the earth.

Conclusion

From a naturalistic perspective, life on earth should be completely unexpected. While simple chemicals could have reacted on an "early" earth, there is no reason to expect that those reactions would produce the type of specific, complex molecules necessary for responding to stimuli, growing, developing, controlling internal conditions, or using energy — and certainly not reproduction.

The Bible says that God created life on earth in the beginning (Matthew 19:4). What we observe confirms that. In life, we see exclusively left-handed amino acids, structurally specific proteins which perform so many precise functions, exact information in DNA for all the protein sequences, complex machines which prepare all the different proteins, and a mind-boggling system of enzymes that copies the three billion letters of DNA precisely.

You can also see evidence for a Creator in the way that these two complex types of molecules, proteins and DNA, work together. It takes the information in DNA to make a protein, and it takes proteins to build DNA. The simultaneous need for two complicated molecules working together is strong evidence of a Creator, and a serious problem for the naturalist.[28]

If you are willing to open your eyes and to search for wisdom from God like hidden treasure, you will find it (Proverbs 2). That is certainly true of the latest discoveries related to proteins and DNA. Evidence for a Creator of life on earth is everywhere — even in the tiniest organisms.

Undoubtedly, God has revealed Himself in all that He has made (Romans 1:20), but He has more completely revealed Himself in Scripture. In the Bible we see that God created you in His image. He loves you more than you can imagine and has given you a clear purpose:

> You shall love the Lord your God with all your heart and with
> all your soul and with all your strength and with all your mind,
> and your neighbor as yourself (Luke 10:27).[29]

So you see, your answer to that simple question about how your life began is critically important. If He made us, we belong to Him. If we choose to ignore that plain truth, we will suffer the eternal consequences of His righteous judgment. On the other hand, if we made ourselves, we decide truth; and death is the end. The evidence is clear, and the consequences are profound.

28. James Watson et al., *Molecular Biology of the Gene*, 7th Ed., Cold Spring Harbor Laboratory Press, 2013, p. 593.
29. Scripture in this chapter is from the English Standard Version (ESV) of the Bible.

> *In essence, atheistic evolutionists substitute natural selection for God Himself!*

WHAT ABOUT NATURAL SELECTION?

DR. NATHANIEL JEANSON holds a BS in molecular biology and bioinformatics from the University of Wisconsin-Parkside and a PhD in cell and developmental biology from Harvard University. At Harvard, he was actively involved in adult stem cell research and published peer-reviewed papers in secular journals. His current research uses DNA comparisons to understand the true origin of species, and he has published groundbreaking results on this question in articles and in a book, *Replacing Darwin: The New Origin of Species*. He serves as a research biologist, author, and speaker with Answers in Genesis.

DR. GEORGIA PURDOM holds a PhD in molecular genetics from Ohio State University. She formerly served as an assistant and associate professor of biology at Mt. Vernon Nazarene University. Dr. Purdom is the Director of Educational Content and actively speaks and writes for Answers in Genesis. She also chairs the ministry's Editorial Review Board.

O n the grassy plains of East Africa, a herd of Grant's gazelles meander slowly in the afternoon sun. Suddenly, the herd dashes off in unison — with a streak of spotted fur in hot pursuit. The healthy gazelles easily escape the hungry cheetah, but a sickly and weak gazelle at the back of the herd pitifully succumbs to the carnivore's devices. Has "natural selection" struck again? And why does it matter to the creation/evolution debate?

Defining Natural Selection

The term *natural selection* has been defined clearly for over 150 years. Charles Darwin put the term in the title to his book *On the Origin of Species by Means of Natural Selection*, and he articulated what he meant in the text of his seminal work:

> But if variations useful to any organic being do occur, assuredly individuals thus characterised will have the best chance of being preserved in the struggle for life; and from the strong principle of inheritance they will tend to produce offspring similarly characterised. This principle of preservation, I have called, for the sake of brevity, Natural Selection.[1]

Evolutionists to this day define it much the same way (but without the Victorian verbosity):

> The differential survival of and/or reproduction of classes of entities that differ in one or more characteristics.[2]

Thus, "survival of the fittest"[3] or "survival of the fittest to reproduce" is the standard definition of the process termed *natural selection*.

Do Biblical Creationists Believe in Natural Selection?

The process of natural selection finds no conflict with the text of Scripture.[4] Ever since the Fall (Genesis 3), living things have been dying and killing each other, and the self-evident fact of natural selection is perfectly consistent with the Bible. Natural selection has happened, and it continues

---

1. Charles Darwin, *On the Origin of Species*, 1st edition, (London: John Murray, 1859), p.127. http://darwin-online.org.uk/content/frameset?itemID=F373&viewtype=text&pageseq=1.
2. Douglas J. Futuyma, *Evolution* (Sunderland, MA: Sinauer Associates, Inc., 2013), p. G-9.
3. Since the "fittest" are sometimes defined retrospectively by those individuals who survive, "natural selection" is occasionally nothing more than a self-evident truth: survival happens.
4. Georgia Purdom, "Is Natural Selection the Same Thing as Evolution?" Answers in Genesis, January 3, 2008, https://answersingenesis.org/natural-selection/is-natural-selection-the-same-thing-as-evolution/.

to happen every day. In fact, the concept of natural selection was first artic-ulated, not by an evolutionist, but by a creationist nearly a quarter century before Darwin published his most significant work.[5]

Furthermore, as biblical creationists, we must affirm that the term *natural* has been used from the earliest days of formal scientific inquiry to describe God's upholding of the universe through the laws of nature. For the Christian, *nature* is simply shorthand for God's providential operation of the creatures and creation we see around us.[6] In our example above, the culling of the sickly gazelle removes its unique genetic contribution from the overall genetic pool of the gazelle population, potentially preventing propagation of its genetic mutations.

In addition, repetition of this predation cycle over time could alter the ratios of genetic varieties in the gazelle species, potentially leading to the formation of a new species. Thus, natural selection is an observable fact that can participate in the process of variation and speciation within the original kinds of animals that God created.

How Do Evolutionists Misuse the Process of Natural Selection?

Unfortunately, evolutionists have taken a straightforward truth and co-opted it for their anti-biblical purposes:

> [Natural selection] provided an entirely natural, mechanis-tic explanation for adaptive design that had been attributed to a divine intelligence.[7]

In the evolutionary worldview, natural selection and mutations are the pri-mary driving forces resulting in the evolution of all living things from a single-celled common ancestor over billions of years — without any divine intervention. In essence, atheistic evolutionists substitute natural selection for God Himself!

The misuse of this term shouldn't intimidate biblical creationists. After all, people have been co-opting terms for anti-biblical purposes for millen-nia. Even today, unbelievers justify gay "marriage,"[8] abortion,[9] and all sorts

---

5.   Paul G. Humber, "Natural Selection — A Creationist's Idea," http://www.icr.org/article/nat-ural-selection-creationists-idea/.

6.   Tommy Mitchell, "Is Natural Selection 'the Devil's Device'?," Answers in Genesis, March 9, 2007, https://answersingenesis.org/natural-selection/is-natural-selection-the-devils-device/.

7.   Douglas J. Futuyma, *Evolution* (Sunderland, MA: Sinauer Associates, Inc., 2013), p. 8.

8.   Steve Golden, "Are There Really 'Gay Christians'?," Answers in Genesis, May 24, 2014, https://answersingenesis.org/family/homosexuality/are-there-really-gay-christians.

9.   Tim Chaffey, "*Roe v. Wade*: 40 Years Later," Answers in Genesis, https://answersingenesis.org/sanctity-of-life/abortion/roe-v-wade-40-years-later/.

of other sins in the name of "Christianity." Yet no Bible-believer would logically conclude that, because sinners wrap the cloak of "Christianity" around their vices, the entire Christian religion should be thrown out. Instead, we would all agree that the abusers of the term should be exposed, and the correct definition should be restored and emphasized to prevent error from spreading.

The same principle holds true in the realm of natural selection. Just because unbelievers co-opt the term for their anti-Christian purposes doesn't mean that natural selection isn't real or that the term should be thrown out. Instead, biblical creationists should point out the ability of natural selection to remove the sickliest individuals from a population and to preserve the least degenerate and most well-adapted organisms,[10] and we should also emphasize the scientific *inability* of natural selection to evolve the diversity of life from a common ancestor.[11]

We should also expose the logical fallacies that evolutionists employ with natural selection in an attempt to buttress their case. For example, when pressed for evidence for molecules-to-man evolution, evolutionists often cite examples of natural selection. This is an equivocation fallacy since *natural selection* has been deftly substituted for *evolution* mid-argument. These two terms have very different definitions.

Furthermore, natural selection — the survival of the fittest to reproduce — actually works in the *opposite* direction of molecules-to-man evolution. Natural selection *eliminates* variety, and goo-to-you evolution requires an ever-increasing growth in variety.[12] Thus, natural selection is a fact, but Darwinian evolution from a universal common ancestor is not — despite the evolutionists' best attempts to use the former to prove the latter.

Examples of Natural Selection

We can illustrate these principles by examining two of the most common examples of natural selection: Darwin's finches and antibiotic resistance in bacteria. Both of these examples show clearly what natural selection is and is not capable of.

---

10. This is a general principle, not an inviolable rule. Occasionally, the weaker members of a population survive over and above the stronger.
11. For example, see (with caution): Michael Behe, *Darwin's Black Box: The Biochemical Challenge to Evolution* (New York: Touchstone, 1996). Sadly, while Behe's critique of Darwin is devastating, Behe accepts evolutionary common ancestry and the secular timeline.
12. Roger Patterson, "Natural Selection vs. Evolution," Answers in Genesis, March 8, 2007, https://answersingenesis.org/natural-selection/natural-selection-vs-evolution/.

Darwin's Finches

Darwin's finches are often portrayed as the textbook example of "evolution in action." The birds' heads are often shown in rows with the most obvious difference being their beak size and shape. Darwin observed these small birds when he visited the Galápagos Islands in the early 1800s. There are now 18 recognized species of finches that mainly differ in their beak size and shape.[13] He proposed that, given enough time (like millions of years), those small differences he observed in the finches could add up to large differences that caused one kind of organism to evolve into a completely different kind of organism (e.g., dinosaurs evolved into birds). Darwin believed natural selection (acting on genetic variation) was a central process allowing evolution to accomplish this.

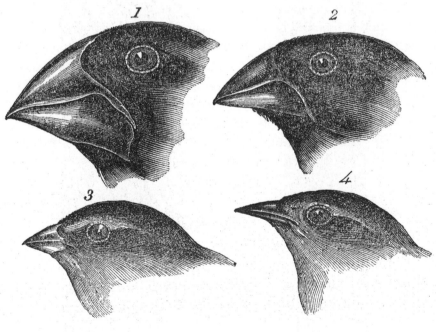

1. Geospiza magnirostris
3. Geospiza parvula
2. Geospiza fortis
4. Certhidea olivacea

While any good biblical creationist would agree that natural selection (which is observable in the present) can and does lead to adaptation and variation within a kind (like the finches), it does not and cannot lead to the

---

13. Sangeet Lamichhaney et al., "Evolution of Darwin's Finches and Their Beaks Revealed by Genome Sequencing," *Nature* 518, no.7539 (2015): 371–375.

types of changes necessary for molecules-to-man evolution. In fact, time is irrelevant. What is needed for evolution to occur is genetic mechanisms, like mutations, that can provide the necessary complexity AND natural selection. But the combination of mutations (discussed in chapter 15) and natural selection is not capable of this.

Genetically speaking, we know that two genes are critical for variation in beak size and shape — BMP4 (bone morphogenetic protein)[14] and calmodulin.[15] Differences in the expression levels and expression locations of these genes lead to short, wide beaks and long, narrow beaks and beak types in between. Within any given finch species there is always some variety. In some years, the seeds available for food favor those finches with wide beaks and in other years it favors those with narrow beaks. Essentially, the beak size within the species oscillates but the beak stays a beak and the finch stays a finch! Again, time is irrelevant because all natural selection can do is select for or against genetic variety that is already present. It (along with mutations) can't produce the variety needed for molecules-to-man evolution.

Over the last four decades, the process of species formation in Darwin's finches has been observed.[16] The resulting new species, called Big Bird, was a hybrid resulting from the mating of a medium ground finch with a large cactus finch. Big Birds have a unique beak size/shape and mating song, so only mate with other Big Birds. The hybrid finches are also larger and may be able to access food choices that other finches cannot, and appear to be surviving well on the island on which they first appeared. Hybridization is one way in which additional combinations can occur within a population and increase its survival. Future weather changes (e.g., El Niño) that affect the typical food source for finches on the island may not affect the food source of the Big Bird species, allowing natural selection to favor it under those conditions. But again, natural selection (along with mutations) simply tweaked the size and shape of the birds; it didn't produce a dramatic increase in complexity.

Antibiotic Resistance in Bacteria

Antibiotic resistance in bacteria is another example of natural selection that is often portrayed as "evolution in action." But, as we will see, natural

---

14. A. Abzhanov et al., "BMP4 and Morphological Variation of Beaks in Darwin's Finches," *Science* 305 (2007): 1462–1465.
15. A. Abzhanov et al., "The Calmodulin Pathway and Evolution of Elongated Beak Morphology in Darwin's Finches," *Nature* 442 (2006): 563–567.
16. Sangeet Lamichhaney et al., "Rapid Hybrid Speciation in Darwin's Finches," *Science* 359 (2018): 224–228.

selection works in conjunction with mutation to bring about variation within bacteria but does not lead bacteria to become a different kind of organism as evolution requires.

Antibiotics are natural products produced by fungi and bacteria, and the antibiotics we use today are typically derivatives of those. Because of this relationship, it is not surprising that some bacteria would have resistance to certain antibiotics; they must do so to be competitive in their environment. In fact, if you took a sample of soil from outside your home, you would likely find antibiotic-resistant bacteria.

A bacterium can gain resistance through two primary ways:

1. By mutation of existing genetic information
2. By using a design feature built in to swap DNA (technically called horizontal gene transfer) — a bacterium gains resistance from another bacterium that has resistance

Let's take a look at the first. Some antibiotics work by binding a protein in the bacterium and prevent it from functioning properly, killing the bacterium. Antibiotic-resistant bacteria have mutation(s) in their DNA which code for that protein. Mutant DNA leads to mutant proteins. The antibiotic cannot bind to the mutant protein, and thus, the bacteria live. Although the bacteria can survive well in an environment with antibiotics, it might come at a cost. If the antibiotic-resistant bacteria are grown with nonmutant bacteria in an environment without antibiotics, the nonmutant bacteria could have an advantage. This is because the antibiotic-resistant bacteria produce a mutant protein that may not allow them to compete well with nonmutant bacteria.

Let's clarify this by looking at the bacterium *Helicobacter pylori* which is a common cause of ulcers. Antibiotic-resistant *H. pylori* have mutation(s) that can result in the inability to produce a protein.[17] This protein normally works to assist with the breakdown of nutrients but also converts the antibiotic to a poison which causes death. When antibiotics are applied to mutant *H. pylori* these bacteria live while the normal bacteria are killed. So, by natural selection the ones that have mutation(s) survive and pass this trait along to their offspring. However, they also cannot produce the protein, so are unlikely to be competitive with normal *H. pylori* in antibiotic-free environments. It's essentially a trade-off for the bacteria — they have

---

17. Toshihiro Nishizawa and Hidekazu Suzuki, "Mechanisms of Helicobacter pylori antibiotic resistance and molecular testing," *Frontiers in Molecular Biosciences* 1 (2014): 1–7.

gained antibiotic resistance but are hampered in their ability to breakdown nutrients. This is not an example of the net gain of genetic variety which is required for evolution.

Now let's take a look at the second method. A bacterium can get antibiotic resistance by gaining resistance genes from another bacterium. Unlike you and me, bacteria can swap DNA. It is important to note that this is still not considered a gain of genetic variety required by evolution since the genes already exist, and while the mutated DNA may be new to a particular bacterium, it is not new or novel overall. The bacterium may now be resistant to the antibiotic, but it's not on its way to becoming a different kind of organism.

What we observe with both of these methods is that bacteria remain bacteria, and natural selection (and mutation) do not lead to the net gain in complexity that is required for the evolution of one kind of organism into a completely different kind of organism.

Conclusion

Both evolutionists and creationists would define natural selection similarly. It is a process that is readily observable in the present. The main difference comes down to the answer to this question — could natural selection (along with mutations) over millions of years produce the types of changes needed to go from molecules to man?

The short answer is No! Natural selection is a process that selects from the variation in populations allowing them to survive and speciate in a fallen world. Simply put, the changes that are observed today show variation within created kinds — a horizontal change, sometimes over the course of very short time spans. For molecules-to-man evolution there must be a change from one kind into another — a vertical change. This is not observed, and the mechanisms of mutation and natural selection can never supply the novel traits required by evolution. We will never see a bacterium like *H. pylori* give rise to something like a finch even if millions of years were available. Instead, we simply observe variation and speciation within each created kind.

Natural selection cannot be a driving force for molecules-to-man evolution when it does not have that power, nor should it be confused with molecules-to-man evolution. It is an observable phenomenon that results in limited variation within a kind — nothing more, nothing less. It is a great confirmation of the Bible's history.

"

No amount of posturing by the evolutionist can change the fact that these moths are still moths and will continue to be moths.

"

13 ARE PEPPERED MOTHS EVIDENCE FOR EVOLUTION?

With an MD from Vanderbilt University School of Medicine, **DR. TOMMY MITCHELL** is also a Fellow of the American College of Physicians (FACP) and Phi Beta Kappa Society. He is a popular speaker and author with Answers in Genesis. In addition to the articles he has written for AiG's website and other publications, he was the featured speaker during AiG's relief efforts after Hurricane Katrina, resulting in a Telly award-winning DVD titled *A God of Suffering?* With his experience as a physician, he is able to connect with people of all ages and educational levels with an innate ability to unveil biblical and scientific truth.

S top me if you have heard this tale before. It's about one of the sacred cows of evolution: the peppered moth. The story of this moth has been set forth for decades as *the* prime example of evolution in action. It is a fascinating story about how, due to a combination of environmental changes and selective predation, a moth turned into, well, a moth.

The peppered moth, scientifically known as *Biston betularia*, exists in two primary forms, one light colored with spots and one almost black. As the tale goes, in the mid 1800s the lighter variety of the moth (*typica*) predominated. During the Industrial Revolution, the lichen on tree trunks died, soot got deposited on trees, and as a result trees got darker. As this change occurred, the population of darker moths (*carbonaria*) increased, presumably due to the camouflage offered by the darker trees. Bird predators could not see the dark moths against the dark bark. As the darker moth population increased, the lighter moth population decreased.[1]

This story has been touted for years as a great example of Darwinian evolution in action. Countless textbooks are lavishly illustrated with photographs of light and dark moths resting on light and dark tree trunks to teach the wonders of evolution. "It is the slam dunk of natural selection, the paradigmatic story that converts high school and college students to Darwin, the thundering left hook to the jaw of creationism."[2]

Much of the "proof" for this evolutionary change came from the work of a man named Dr. Bernard Kettlewell, a medical doctor-turned-entomologist, at Oxford University. Dr. Kettlewell had been intrigued by changes in the relative populations of the moths. In his experiments he set out to show

---

1. This darkening of the wings is due to the increased amount of the pigment melanin in the wings of the *carbonaria* variety and is known as "melanism."
2. Judith Hooper, *Of Moths and Men: An Evolutionary Tale* (New York: W.W. Horton, 2002), p. xvii.

that the changes were a result of natural selection in response to environmental change and selective predation.

The Work of Kettlewell

First of all, Kettlewell had to show that birds were indeed predators of these moths. Up to that time, many biologists did not consider birds the primary predators of *Biston*. Kettlewell released moths into an aviary and observed the moths being eaten as they rested. This observation settled the issue of bird predation, at least to Kettlewell's satisfaction.[3]

For the next phase of his study, Kettlewell went to a polluted woodland area near Birmingham, England. There the trees had become darkened due to pollution. In the woods, Kettlewell undertook the first of his release-recapture experiments. He released moths, 447 of the *carbonaria* variety and 137 of the *typica* variety. Traps were set to recapture the moths that night, and the numbers of each variety were assessed the next morning. A much higher percentage of darker moths than lighter moths were recovered. Kettlewell recaptured 27.5% of the *carbonaria*, but only 13.0% of the *typica*. From this data, Kettlewell concluded that "birds act as selective agents,"[4] and subsequently felt that this represented evolution by natural selection.

To further examine this, Kettlewell then undertook another release-recapture experiment. This was done in a wooded area near Dorset, England. Here the trees had not been darkened by pollution. As before, both light and dark moths were released and then recaptured and counted. Here 12.5% of the *typica* were recaptured but only 6.3% of the *carbonaria*. Kettlewell anticipated this result because he hypothesized that birds would more easily prey upon the darker moths than the lighter moths due to the lighter color of the trees.

Adding credence to Kettlewell's theory, others noted that as pollution decreased, the population of lighter moths increased in some areas. In the late 1950s, pollution control laws were enacted and air quality improved. In some places, as the lichen returned to the trees, the expected increase in the population of the *typica* variety of moth occurred.[5] Scientists believed this increase further confirmed this living example of evolution.

---

3. H.B.D. Kettlewell, "Selection Experiments on Industrial Melanism in the Lepidoptera," *Heredity* 9 (1955): 323–342.
4. Ibid., p. 342.
5. Jonathan Wells, "Second Thoughts about Peppered Moths," The True.Origin Archive, http://trueorigin.org/pepmoth1.asp.

From this point on, there was no stopping the peppered moth bandwagon. High school and college biology textbooks heralded the peppered moth as the classic example of evolution in action. The peppered moth story has been presented to students for years as a classic case of evolution, the process by which molecules eventually turned into man.

Trouble in Paradise

Scientific claims must be confirmed through repetition, but over the years many attempts to repeat Kettlewell's studies have failed to confirm his results. These contradictory reports showed high populations of *typica* in polluted areas[6] or inordinately high numbers of *carbonaria* in lightly polluted areas.[7] Some studies failed to confirm the observation that the lighter moths increased as the lichen cover of the trees recovered. Nonetheless, the challenges failed to remove the vaunted moth from its lofty perch.

The major challenge to Kettlewell's work came in 1998 when Michael Majerus, a geneticist from Cambridge published a book entitled *Melanism: Evolution in Action.*[8] Although many of the criticisms of Kettlewell's work had been around for years, Majerus's critique of Kettlewell's methods caused quite a stir in evolutionary circles. In a review of this book in the journal *Nature*, Dr. Jerry Coyne said this; "My own reaction resembles the dismay attending my discovery, at the age of six, that it was my father and not Santa who brought the presents on Christmas Eve." He further commented, "It is also worth pondering why there has been general and unquestioned acceptance of Kettlewell's work."[9] Things were starting to look bad for our friend, *Biston betularia.* Then things got worse.

In 2002, a journalist named Judith Hooper published the book *Of Moths and Men: An Evolutionary Tale.* This book detailed the story of the research involving the peppered moth, including an exploration of the lives of the principal people involved. She described the lives and backgrounds of not only Kettlewell but also of E.B. Ford, Kettlewell's mentor at Oxford. The somewhat unflattering portraits of these men were disturbing and, in one sense, made for good reading — if by good reading one likes reveling in the shortcomings of other human beings.

6.   R.C. Stewart, "Industrial and Non-industrial Melanism in the Peppered Moth, Biston betularia (L.)," *Ecological Entomology* 2 (1977): 231–243.

7.   D.R. Lees and E.R. Creed, "Industrial Melanism in Biston betularia: The Role of Selective Predation," *Journal of Animal Ecology* 44 (1975): 67–83.

8.   M.E.N. Majerus, *Melanism: Evolution in Action* (Oxford: Oxford University Press, 1998).

9.   J.A. Coyne, "Not Black and White," *Nature* 396 (1998): 35–36.

However, it was Hooper's detailed examination of Kettlewell's experimental techniques that fueled the most controversy. She thoroughly described the method used by Kettlewell in each of his field studies, along with an analysis of the data he collected. Her conclusions were shocking in that she suggests that Kettlewell, after obtaining disappointing data in the early phase of his study, manipulated his collection of data later in the study in order to obtain the desired result. The possibility of outright fraud was even mentioned. The scientific community was aghast. The first and foremost evidence for evolution in action, "the prize horse in our stable,"[10] was apparently in jeopardy.

What's the Problem?

Although there have been many concerns raised about Kettlewell's experimental techniques, the biggest issue seems to revolve around where moths rest during the day. In his study, Kettlewell released moths during the daytime and watched them take resting places on the trunks of trees. He then observed birds preying on the moths. During the night, he collected and counted the moths. He concluded that birds preyed more readily on the more visible moths than on the ones better hidden by their surroundings. The problem with this conclusion is that, over many years of study, it had been determined that *these moths don't rest on tree trunks during the day!* They fly only at night, and they take resting places high in the trees on the underside of branches. In these places they are much better concealed from birds than were the moths in Kettlewell's experiments. According to Howlett and Majerus, "Exposed areas of tree trunks are not an important resting site for any form of B. betularia."[11]

This is more than an insignificant criticism. Abnormal placement of the moths into a location rendering them much more visible would bring into question the validity of Kettlewell's results. First of all, the distinction between light and dark moths would be much less on the shadowy underside of a branch. Secondly, the unnaturally high concentration of moths in an unusual area might have changed the normal feeding pattern of the birds. In fact, some researchers are not convinced that birds are the primary peppered moth predators in nature — James Carey of the University of California, for example.[12] Also, some researchers (although not Kettlewell

10. Ibid., p. 35.
11. R.J. Howlett and M.E.N. Majerus, "The Understanding of Industrial Melanism in the Peppered Moth (Biston betularia) (Lepidoptera: Geometridea)," *Biological Journal of the Linnean Society* 30 (1987): 40.
12. J. de Roode, "The Moths of War," *New Scientist* 196 no. 2633 (2007): 49.

himself) have conducted experiments by using dead moths glued to tree trunks,[13] a practice that has been criticized by some observers. Furthermore, many researchers considered the method by which Kettlewell assessed the degree of moth camouflage to be overly subjective. This bias would call into question the entire body of data.

These criticisms bring into question the entire issue of selective bird predation being the driving force behind this so-called splendid example of natural selection. Without an observable, defined environmental factor to push the peppered moth to "evolve," the famous moth could not even be a candidate to be used as evidence to support Darwin's theory.

Was Kettlewell Wrong?

So was Kettlewell wrong? One major figure in this discussion has come to Kettlewell's defense, and that person is none other than Majerus, the man whose book fueled much of the recent controversy.

Over the last few years, Majerus has reexamined this question. He has conducted a study that apparently does not suffer from some of the supposed deficiencies of Kettlewell's experimental techniques. He was very careful to ensure that the moth's resting places mimicked those seen in nature, and the moths were released at night.[14] Also, using binoculars, he observed birds eating the moths. He claims that the results of his study validate Kettlewell's work. De Roode concludes, "The peppered moth should be reinstated as a textbook example of evolution in action."[15]

Good scientists must examine and reexamine the methods and techniques used to study our world. The experimental method itself relies on others conducting the same or similar types of investigations to see if previous conclusions are indeed valid. As part of this quest for knowledge, flaws in the methods used by prior investigators are sometimes uncovered. After all, no one makes a perfect plan. Shortcomings in methodology can be corrected and further data collected to ensure proper conclusions are reached. To that end, all those who have questioned Kettlewell's methods should be commended. If there were problems with his methods, and apparently there were, those problems seem to have been corrected in subsequent evaluations.

Further, those who would be too critical of Kettlewell should proceed with some caution. There has been much written in both the pro-evolution and the pro-creation camps that has been very critical of Kettlewell. Some of

13. Wells, p. 7.
14. de Roode, p. 48.
15. Ibid., p. 49.

this seems justified, but much of it does not, particularly the accusation that he falsified his data. There can be no more serious accusation made against a scientist, so it would seem that more proof is needed before that charge be made. After all, others involved in this area have collected data which validates Kettlewell's original conclusions. No one can know another's heart, so some measure of charity needs be given here. Perhaps Kettlewell's shortcomings can best be measured by this quote from a colleague who characterized him as "the best naturalist I have ever met, and almost the worst professional scientist I have ever known."[16]

So Where Are We?

Does all this debate about the validity of Kettlewell's peppered moth data really pose a problem for creationists? The evolutionist claims that the peppered moth story is such a shining example of evolution in action that to question it is to demonstrate unwillingness to accept proven science. Majerus has said, "The peppered moth story is easy to understand because it involves things that we are familiar with: vision and predation and birds and moths and pollution and camouflage and lunch and death. That is why the anti-evolution lobby attacks the peppered moth story. They are frightened that too many will be able to understand."[17]

Exactly what is it that we should be able to understand? To the creationist, it is very, very simple. Over the last 150 years, moths have changed into moths! The creationist has no difficulty with this process. The issue of Kettlewell's shortcomings notwithstanding, the creationist has no problem with the results of his (and other subsequent researchers') work. The concept that a less visible organism would survive better than a more visible one seems obvious in the extreme. What is not to understand here? According to de Roode, "The peppered moth was and is a well understood example of evolution by natural selection."[18] The creationist would agree that this population change represents natural selection. However, this change is most certainly *not* molecules-to-man evolution. Natural selection and molecules-to-man evolution are not the same thing, and many are led astray by the misuse of these terms.

Natural selection can easily be seen in nature. Natural selection produces the variations within a kind of organism. Thanks to natural selection, we have the marvelous variety of creatures that we see in our world.

16. J.A. Coyne, "Evolution Under Pressure," *Nature* 418 (2002): 19.
17. Ibid., p. 49.
18. de Roode, p. 49.

However, in this process, fish change into (amazingly) fish, birds change into birds, dogs change into dogs, and moths change into moths. If, during the process of the study of peppered moths, the moths had changed into some other type of creature, a bird perhaps, then we might have something to talk about.

No amount of posturing by the evolutionist can change the fact that these moths are still moths and will continue to be moths. The variation seen is simply the result of sorting and resorting of the genetic material present in the original moths. At no time has there been any new information introduced into the genome of the moth (which is what molecules-to-man evolution would require). There is no evidence of the beginnings of an intermediate form between the present moth and the creature it is destined to evolve into. Moths stay moths, fish stay fish, and people stay people, regardless of the great variety seen within each.

Ultimately, the peppered moth story is more of the same. Although much of the clamor surrounding Kettlewell's work has made for good reading and, in some ways, has made for good science, the results are clear. There is nothing here, in even the smallest way, to provide evidence for the process of molecules-to-man evolution. That is what the creationist is "able to understand."

> *Species is a man-made term and, frankly, the word species is difficult to define, whether one is a creationist or an evolutionist!*

IS A SPECIES THE SAME THING AS A BIBLICAL KIND?

With a PhD in molecular genetics, **DR. GEORGIA PURDOM** is a researcher, speaker, and writer with Answers in Genesis in Petersburg, Kentucky. She is the co-founder of the Microbe Forum, served as a member of the Executive Council of the Creation Biology Society, as well as serving as a peer reviewer for the *Creation Research Science Quarterly* and the *Answers Research Journal*. Her specialty is cellular and molecular biology and she has published papers in the *Journal of Neuroscience*, the *Journal of Bone and Mineral Research*, and the *Journal of Leukocyte Biology*.

With a master's degree in mechanical engineering from Southern Illinois University at Carbondale, **BODIE HODGE** is a speaker, writer, and researcher for Answers in Genesis. With experience in apologetics, he has contributed to and written a number of books and articles.

Although not exactly the same mantra that the travelers in the classic *Wizard of Oz* repeat, "Zonkeys, Ligers, and Wholphins, Oh My!" these names represent real life animals just the same. In fact, two of these strange-sounding animals, a zonkey and a zorse, can be seen at the Creation Museum petting zoo (figure 1). But what exactly are these animals and how did they come to be? What is the difference between a "kind" and a species? Can the Bible explain such a thing?

Figure 1. Zonkey and zorse at the Creation Museum

What Is a "Kind"?

The first thing that needs to be addressed is: "What is a kind?" In biology textbooks, you will find this taxonomic classification of plants and animals: *Kingdom, Phylum, Class, Order, Family, Genus, Species.* The Swedish physician, botanist, and zoologist Carl Linnaeus (1701–1778) is known as the father of modern taxonomy for creating this system of classification. And he was also a creation scientist! Often, people are confused in thinking that the modern "species" is the same as the original created "kind" discussed in Genesis 1.

But these two categories are not necessarily the same. *Species* is a man-made term and, frankly, the word *species* is difficult to define, whether one is a creationist or an evolutionist! For example, species are usually defined as a group of organisms that can produce fertile offspring. However, the coyote (*Canis latrans*) and domestic dog (*Canis lupus*) can mate and produce coy-dogs that are fertile even though they are different species. Thus, we can see the difficulty in defining what a species is.

The Old Testament was originally written in Hebrew. In Genesis 1, the Hebrew word *min* is translated in English Bibles as *kind*. Genesis 1 tells us that God created plants and animals "according to their kinds." That same Hebrew word, *min*, is used again in Genesis 6 and 7 when God instructed Noah to take two of every kind (*min*) of land-dwelling, air-breathing animal onto the Ark (Genesis 6:19–20 and 7:14).

Figure 2. Wild and domestic dogs all belong to the same dog kind.

A plain reading of the text infers that plants and animals were created to reproduce within the boundaries of their kind. Evidence to support this concept is clearly seen (or rather not seen) in our world today as there are no reports of dats (dog + cat) or hows (horse + cow)! So, a good rule of thumb is that if two things can breed together then they are of the same created kind. It is a bit more complicated than this, but for the time being this is an adequate definition of a "kind."

As an example, dogs can easily breed with one another, whether wolves, dingoes, coyotes, or domestic dogs. When dogs breed together you get dogs, so there is a dog kind (figure 2). It works the same with landfowls. There are

LANDFOWL VARIATIONS

Figure 3. The amazing variety of landfowl species and breeds all belong to the same kind.

many species of landfowls, but landfowls breed with each other and you still get landfowls. So, there is a landfowl kind (figure 3). The concept is fairly easy to understand.

But in today's culture where evolution and millions of years are taught as fact, many people have been led to believe that animals and plants (that are classed as a specific species) have been like this for tens of thousands of years and perhaps millions of years. So, when they see things like lions or zebras they think they have been like this for an extremely long time.

From a biblical perspective though, land animals like wolves, zebras, sheep, lions, and so on have at least two ancestors that lived on Noah's Ark only about 4,300 years ago. These animals have undergone many changes since that time. But dogs are still part of the dog kind, cats are still part of the cat kind, and so on. God placed a great deal of genetic diversity (genetic variations in the DNA) within the original created kinds, and some variation has occurred since the Fall due to genetic alterations and other mechanisms.[1]

Variety within a Kind

Because of the confusion of scientific and biblical terms for this topic and so that we can grasp the truth regarding the question of origins, creation

---

1. Nathaniel T. Jeanson, "The Origin of Species after the Flood" (article series), https://answers-ingenesis.org/noahs-ark/origin-of-species-after-flood/ (2016).

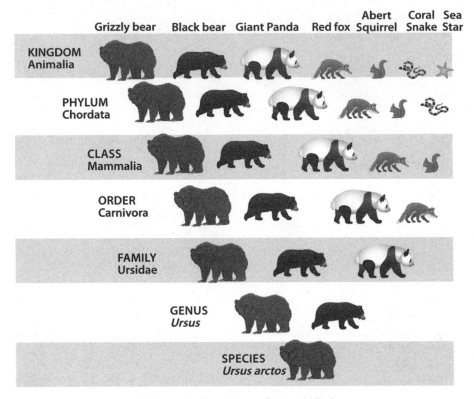

Figure 4. Baramin — Created Kind

scientists have created a scientific term, *baramin,* to refer to a created kind as discussed in Genesis 1. Baramin comes from the Hebrew verb *bara* ("create," used in Genesis 1:1) and *min* ("kind," used ten times in Genesis 1:11–12, 21, and 24–25). Because none of the original ancestors of birds and animals are alive today, creation scientists have been trying to determine baramins and classify living organisms and those organisms known only from the fossil record into those baramins. This field of study is known as baraminology. As a result of research, creation scientists think that for many animals baramin is equivalent to the level of family and possibly order in the modern scientific classification system (figure 4). On rare occasions, a baramin may be equivalent to genus or species.

Classification into baramins is done based on several criteria. For living creatures, hybridization is a key criterion. If two animals can mate and produce offspring (known as a hybrid), then they are considered to be of the same kind.[2] Linnaeus held to this idea as well and believed that God created distinct kinds that were fixed.[3] He observed variation within the kinds but did not think one kind could evolve into a different kind.[4] However, it should be noted that the inability to produce offspring does not necessarily rule out that the animals are of the same kind since this may result from the difficulty of finding hybrid data for wild animals or mutations or other differences (since the Fall).[5]

Zonkeys (male zebra and female donkey) and zorses (male zebra and female horse) are all examples of hybrid animals. They have a mixture of their parent's traits including the beautiful striping patterns of the zebra parents. Hybrid animals are the result of the mating of two animals of the same kind. Perhaps one of the most popular hybrids of the past has been the mule, the mating of a horse and donkey. So, seeing something like a zorse or zonkey shouldn't really surprise anyone, since donkeys, zebras, and horses all belong to the horse kind (family *Equidae*) (figure 5).

Liger and tigons are hybrids that result from mating within the family *Felidae*. Ligers (male lion and female tiger) are the largest cats in the world weighing in at over 1,000 pounds (450 kg). Tigons are the result of mating

Figure 5. Horses of all shapes and sizes are of the same kind (baramin).

2. Jean K. Lightner et al., "Determining Ark Kinds," *Answers Research Journal* 4 (2011): 195–201.
3. Per Landgren, "On the Origin of 'Species,'" in S. Scherer, ed., *Typen des Lebens* (Berlin: Pascal-Verlag, 1993), p. 47–64.
4. J. Ramsbottom, annual presidential address to the Linnaean Society, published in *Proceedings of the Linnaean Society*, 1938, p. 197.
5. Lightner, 2011.

a female lion and a male tiger. These matings only occur in captivity, since lions live in Africa, tigers live in Asia, and the two are enemies in the wild.

Other hybrids in this family include bobcats that mate with domestic cats and bobcats with lynx (blynx and lynxcat). There have been mixes of the cougar and the ocelot as well as many others. This shows that large, midsize, and small cats can ultimately interbreed, and suggests that there is only one cat kind.

Turning to the ocean, a wholphin is a hybrid resulting from mating a false killer whale and bottlenose dolphin. Both belong to the family *Delphinidae*. Such a mating occurred in captivity at Hawaii's Sea Life Park in 1985.[6] This hybrid shows the difficulty of defining a species since a major criterion is the ability to interbreed and produce fertile offspring. Even though the whale and dolphin are considered separate species and genera, they can interbreed and produce offspring. Of course, from a biblical perspective it is easy to say they both belong to the same kind (baramin)!

Many times, hybridization data is unknown. This is especially true for animals that are only known from the fossil record (because they are not living, we don't know if they can mate and produce offspring). In these cases, the key criterion that is used is called the cognitum.[7] The cognitum is a perception-based concept that naturally groups organisms together through human cognitive senses.[8] For example, if a person was given a picture showing kangaroos, squirrels, and rabbits all mixed together in a photograph, the person would likely separate the animals into three groups based on their shared physical characteristics. Kinds have retained distinctiveness even as diversification within the kinds has occurred, and there is a strong cognitum at the family level. Both hybridization and cognitum strongly indicate that kind is at the family (and sometimes order) level (figure 4).

The concept of kind is important for understanding how Noah fit all the animals on the Ark. If kind is at the level of family/order, there would have been plenty of room on the Ark to take two of every kind and seven pairs of some (figure 6).[9] For example, even though many different dinosaurs have been identified, creation scientists think there are only about 60–80 kinds

6. Stephen Adams, "Dolphin and Whale Mate to Create a 'Wholphin,'" Telegraph.co.uk, April 2, 2008, www.telegraph.co.uk/news/uknews/1582973/Dolphin-and-whale-mate-to-create-a-wolphin.html.

7. Lightner, 2011.

8. Ibid.

9. Andrew Snelling, ed., *Extant Ark Kinds: Mammalian and Avian Kinds* (Petersburg, KY: Answers in Genesis, 2018) and Andrew Snelling, ed., *Extant Ark Kinds: Amphibian and Reptile Kinds* (Petersburg: KY: Answers in Genesis, 2018).

ANIMALS ON THE ARK

	Kinds	Animals
Mammals	468	1,488
Synapsids	78	156
Birds	284	3,676
Reptiles	320	928
Amphibians	248	496
Total	1,398	6,744

Figure 6

of dinosaurs. Even though breeding studies are impossible with dinosaurs, by studying fossils one can ascertain that there was likely one Ceratopsian kind with variation in that kind, and so on (figure 7).

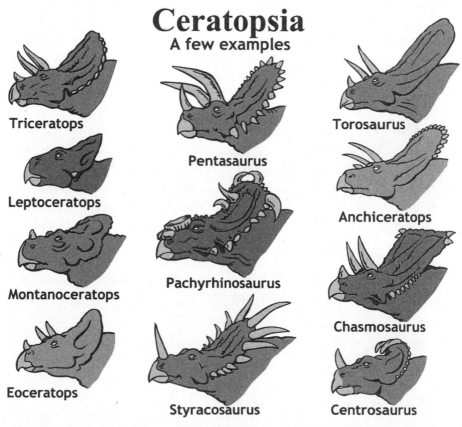

Ceratopsia
A few examples

Triceratops

Pentasaurus

Torosaurus

Leptoceratops

Anchiceratops

Montanoceratops

Pachyrhinosaurus

Chasmosaurus

Eoceratops

Styracosaurus

Centrosaurus

Figure 7. All these varieties are in one kind (baramin) of dinosaur — Ceratopsia.

After the Flood, the animals were told to "be fruitful and multiply on the earth" (Genesis 8:17). As they did this, natural selection, mutation, and other mechanisms acting on created genetic diversity within organisms allowed speciation within the kinds to occur.[10] Speciation was necessary for the animals to survive in a very different post-Flood world. This is especially well illustrated in the dog kind in which current members (e.g., coyotes, dingoes, and domestic dogs) are confirmed to be descended from an ancestral type of dog.[11]

So Many Dogs, So Little Time?

Some people might object and say, "But think about all the different species of dogs there are. It seems like there would need to be a lot of change in a short period of time (it's been around 4,000 years since the Flood). Is that reasonable? Are you suggesting some kind of hyper-evolution?" Keep in mind that dogs are still dogs (and this is true regardless of the animal kind — cats are still cats, horses are still horses, and landfowls are still landfowls). For molecules-to-man evolution, one kind of organism would need to change into a completely different kind of organism (e.g., dinosaurs into birds), and that is not what we observe. We observe speciation (change within a kind) and not evolution (change between kinds).

Great Dane
C. lupus

Yorkshire Terrier
C. lupus

Figure 8

Let's continue with our dog example. There are approximately 35 species of dogs in the world today. Within *Canis lupus* (wolves and domestic dogs), there are approximately 338 breeds. Many of the dog breeds look very different from one another, like a great dane vs. a Yorkshire terrier (figure 8), however, they are all *Canis lupus*. On the other hand, the wolf (*Canis lupus*) and coyote (*Canis latrans*) look very much alike yet they are different species. (figure 9) Breeds obviously came about through artificial selection. People chose traits they wanted or didn't want and bred the dogs accordingly. Most dog breeds have only come

10. Jeanson, 2016.
11. Robert K. Wayne, "Origin, Genetic Diversity, and Genome Structure of the Domestic Dog," *Bioessays* 21 (1999): 247–257.

Wolf
C. lupus

Coyote
C. latrans

Figure 9

into existence in the last 500 years. So, if people can selectively breed and obtain this great variety of dog breeds within several hundred years, it's quite plausible that a mere 35 species of dogs with seemingly much less variety among them could have come into existence through natural processes in just a few thousand years (since the Flood).

Remember, too, that natural processes such as natural selection, genetic drift, migration, etc. are acting on pre-existing genetic diversity that God created within the kinds.[12] The reshuffling and limited alteration of that genetic diversity through reproduction plus natural processes leads to many possibilities for organisms and the variety of species we observe within the kinds in our modern world.[13]

Modern Examples of Rapid Change/Speciation

Current scientific literature is replete with examples of rapid and observable changes, including speciation in organisms in very short time frames. For example, Italian wall lizards have developed larger heads and cecal valves in just 40 years.[14] Green lizards have developed bigger toe pads in 15 years,[15] and guppies have been shown to produce more embryos per reproductive cycle in just eight years.[16] Even a new species of Galápagos finch (Big Bird)

12. Jeanson, 2016, ibid.
13. Jeanson, 2016, ibid.
14. Kimberly Johnson, "Lizards rapidly evolve after introduction to island," nationalgeographic. com, April 21, 2008, https://www.nationalgeographic.com/animals/2008/04/lizard-evolution-island-darwin/.
15. Rachel Feltman, "Competition drove these lizards to evolve big, sticky feet in just 15 years," washingtonpost.com, October 23. 2014, https://www.washingtonpost.com/news/speaking-of-science/wp/2014/10/23/competition-drove-these-lizards-to-evolve-big-sticky-feet-in-just-15-years/?utm_term=.3316585ed5c4.
16. "When evolution is not so slow and gradual," sciencedaily.com, June 3, 2009, https://www.sciencedaily.com/releases/2009/06/090602133551.htm.

has been observed to form from a mating of two different finch species in just 36 years.[17]

These studies show that it doesn't take millions of years for species to form as evolutionists theorize. Instead, as one science journalist stated when reporting on this topic, "Researchers who once assumed evolution required millennia are documenting species adapting in mere decades, or even shorter time frames. . . . Adaptation is happening right under our noses, in our lifetimes."[18]

A Great Place for Creation Research

Great variety can be observed in the offspring of animals of the same kind, just as the same cake recipe can be used to make many different cakes with various flavors and colors. What an amazing diversity of life God has created for us to enjoy!

The study of created kinds is an exciting area of research, and our hope is to help encourage others to get involved. Whether studying the duck kind, elephant kind, camel kind, or others, the field of baraminology is a great place for biologists, zoologists, geneticists, and paleontologists (in the case of extinct kinds) to get immersed in creation research.

---

17   "Galapagos study finds that new species can develop in as little as two generations," phys. org, November 23, 2017, https://phys.org/news/2017-11-galapagos-species.html.

18   Jane Braxton Little, "Rapid evolution change species in real time," *Discover Magazine,* January 22, 2015, http://discovermagazine.com/2015/march/19-life-in-the-fast-lane.

"———————————————————

. . . any claims that mutations provided the raw material for the Darwinian evolution of new, increasingly complex life forms is based not on observational science but on wishful thinking.

———————————————————"

ARE MUTATIONS THE MAGICAL KEY THAT MAKES EVOLUTION POSSIBLE?

DR. ELIZABETH MITCHELL received a Bachelor of Science degree in chemistry from Furman University in 1980, graduating *summa cum laude*. She graduated from Vanderbilt University School of Medicine in Nashville in 1984 and completed her residency in obstetrics and gynecology at Vanderbilt University Affiliated Hospitals in 1988. She earned board certification and fellowship in the American College of Obstetrics and Gynecology. Dr. Mitchell practiced medicine near Nashville, TN, but in 1995 she retired from private practice to devote herself to the needs of her three children and their homeschooling. She is a talented researcher and writer for Answers in Genesis (AiG), operating under the conviction that accurate history never violates biblical history, that correct scientific understanding of our past will never contradict God's eyewitness account in the Bible, and that genuine understanding of God's Word builds faith in Jesus Christ.

A single-celled organism was supposedly the first life form. Then that initial creature had to evolve over billions of years into a diverse array of creatures including dogs, trees, humans, and dinosaurs. It had to change for evolution to be possible. But how?

Introduction

In the 1800s, Charles Darwin proposed that natural selection was the driving force for evolution — a process that filters organisms according to "survival of the fittest." However, that didn't explain where new kinds of organisms came from in the first place. So modern evolutionists, with the knowledge of genetics, looked for a mechanism to add the genetic information needed to form novel traits so that, for example, a dinosaur could evolve into a bird.

Mutations are often called the "engines of evolution." Why? Because mutations, unlike natural selection, are seen as the genetic generators of new information for new traits. And the randomly produced information mutations presumably produce, is believed to be building blocks for new kinds of organisms from which natural selection can select the fittest to survive.

The evolutionary worldview holds that new kinds of living things arise from existing, and often less complex, ones. As in the instance above, evolutionary scientists would have us believe that single-celled organisms evolved over time into multicellular organisms and, subsequently, that ape-like creatures evolved into humans. That would require drastic changes in the informational blueprints from which organisms develop. Could mutations supply that information?

Because observable mutations can introduce more variety into a population of organisms, evolutionary scientists believe that mutations have provided raw material for novel traits for the evolution of new kinds of countless organisms over millions of years. Is this possible? Have mutations been the engine that drove evolution, producing an almost infinite variety of organisms from which Darwinian evolution could select the fittest to climb the evolutionary ladder?

What Are Mutations?

Before we can know what mutations might be capable of supplying for the biological tree of life, we must understand what mutations are. Mutations are errors in an organism's genetic material. Every living organism — from bacterium to human — has a genetic blueprint by which it develops and functions. This blueprint, written in genetic code on DNA, is a complex storehouse of information. That DNA is copied and passed on when cells divide. And the genetic blueprint — or *genome* — for a particular kind of organism is passed to offspring during reproduction.

Living things were created after their own kinds and reproduce accordingly — as described in Genesis chapter one and observed in all of biological science — because each kind has its own genome. This genome is the genetic blueprint that produces that kind of organism.

Within an organism's genome, there are many possible variations, such as those that determine our eye color and skin pigmentation. Many genes — which are the DNA instructions to make particular proteins and the traits associated with them — exist in varying forms, called *alleles.*

God designed all living things, including humans, to vary a great deal within their created kinds. The shuffling and mixing of these alleles during reproduction produces amazing variety, but never a new and different kind of organism. And never a more complex one.

But if something goes wrong when DNA is being copied — if some information is left out, damaged, scrambled, substituted, or even duplicated — then this change, a *mutation,* may also be passed on. If a mutation — a DNA copying error — occurs during reproduction, then the mutation may be passed on to offspring. Just as the genetic variant for eye color may be passed on to offspring, so may a mutation for a trait like color-blindness or sickle cell hemoglobin.

Mutations — Harmless, Harmful, or Helpful?

Many mutations are harmless and produce no discernible difference in an organism, human or otherwise. These often occur in the parts of DNA that do not specifically encode a protein product. Such mutations, because they can still be passed on to offspring, are used to trace population movements. By DNA testing populations, scientists can follow the path of even an inconsequential mutation across the globe.

Some mutations cause problems but do not limit the chances for survival and reproduction. An example would be color-blindness. Other mutations cause devastating problems. Tragic examples include Tay-Sachs disease, an inherited disease that destroys nerve cells in an affected child, and Huntington's chorea, an inherited disease that causes neurological degeneration manifested later in life.

Mutated genes, like all genes, must be expressed to have an effect. Some mutated genes have no effect because the organism has a corresponding gene of a different variety that is dominant over it. If no such dominant overriding gene is present, the mutation is expressed as a particular characteristic.

For instance, most mutations causing human color blindness are carried on the X-chromosome. And males have only one X chromosome. Therefore, males whose X-chromosome carries such a defect fail to properly develop some of the color-sensing cones in the eye and are unable to distinguish certain colors. Female carriers of a color blindness mutation, on the other hand, usually have normal color vision because they have a corresponding normal gene on their other X chromosome.

Some mutations are expressed when two corresponding genes both have the mutated form. An example occurs in Tay-Sachs disease. The mutated gene in Tay-Sachs disease causes an abnormality in a vital nerve cell enzyme, resulting in the build-up of toxic molecules inside nerve cells. This disease occurs in a child that inherits the mutated form of the gene from both parents. Other mutations, such as the mutation causing Huntington chorea, another neurological wasting disease, are expressed even if the abnormal gene is inherited from only one parent.

Some mutations, though not most, even offer some benefit. Could such "beneficial mutations" be the sort of mutations evolutionists need in vast numbers to justify their claims?

Beneficial Mutations: A Basis for Evolutionary Advances?

Let's examine the claim that beneficial mutations could fuel evolutionary advancement. A prevalent example of a beneficial mutation is the mutation that enables adult humans to continue making the enzyme needed to properly digest milk.

The gene is active in infants, but it is designed to shut down over time. However, many people — probably most people you know — carry a mutation causing the gene to remain active. They continue to produce the enzyme needed to fully digest the lactose in milk on into adulthood. Such a mutation certainly could have survival advantages in a locale where food was limited but dairy products readily available. Yet this mutation, however convenient for lovers of ice cream and fine cheeses, does not create any new information. It only allows the continued expression of existing genetic information.

Another commonly cited example of a beneficial mutation is sickle cell trait. Hemoglobin is the oxygen-carrying protein found in red blood cells. The mutated gene in sickle cell causes production of an abnormal hemoglobin. Sickle cell hemoglobin still works, but due to its defects it twists itself into abnormal shapes that deform the red blood cells carrying it.

Sickled red blood cells are fragile and have trouble squeezing through tiny capillaries. People who inherit two copies of the mutant sickle cell allele from their parents suffer from sickle cell anemia, a disease associated with many health problems, including a high death rate from malaria.

People who inherit only one copy of the sickle cell allele make enough normal hemoglobin with their un-mutated allele to get along well enough. However, the abnormal hemoglobin their cells carry interferes with the life cycle of the malaria-causing parasite, thanks to the same defect that makes blood cells twist.

Therefore, carriers of a single sickle cell gene resist malaria better than people with normal hemoglobin. Furthermore, in regions where deadly malaria is endemic, there is a high prevalence of people carrying one copy of the sickle cell mutation in the population. Being a carrier of the sickle cell trait appears to offer a survival advantage under these specific circumstances.

Does that mean the sickle mutation produces new information? Not at all. The abnormal hemoglobin is just defective hemoglobin, not a new kind of oxygen-carrying molecule. This defective hemoglobin does not work better. It merely has a defect that hurts the parasite's ability to reproduce. People with sickle cell trait have lost some of their hemoglobin-making information, and carriers only survive malaria better if they also retain the correct hemoglobin-making information elsewhere in their DNA.

Natural selection is the tendency for organisms best suited to survive and reproduce, thereby increasing the prevalence of their characteristics in a population. Natural selection of people carrying a single copy of the mutated gene is the reason we find a higher prevalence of sickle cell carriers in malaria-cursed regions than in comparable populations elsewhere.

But nothing in this process involves production of new information. The sickle cell mutation is not an evolutionary advance toward a new kind of organism, nor even a new kind of oxygen-carrying molecule. The beneficial nature of the sickle cell mutation under certain circumstances, like the beneficial nature of the lactose tolerance mutation, illustrates natural selection. It is not, however, a model for Darwinian evolution.

Genetic Information

We've been using the word *information* a lot. In biological terms, just what is information? Cells are the building blocks of all living things. The information contained in living cells — be they single-celled organisms or components of multicellular organisms like hyacinths, honeybees, or humans — is written in coded form in the organism's DNA molecules.

That information includes the instructions for the development of that organism as well as the instructions for the many things that organism's cells can do. The information in DNA is expressed using intracellular machinery that decodes and carries out the instructions, making countless proteins that function in particular ways. DNA is a complex information-containing molecule that is copied in order to pass on that information to copies of the cells containing it.

The information encoded on DNA is written in *genes*. Genes are simply the units of DNA instructions that direct how a living organism is made and how its cells function. All the functions of a cell are ultimately carried out or made possible by the proteins encoded in its DNA.

Therefore, we can say that a gene's instructions are decoded into "words" — the amino acids that are strung together to make a protein. The individual components of a gene — called nucleotides — are then like the "alphabet" of the genetic code in which these instructions are written.

Changing a nucleotide to a different one is a sort of mutation, an error analogous to a spelling error. Just as some spelling errors can be overlooked without misunderstanding the sense of a sentence, some mutations are inconsequential.

Likewise, other spelling errors or complete omissions or duplications of words can completely change the meaning of a sentence or turn it into nonsense. Analogously, some mutations result in defective protein products — like sickle cell hemoglobin — and others result in a completely nonfunctional protein product — like a nonfunctional enzyme that leaves toxic byproducts to build up in an organism's cells.

Sometimes multiple copies of certain genes are found in an organism's normal genome. Yet a duplication mutation that results in additional copies of the gene may cause disease. This is the case with Huntington's chorea.

Even if the duplication of a gene were to be harmless or beneficial, the information produced by the duplication would not be new, any more than the presence of ten copies of a particular book in a library would represent more actual information than the presence of one.

But What About Genetic Differences?

Are differences in the genomes of different kinds of organisms always the result of mutations? No, they are typically just created differences, often in the midst of common designs. But what about the similarities between the genomes of different kinds of organisms? Don't they show that mutations accumulated to evolve each from a common ancestor? Not at all!

The similarity between ape and human genomes is often touted as an example of this evolutionary claim. Just how similar the chimpanzee and human genome are is itself difficult to nail down. Some sources have claimed up to 97–99% similarity, while other sources come up with much lower estimates, even in the neighborhood of 70–80% (see chapter 22 for more information on this topic).

Differences in estimates depend largely on differences in the way similarity is assessed. The DNA content of a genome is enormous. Despite the appearance on science fiction programs, there is no quick and easy way to compare the genomes of different kinds of organisms.

Some methods even assume the genomes share a common ancestry and try to assess how much they have diverged from it. In any case, even the lowest estimates of genetic similarity between chimps and humans show that there is a lot of similarity there.

So why isn't this genetic similarity evidence for Darwinian evolution? Why aren't those shared genes the obvious legacy of a shared ancestor? Well, to make such a claim is to *assume* that genetic information resulted from Darwinian evolution in the first place. It is to *assume* that genetic differences must result from mutations! That is a worldview-based assumption, not scientific evidence.

Such an assumption — that genetic differences must represent mutations and divergence from a common ancestor — ignores the fact that genetic differences can be the result of common designs by a Creator.

The Creator God is the common designer of all life. We observe in science that living things do indeed vary and reproduce only within their created kinds. Indeed, God — the only actual eyewitness to the origin of life — has told us in His Word that He made all kinds of living things in the beginning. Then they were to reproduce in a good world, uncursed by God for man's sin.

Sin, of course ruined this creation, but what we observe is a brilliant confirmation of what we read in Scripture. We would therefore expect that many kinds of living things — designed as they are to live in the same world, utilizing the same sorts of biochemical and biological resources — would share many common designs.

Common designs include many sorts of things, from the existence of four limbs and a vertebral column to the general plan of the digestive system to the presence of many common enzymes in the metabolic processes that process food. And each of these designs is encoded in the genome.

Thus, it is no surprise to find similar genes in different kinds of organisms that have some similarities to each other. *Those similarities are evidence of common design and a common Designer.* They are not footprints of a common evolutionary ancestor from which each organism diverged through accumulated mutations and evolutionary processes.

Conclusion: Mutations — Mistakes, Not Evolutionary Raw Material

Mutations are errors. They can be inconsequential, or they can — and often do — result in a loss of a cell's genetic information.

Mutations can even produce variations that are beneficial under certain conditions. But observational science has never demonstrated that mutations can produce the sort of new information and novel traits that would be required to produce a new kind of organism.

Even when natural selection favors the persistence of a particular mutation in a population, no new kind of organism is evolving. Thus, any claims that mutations provided the raw material for the Darwinian evolution of new, increasingly complex life forms is based not on observational science but on wishful thinking.

> *Though it took textbook publishers almost 100 years to remove the horse evolution information from the curriculum, the scientific community started questioning the fossil evidence in the early 1900s.*

16 A Horse Will Always Be a Horse, of Course!

In addition to her work as a forensic science educator, speaker, and author, **DR. JENNIFER HALL RIVERA,** has also contributed articles to *Answers in Depth* and *Answers Magazine*. Now serving as Education Specialist at the Creation Museum, Dr. Rivera presents daily workshops and develops children's educational programs. Her interest in the forensic sciences started at an early age and is credited to the godly instruction of her father, a renowned fingerprint expert. Her experience in the field of forensic science includes employment in a crime scene unit, over a decade of teaching, journal publications, and numerous speaking events.

From the earliest artistic representations to modern photography, the beauty and majesty of the horse have long captivated the interest of mankind. Beginning thousands of years ago, the horse has been one of the most painted animals depicted on the walls of caves. Archaeologists have discovered cave paintings displaying a variety of horse species, making it the primary animal image (over 30%) found in archaeological sites.[1] These paintings show great variability in color and detail and have been found all over the world.

Horses — Our New Best Friend

God created horses (equids) on the sixth day of the creation week with vast genetic diversity, adaptability, and complexity, which appears to be more diverse in the past than once believed by scientists. After genetic testing of bone and teeth fragments dated to the Pleistocene period (post-Flood period), horses (primarily the spotted horse), once believed to be only symbolic in early cave paintings, have now been matched to the physical characteristics represented in these paintings.

This discovery verified the paintings were accurate representations of horse species alive during that era of history.[2] Additionally, scientists stated, "Genetic variability was much larger in the Pleistocene animal populations compared with their modern counterparts. . . and extended to color phenotypes as well."[3] Vast diversity in a relatively short past contradicts evolutionary theories, but fully supports biblical creation.[4]

Why are discoveries like this significant? The horse has been used as one of the primary examples of evolution for over 100 years. A renowned paleontologist once wrote, "One's mind inevitably turns to that inexhaustible textbook example, the horse sequence. This has been cited — incorrectly more often than not — as evidence for practically every evolutionary principle that has ever been coined."[5]

1. M. Pruvost, R. Bellone, N. Benecke, E. Sandoval-Castellano, M. Cieslak, T. Kuznetsova, A. Morales-Muniz, T. O'Connor, M. Reissmann, and M. Hofreiter, "Genotypes of Predomestic Horses Match Phenotypes Painted in Paleolithic Works of Cave Art. *PNAS*, 2011, 108(46), 18626–18630.
2. Ibid.
3. Ibid.
4. N. Jeanson, "Getting Enough Genetic Diversity: How Species Arose After the Ark," 2016, https://answersingenesis.org/creation-science/baraminology/getting-enough-genetic-diversity/.
5. B.J. MacFadden, "Horses, the Fossil Record, and Evolution," in M.K. Hecht, B. Wallace, G.T. Prance, editors, *Evolutionary Biology*, vol. 22 (Boston: Springer, 1988).

Horse Evolution

The history of horse evolution began in 1839, when Sir Richard Owen, the originator of the word "dinosaur," discovered a fossil resembling a rabbit/hare-like creature or hyrax-type creature. He rightly didn't lump them with either. Owen named this animal a *Hyracotherium*.[6] See figure 1.

Owen never associated the *Hyracotherium* with horse lineage either, and his discovery remained largely unnoticed for 20 years. During this 20-year period, Charles Darwin published his famous work, *Origin of Species,* which fueled a debate concerning the origins of life and whether biblical creation of animal kinds or slow, gradual evolutionary processes over millions of years explained the fossil record and animal species.

The publication of *Origin of Species* had a dramatic impact on the way scientists viewed fossil evidence. Many scientists began to abandon the idea of a young earth and biblical created kinds (Genesis 1) and turned their attention toward a search for transitional (in-between) animal species in support of evolution. This fervent search continues to this day.

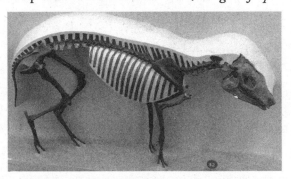

Figure 1 — Hyracotherium fossils are often displayed in a horse-like manner to support evolutionary theories, as seen in Figure 1. But it is important to remember, the hyracotherium was named after its rabbit-like anatomical structure and should resemble a pose similar to the Cave Hyrax in Figure 2.

The next progression in horse evolution was the discovery of numerous horse fossils located in Europe and North America in the 1870s.[7] These discoveries include a fossil in North America about the size of a small dog, which was named Eohippus (later changed to *Hyracotherium*). At this time, the discovery of Owen's fossil, *Hyracotherium,* had not been equated as being the same fossil as the Eohippus.

Coinciding with this discovery is the growing popularity of Darwinian evolution — which largely influences the way scientists begin to view fossil evidence and animal species. The Eohippus, which was a small creature with

---

6. D. Bennett, "The Evolution of the Horse," *The Elsevier World Animal Science Encyclopedia,* 1992 (7), 1–37.
7. Ibid.

Figure 2 — Cave Hyrax

three toes on the front legs and four toes on the hind legs, was labeled the "dawn horse," since proponents of evolution believed it was the earliest known horse example.[8]

Meanwhile in Europe in 1873, Russian paleontologist Vladimir Kovalesvsky was the first to suggest that the *Hyracotherium* (discovered in Europe) is a relative of the horse family and attempted to show a relationship between the two species.

In 1876, a renowned paleontologist from Yale University, O.C. Marsh, collected a vast array of American horse fossils. His collection included bones and teeth that he theorized were from 30 different types of horses. Marsh's private collection included an Eohippus, or *Hyracotherium*, specimen which was then followed by a gradual "evolution" of the horse based on his fossil evidence.

One of the greatest supporters for Darwinian evolution, T.H. Huxley, visited Marsh to view his collection and was so impressed at what he believed to be the vast "evidence" for horse evolution, he decided to include Marsh's research on horses in his famous talk at the New York Academy of Sciences.[9]

Huxley was convinced that the gradual changes in horse fossils verified the Darwinian evolutionary processes he was propagating. Marsh, in support of Huxley's Darwinian evolutionary belief system, created a drawing (sketch) for Huxley's lecture which simply showed a change in general size, decreasing number of horse toes, and an increase in sizes of horse teeth over time[10] (see figure 3).

Proponents of Darwin's theories, overly zealous at this "proof" of transitional species through evolutionary processes, marveled at this drawing. This hypothetical sketch was accepted in the scientific community as "evidence" of horse evolution and they lobbied for the printing of the diagram in every

8.   J. Sarfati, "The Non-evolution of the Horse: Special Creation or Evolved Rock Badger," Creation.com.

9.   B. MacFadden, "Fossil Horses — Evidence for Evolution," *Science*, 2005, 307(5716), 1728–1730, DOI: 10.1126/science.1105458.

10   S. Keep, "A Horse Is a Horse of Course, of Course . . . As long As You Know What a Horse Is," Part 1, National Center for Science Education, 2014, https://ncse.com/blog/2014/09/horse-is-horse-course-course-as-long-as-you-know-what-horse-0015872.

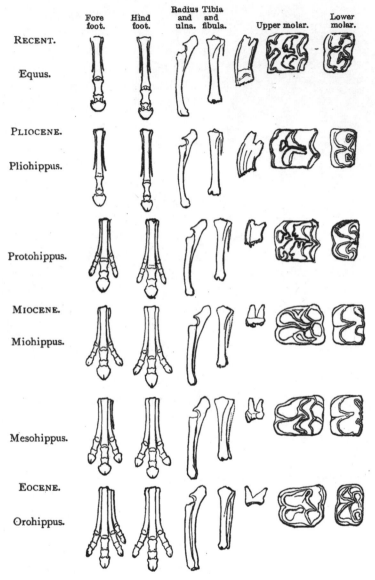

Figure 3 — Diagram by O.C. Marsh showing evolution of horse feet and teeth over time. (United States public domain)

biology textbook of the era, in addition to the creation of numerous museum exhibits[11] (see figure 4).

The following quote is found in an animal biology textbook from 1931: "Before concluding our survey of the paleontological evidence for evolution, it will be well to review in somewhat greater detail the changes undergone by a few representative forms. . . . Perhaps the best-known and most complete

11. MacFadden, " Fossil Horses — Evidence for Evolution."

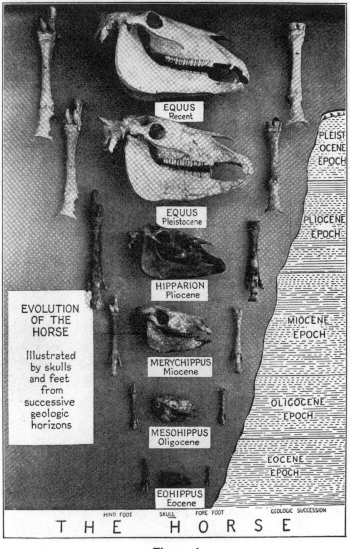

Figure 4

fossil pedigree among vertebrates is that of the horse.[12] This textbook provided students with a chart depicting horse evolution (see figure 5).

Again, in 1970, a high school biology textbook stated, "At present, perhaps the most completely known fossil record of any evolutionary line is that of the horse family," and provided students the diagram in figure 6.[13] Take a moment here to study the diagram of the *Hyracotherium* in figure 6.

---

12. *Animal Biology*, (New York: Harper and Brothers, 1931).
13. *High School Biology* (Chicago: Rand McNally & Company, 1970).

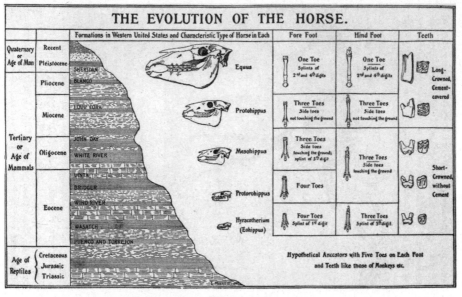

Figure 5

Does this diagram resemble the fossil skeleton in figure 1 or is it modified and shaped to fit the horse evolution theory? Interestingly, in the 1980s, an important shift occurred in the theory of horse evolution. Scientific publications began to acknowledge there was no reliable proof for horse evolution in the fossil record.[14] Yet, the narrative was in place and science textbooks continued to print this theoretical view of horse evolution until as recently as the mid-2000s.

In 2005, a Glencoe high school biology text stated, "One of the best-studied cases in the fossil record concerns the evolution of horses"[15] Pay attention to the differences in the horse representations between the examples in 1970 (figure 6) when compared to 2005 in figure 7. Remember, these are artists' representations of the fossil record, not fact — they attempt to make the *Hyracotherium* appear as horse-like as possible.

Do you see a pattern? Theoretical drawings, misinterpretations of the fossil record, and the misidentification of adaption as evolution, have driven horse evolution for decades. Thousands of students have been exposed to this false ideology. With the discovery of additional evidence, many scientists now recognize that the *Hyracotherium* is not a horse, but more akin to a rock badger or Hyrax, which is how the fossil received its

14. *National Geographic*, January 1981: 74.
15. *Biology* (7th ed.) (Glencoe: McGraw Hill, 2005).

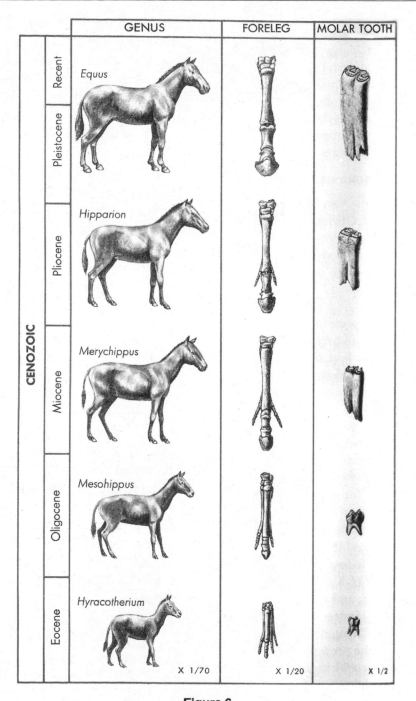

		GENUS	FORELEG	MOLAR TOOTH
CENOZOIC	Recent / Pleistocene	Equus		
	Pliocene	Hipparion		
	Miocene	Merychippus		
	Oligocene	Mesohippus		
	Eocene	Hyracotherium	X 1/20	X 1/2

X 1/70

Figure 6
Credit: _High School Biology: BSCS Green Version_, 2nd ed (1968). Rand
McNally & Company: Chicago, IL.

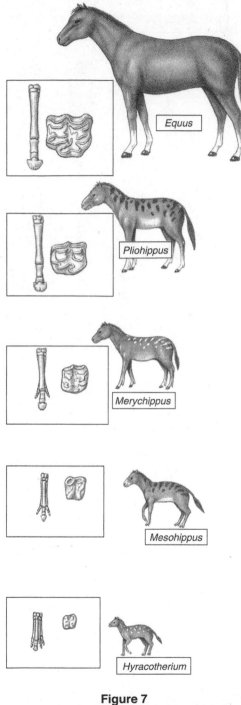

Figure 7
Credit: *Biology*, 7th ed. (2005). McGraw-Hill
Higher Education. Boston: MA

original name,[16] or it may even be its own kind.

An important observation should be noted — in every diagram, drawing, or sketch throughout the secular textbooks and research-related materials, the artistic representations of horses over the supposed millions of years still resembles a horse, with the exception of the *Hyracotherium,* which is not a horse but made to look horse-like. Minor adaptions and changes in features have not skewed the fact that they are all horses and members of the equid family.

There are distinguishable differences in horse fossils that evolutionists believe support their theories. A few of these include size, number of ribs, and number of toes. Horses come in a variety of sizes, ranging from the smallest recorded horse in the world (Thumbelina) with a height of 17 inches to the largest recorded horse (Big Jake), which stands almost 7 feet tall.[17]

Early proponents of horse evolution claimed there was progressive increase in horse

16. J. Morris, "The Mythical Horse Series," *Acts & Facts,* 2008, 37(9): 13.
17. Guinness World Records, September 13, 2012, *Big Jake the World's Tallest Horse,* http://www.guinnessworldrecords.com/news/2012/9/record-holder-profile-big-jake-worlds-tallest-horse-video-4474big.

size in the fossil record, but this is not the case. "There is no consensus on horse ancestry among paleontologists, and more than a dozen different family trees have been proposed, indicating that the whole thing is only guesswork."[18] The fossil record has revealed that there is not a linear pattern within the horse fossil record, but more like a complex bush of genetic diversity. This has caused evolutionists to abandon many of their previous beliefs on horse evolution,[19] but at the same time lends support to the created kinds described in Genesis 1. This range of genetic diversity in size is evident in the fossil record and continues to be evident in present-day horses.

Horse fossils also vary in their number of ribs. Within the fossil record, there is evidence of horses with 18 ribs, then a later horse having 15 ribs, then 19 ribs, and then in an upper layer, 18 ribs.[20] This is not the same animal evolving over long periods of time, and would require a genetic reversal of information, which contradicts the gain of information required for evolution. Rather, this evidence supports different species of horses that would have reproduced over the years with mere variation within their kind after the global Flood.

Additionally, horses in the past exhibited varying numbers of toes. Some evolutionists believe that horses and humans evolved from a single, five-toed common ancestor.[21] But, once again, horse toe fossils have not represented a linear progression from a five-toed horse to a three-toed horse and finally the modern one-toed horse, as would be expected if you believe in evolutionary processes.

Rather, these fossils have revealed sporadic numbers of toes throughout the fossil record, suggesting they were living alongside one another at the same time ("ancient" horses alongside modern horses). An example of this was when the three-toed *Neohipparion* was found in Oregon alongside a one-toed *Pliohippus*.[22] A recent study on horse fossils found that the *Hyracotherium* was the only extinct "equid" to show a difference in the number of digits (or toes) in the forelimb and hindlimb[23] — further evidence that the *Hyracotherium* is not a horse.

18. G. Chapman, "Horse Non-Sense," *Creation*, 1991, 14(1): 50.
19. Ibid.
20. Ibid.
21. New York Institute of Technology. (2018). "Researchers Pose Revolutionary Theory on Horse Evolution," *Science Daily*, retrieved from: https://www.sciencedaily.com/releases/2018/01/180125135537.htm.
22. *National Geographic*, January 1981: 74.
23. N. Solounias, M. Danowitz, E. Stachtiaris, A. Khurana, M. Araim, M. Sayegh, J. Natale, "The Evolution and Anatomy of the Horse Manus with an Emphasis on Digit Reduction,"

Additionally, evidence showing the *Hyracotherium* is not a horse is in the structure of its limbs. The *Hyracotherium* has distinctly tetradactyl forelimbs and tridactyl hindlimbs. This is in contrast to horse fossils where there are monodactyl forelimbs and hindlimbs. The authors go on to say, "Unlike the limbs of *Hyracotherium*, the forelimbs and hindlimbs of the other described equids are notably similar, both in number of digits and overall morphology."[24] For biblical creationists, these distinct similarities in the equid fossils in relation to the *Hyracotherium* is expected, because the *Hyracotherium* is a separate biblical kind than that of the horse.

Fortunately, the linear diagram of horse evolution so popular in science textbooks for 100 years is slowly fading away. Evolutionists now recognize there is no distinguishable order or pattern for horse evolution in the fossil record nor can they agree on the horse family tree.[25] Though it took textbook publishers almost 100 years to remove the horse evolution information from the curriculum, the scientific community started questioning the fossil evidence in the early 1900s.

As the equid fossil evidence increased, scientists had to acknowledge the lack of linear progression evident in the fossil record. Quotes such as this one by Raup (1979) began to surface throughout academia, "Some of the classic cases of Darwinian change in the fossil record, such as the evolution of the horse in North America, have to be discarded or modified as a result of more detailed information."[26]

Slowly, museums began to modify their horse evolution exhibits, although 55% of popular museums still depict the linear model.[27] When the Field Museum in Chicago opened its new Evolving Planet display in 2006, the horse evolution exhibit no longer depicted a linear form of evolution that popularized science textbooks, though it still implies a form of horse evolution.

The American Museum of Natural History also shows "ancient" horses living together side-by-side, and no longer in a linear evolutionary progression (figure 8). A similar exhibit is also depicted at the Kentucky Horse Park.

Textbook publishers have been the last to catch up to current research on horse evolution. One of the most visible removals of horse evolution

Royal Society Open Science, 5: 171782, 2018, http://dx.doi.org/10.1098/rsos.171782.
24. Ibid.
25. Chapman, "Horse Non-Sense."
26. D.M. Raup, "Conflicts between Darwin and Paleontology," *Field Museum of Natural History Bulletin*, 1979.
27. B. Macfadden, (2012). "Fossil Horses, Orthogenesis, and Communicating Evolution in Museums," 2012, https://link.springer.com/article/10.1007/s12052-012-0394-1.

Figure 8

occurred in 2012. South Korea mandated that horse evolution be removed from the textbooks as evidence for evolution.[28] The major textbook distributors have removed the topic of horse evolution and have replaced it with other animals, such as the camel.

And the debate continues, as secular scientists today still acknowledge the flaws of horse evolution. In a current call for research from scientists interested in further studying horse evolution, they acknowledge in their literature, "The evolutionary biology of *Equus* evolution across its entire range remains relatively poorly understood and often highly controversial."[29]

Despite the flaws, misinterpretations, and the acknowledgement of famous evolutionists that there is no evidence of horse evolution, there is still a fervent effort to find evidence to support their beliefs. Therefore, the topic remains at the forefront of the creation/evolution debate.

Though evolutionists continue to the search for evidence of horse evolution, creationists have found the answer in the inerrant Word of God. Both evolutionists and creationists look at the same evidence in the fossil record — it is just how they interpret that evidence that is different. Evolutionists rely on man's constantly changing flawed word, while creationists rely on God's perfect Word.

The Bible states ten times in Genesis 1 that God created everything according their kind. The Bible also describes God creating the land animals on day 6 of the creation week, just 6,000 years ago. Genesis 1:24–31 states,

28. S. Park, "South Korea Surrenders to Creationists Demands," 2012, https://www.nature.com/news/south-korea-surrenders-to-creationist-demands-1.10773.

29. R. Berner, G. Semprebon, F. Rivals, L. Avilla, and E. Scott, "Examining Evolutionary Trends in *Equus* and Its Close Relatives from Five Continents," https://www.frontiersin.org/research-topics/8057/examining-evolutionary-trends-in-equus-and-its-close-relatives-from-five-continents.

> And God said, Let the earth bring forth living creatures according to their kinds – livestock and creeping things and beasts of the earth according to their kinds. . . . And God saw everything that he had made, and behold, it was very good. And there was evening and there was morning, the sixth day.[30]

When God finished His creation, it was very good. *Very good* means there was no death, disease, or suffering, but Adam's sin changed everything. Sin became so common nature that man did evil continually. A perfect, righteous God demanded judgment and sent a global flood to destroy all living things with breath in their lungs.

As a result of catastrophes, the fossil record provides clues to the vast diversity and variety of horses that once roamed the earth. These clues also offer insight into the original created kind of equid. Whether the original created kind of equid had 5 toes, 3 toes, or 1 toe, or 15, 18, or 19 ribs — or all of the above, we can be assured that God created the horse with the potential for vast genetic diversity.

The examples of horses we see in the fossil record, documented in history, and living today are just a small part of the genetic variation created in horses by an all-powerful Creator God. Though we may see changes in characteristics, number of toes and ribs, or size of horses, this is not evidence of evolution, but simply adaption and genetic variation. And one thing is for certain, a horse will always be a horse of course, unless you were never a horse to begin with!

---

30. Scripture in this chapter is from the English Standard Version (ESV) of the Bible.

" *In light of how much attention evolutionary textbooks pay to whale evolution and its iconic status, it seems uncanny that newer college courses on the subject go to great pains to strip away the notion that there is a linear progression of transitional whale ancestors in the fossil record.* "

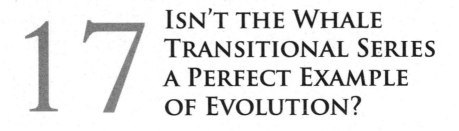

17

ISN'T THE WHALE TRANSITIONAL SERIES A PERFECT EXAMPLE OF EVOLUTION?

With a B.S. in Natural Sciences degree from the University of Cincinnati, **TROY LACEY** works at Answers in Genesis, answering questions of science and faith sent to the ministry as the correspondence representative (answering questions of science and faith sent to the ministry), science writer, and content support. As a Science Writer working on Content Support, you can find many of his articles at the Answers in Genesis website, including cultural topics, reviews, information for children, science topics, biblical questions, and many others.

F or those who remember sitting in 10th grade biology class in high school, or freshman biology in college, if asked which animal showed the most clear and definitive case for evolution, including transitional (or intermediate) forms, the whale evolution series would be among the first to spring to mind.

Introduction

The images of hyena-like terrestrial animals, whose feet morph into webbed feet and then flippers, who gradually lose their hind limbs, grow larger, develop fins and flukes, and whose nostrils shift from the front of their heads onto the top of their heads can readily spring to mind. Even those who have long forgotten their biology classes can recall seeing these representations in museums, zoos, or aquariums.

But how watertight is this transitional series? And what of new genetic claims that hippos share more common DNA with whales? Is this a slam dunk for evolution, proving that one kind of animal can change into another via natural selection and mutations? It sure is presented that way! But let's take a closer look at the "steps" in this transitional series. Let's examine some of the problems which are glossed over and the select anatomy which is touted as being proof of common ancestry.

Pakicetus

One of the first animals encountered in this series is *Pakicetus*. Initially it was presumed to be a semi-aquatic mammal based on having triangular teeth and a bony wall around its ears (which is unlike other terrestrial mammals). In 2001, an almost complete skeleton was discovered, and it was an entirely terrestrial animal. But it is still listed as the first whale in most textbooks.

One of the characteristics which is listed as being whale-like (its triangular teeth) have been found in other terrestrial mammals not considered ancestral to whales, like *Zhangheotherium quinquecuspidens*[1] an extinct symmetrodont[2] and *Cynogale bennettii*,[3] a living type of civet. Additionally, further studies of Pakicetus' ear (even while proclaiming it a transitional form) have shown that it was more suited for hearing sounds in the air rather than in water.[4]

---

1. https://www.cell.com/current-biology/pdf/S0960-9822(98)70174-5.pdf, p. r-285.
2. https://pdfs.semanticscholar.org/f49e/b498515c8cf669c24884e66dc55246d0219a.pdf, p. 168.
3. Richard Owen, *On the Anatomy of Vertebrates . . . Mammals* (London, England: Longmans, Green and Company, 1868), p. 131.
4. https://www.nature.com/articles/361444a0.

Ambulocetus

The next animal usually shown in the whale evolution series is *Ambulocetus*. Even though it is a quadruped, it is often depicted as semi-aquatic and often (like a crocodilian) as an ambush predator grabbing animals which venture near the water for a drink. But even sites promoting *Ambulocetus* as semi-aquatic admit that it could walk on land and are unsure of its aquatic mode of locomotion:

> *Ambulocetus* also had front limbs ending with flexible wrists and fingers, and its strong hind limbs had even bigger feet. In water it may have swum like an otter, or like a dog. Or it may have walked like modern hippos along the bottom. Its legs could have supported its full weight, but on land *Ambulocetus* was probably clumsy and slow.[5]

Ambulocetus is listed as whale-like due to supposedly having a similar (to whales) sigmoid process on the auditory bulla and a reduced zygomatic arch (cheekbone). But both of these characteristics may have been overstated and other researchers have questioned whether these characteristics might not be unique to *Ambulocetus* and might be characteristic of other mesonychids.[6]

Protocetids: *Maiacetus, Rodhocetus,* and *Kutchicetus*

Another group often portrayed in this series are the protocetids. One of these protocetids is *Maiacetus inuus* (mother whale) whose fossil thus was named because a baby *Maiacetus* was found inside the mother's fossilized ribcage.

Based on the position of the baby, it appeared that it was going to be delivered head-first (not tail-first as in whales) suggesting that the *Maiacetus* might have given birth on land (like modern pinnipeds).[7] Additionally, *Maiacetus* was a quadruped, and in some fossil specimens which were more complete, still had hips that were attached to its vertebral column.[8]

Next on the list are Rodhocetus and Kutchicetus, both of which are now usually depicted as otter-like and semi aquatic.[9] *Cetus* and *Cetids* come from the Latin for whale by the way.

---

5.   http://stories.anmm.gov.au/whale-evolution/.

6.   Annalisa Berta, "What Is a Whale," *Science* 263 (January 14, 1994): 180–181

7.   http://scienceblogs.com/laelaps/2009/02/03/maiacetus-the-good-mother-whal/.

8.   Ibid.

9.   http://pages.geo.wvu.edu/~kammer/g231/Whales.pdf.

Rodhocetus was touted as having a fluke (whale tail), and yet four legs. This initially sounds like a great missing link. However, the University of Michigan's display of *Rodhocetus* (one of the only places to see the fossil in the world) doesn't have the end of the tail! There is no typical ball vertebra to be observed, which is necessary for fluke tails.[10]

The discoverer of *Rodhocetus* even made a glaring admission. He said, "I speculated that it might have had a fluke. . . . I now doubt that *Rodhocetus* would have had a fluked tail."[11] Furthermore, the hand and feet fossils of *Rodhocetus* were also missing, which causes a problem for interpreting them as flippers.[12] So the essential features that most paleontologists tout as being whale-like on *Rodhocetus* are interpretive and have no evidence to back them up. That's a big problem.

Though rarely mentioned, and rightly so, *Kutchicetus* was very similar in size and anatomy to otters. The primary reason that it is sometimes included in a whale series is to try to provide a transitional series for swimming motion — undulatory movements. So it isn't the anatomy that transitionalists are looking at with this creature (as the skeleton appears to show that it was fully capable of walking on land[13]), but instead its method of locomotion. But in this case, apparently the fossils don't tell the whole tale and a heavy dose of evolutionary interpretation must be added.

Basilosaurus and *Durodon*

Basilosaurus is often depicted next in the whale evolution series along with *Dorudon*. Unlike all the previous "early whales" on the list, both *Basilosaurus* and *Durodon* were fully aquatic. Creationists and evolutionists totally agree here.

Evolutionists are divided though on these basilosaurids and their place in whale evolution. Evolutionist Barbara J. Stahl stated, "The serpentine form of the body and the peculiar serrated cheek teeth make it plain that these archaeocetes could not possibly have been ancestral to any of the modern whales."[14]

---

10. Carl Werner, *Evolution: The Grand Experiment* (Green Forest, AR: New Leaf Press, 2007), p. 139–143.
11. Ibid. and Interview with Dr. Phil Gingerich, Paleontologist, University of Michigan, for video series "Evolution: The Grand Experiment," conducted by Dr. Carl Werner, on August 28, 2001.
12. Ibid.
13. For example, see https://commons.wikimedia.org/wiki/File:Kutchicetus_minimus.jpg.
14. B.J. Stahl, *Vertebrate History: Problems in Evolution* (New York: Dover Publications, Inc., 1985), p. 489.

Dr. Lawrence Barnes has said, "*Basilosaurus* existed at a time when baleen-bearing mysticetes are known to have existed and echo-locating odontocetes are presumed to have existed."[15]

Creation scientists also are divided on Basilosaurus and Durodon. Some think it is possible that the extinct Basilosaurids were of the same created kind as today's toothed whales, or perhaps they were another created kind that has become extinct.

Both of the above basilosaurids have greatly reduced hind limbs. These are mentioned as being functionless and used as proof that as whale ancestors became more aquatic, they lost their hind limbs and evolved fins and flukes. Modern whales are often described in evolutionary textbooks as having "vestigial hipbones," which is often touted as proof of the whale evolution series. But a 2014 article in the journal *Evolution* showed that there is a perfectly designed function after all.[16]

Researcher Brian Thomas of the Institute for Creation Research, commenting on this *Evolution* article, says, "These results show that male whales use pelvis bones that were well crafted for anchoring reproductive organs — not for anchoring limbs. Whale hips are not vestigial."[17]

Discussion and Conclusion

In light of how much attention evolutionary textbooks pay to whale evolution and its iconic status, it seems uncanny that newer college courses on the subject go to great pains to strip away the notion that there is a linear progression of transitional whale ancestors in the fossil record. A course at the University of Indiana has this warning:

> CAUTION: Unfortunately, students may come away from this lesson with the mistaken conclusion that each of the intermediate whale forms were in the direct (lineal) line of descent between the land-dwelling tetrapods and fully aquatic whales. IN REALITY, it is most likely that these "transitional forms" were only "collateral" (cousin-like) ancestors, but showing features that were likely found in their "cousins" that did evolve into modern whales. This subtle distinction may seem unimportant, but to assume that fossils generally fit into a lineal (direct) line of descent

---

15. As recorded in an interview in Carl Werner, *Evolution: The Grand Experiment*, Vol. 1, 3rd edition (Green Forest AR: Master Books, 2014), p. 144.
16. https://onlinelibrary.wiley.com/doi/epdf/10.1111/evo.12516.
17. http://www.icr.org/article/vital-function-found-for-whale-leg.

conveys the erroneous impression of the long-outdated "Ladder of Evolution" concept. Rather, students should recognize that what we are seeing are the vestiges of many side branches in a diverse BRANCHING TREE of evolution.

Furthermore, students should focus more on the mosaic accumulation over time of a series of new *features* modified (derived) from ancestral features over time, not the species *per se*. The fossil remains collected simply reveal that those respective *features* existed in those related species at that period of time.[18]

They even offer a provisional phylogeny diagram[19] which shows these "relationships." Likewise, the University of West Virginia includes several "evolutions" of the whale evolution series on their online course page.[20] However, even in these newer branching tree diagrams, they tend to gloss over how toothed and baleen whales separated, and what they do show seems contradictory. It also appears from the UI provisional phylogeny diagram that modern baleen whales gave rise to modern toothed whales, when all of the older "cousins" on the evolutionary tree were toothed. Even new research has shown that toothed suction feeders[21] and gap-toothed (but still having plenty of teeth) "filter" feeders[22] were (supposedly) the direct ancestors of modern baleen whales. This is certainly not the smooth and neat transitional picture which is painted for the average high school and college student.

As biologist Richard Sternberg has noted, many changes would have been necessary to convert a land-mammal into a whale, including:

- Emergence of a blowhole, with musculature and nerve control
- Modification of the eye for permanent underwater vision
- Ability to drink sea water
- Forelimbs transformed into flippers
- Modification of skeletal structure
- Ability to nurse young underwater
- Origin of tail flukes and musculature
- Blubber for temperature insulation[23]

---

18. http://www.indiana.edu/~ensiweb/lessons/whale.ev.html.
19. http://www.indiana.edu/~ensiweb/lessons/whale.phylog.pdf.
20. http://pages.geo.wvu.edu/~kammer/g231/Whales.pdf.
21. https://phys.org/news/2017-05-baleen-whales-ancestors-toothy-suction.html.
22. https://www.cell.com/current-biology/fulltext/S0960-9822(17)30704-2.
23. https://evolutionnews.org/2015/01/problem_5_abrup/.

Most of these are multi-step processes, and ones which would need to be coordinated in order for the organism to survive and reproduce. However, another drastic change which is completely overlooked in the secular literature is that the newest hypotheses on whale evolution point to an evolutionary lineage with artiodactyls (even-toed ungulates, with hippos being the closest living relative) the vast majority of which are herbivores. The only omnivores (pigs and peccaries) are considered the furthest removed from whale ancestry.

In addition to having to account for drastic morphological differences between medium-sized land animals to large marine ones, we are left with the added problem of why a primarily herbivorous group of animals would venture to the water in order to eat fish (or other aquatic animals), and why all of the subsequent descendants would be obligate carnivores. Indeed, the hypothesized closest living relatives after hippos are the ruminants, all of which have specialized stomachs for digesting plant matter.

Therefore, a complete redesign of the gastrointestinal tract had to have occurred before these "early whales" took to the water. This extremely drastic physiological change is either ignored or just acknowledged as occurring in secular literature. Alternatively, mention of opportunistic carnivory in some hippopotamuses is viewed as being potentially evolutionary linkage to the carnivory seen in whales.[24] But there is a vast difference between opportunism and obligate carnivory, and there is also a vast difference between the digestive system of hippos and whales (especially toothed whales). Hippos utilize fermentation digestion in the first two stomachs,[25] whereas whales utilize muscular contractions in their first stomach to break down food.[26]

Another such irreducibly complex set of features (in addition to the ones listed above) was the coordination among:

> . . . the comb-like baleen to filter out food, expandable "ventral groove blubber" with cartilaginous support bars that open like a Chinese fan, a newly discovered sensory organ, a split jaw that is loosely connected to the skull, and *vibrissae* (long stiff hairs) along the chin to sense prey. The whale's sensory organ detects pressures that its lower jaws endure when taking on so much water in their mouths. Without this key sensor, the animal's jaw could rip apart.

24. https://www.researchgate.net/publication/286035324_Carnivory_in_the_common_hippopotamus_Hippopotamus_amphibius; Implications_for_the_ecology_and_epidemiology_of_anthrax_in_African_landscapes, p. 196.
25. https://onlinelibrary.wiley.com/doi/pdf/10.1111/j.1365-2028.1973.tb00070.x.
26. https://bluewhaleztt.weebly.com/digestive-system.html.

Arctic and Antarctic oceans supply some of the best feeding areas for rorqual species. How do these enormous sea creatures keep from freezing as they engulf hundreds of gallons of cold ocean water? A countercurrent heat exchange arrangement of blood vessels throughout their enormous tongues protects their core body temperature.

What if all these whale feeding features were in place, but the creature had standard nerve packing? If this were the case, then when the whale's mouth ballooned and its tongue extended the nerve would break, severing the vital pressure signal from that special sensory organ.[27]

It seems like the whale benefitted from some extraordinary "luck" in the evolutionary paradigm. All of the necessary components (just to feed) came together by random processes, and they came at just the right time. And all of this "guided natural selection" came about with no clear direct lineage pointing to modern whales, just lots of disconnected side branches.

Unlike the current story of whale evolution, which features lots of "cousins" but no "parents," the biblical picture is clear. Whales, both toothed and baleen were created on day 5 of creation week. They did not evolve from a land ancestor, they actually predated land animals (by a single day). And while some whales may have grown larger[28] since the Ice Age, they are still whales.

---

27. http://www.icr.org/article/clever-construction-rorqual-whales.
28. https://answersingenesis.org/aquatic-animals/how-and-when-did-baleen-whales-get-so-large/.

A big challenge for evolutionists is why would feathers have evolved on dinosaurs? What would be the selective advantage of a reptile evolving feathers?

18 WHAT ABOUT BIRD EVOLUTION — AREN'T THEY DINOSAURS?

DR. DAVID MENTON studied biology and chemistry at Minnesota State University in Mankato, where he graduated with a BS degree in 1959. He worked two years as a research laboratory technician at the Mayo Clinic in Rochester, MN, leaving to do graduate work at Brown University in Providence, RI, where he received a PhD in biology in 1966. Dr. Menton accepted a position in the department of anatomy at Washington University School of Medicine in St. Louis, where he received awards both for his research and teaching. While there, Dr. Menton served as the histology consultant for five editions of *Stedman's Medical Dictionary* and was a guest lecturer in histology at Stanford University Medical School. He also studied sea cucumbers at Woods Hole Marine Biology Laboratory. He retired in 2000 as an Associate Professor Emeritus after 34 years on the faculty.

It is hard to imagine two walking vertebrates that differ more than birds and dinosaurs, and yet not only do evolutionists claim that birds evolved from dinosaurs, they now insist that birds are dinosaurs! You might want to pause here to reflect on all the similarities between a humming bird and a *Tyrannosaurus rex*.

There are, of course, similarities between birds and reptiles, as there are between any two classes of walking vertebrates, but as we will see, the differences between them are substantial. If birds are dinosaurs and their closest living relatives are reptiles like crocodiles and alligators, we might ask if birds are also considered to be reptiles? Incredibly, some evolutionists say birds are indeed technically reptiles,[1] while others insist that there is no longer such a thing as a reptile![2]

In fact, there may eventually be no such thing as a bird! Evolutionists now speak of "non-avian dinosaurs" (dinosaurs) and "avian dinosaurs" (birds). So how on earth did we ever get into this taxonomic chaos?

It All Began with Archaeopteryx

In 1860, only a year after Charles Darwin published *On the Origin of Species*, a fossilized feather was discovered in the "150 million-year-old" late Jurassic strata of a Bavarian quarry.[3] The rock in this quarry is a very fine-grained limestone that was often used to make stone lithographic plates. This preserved the fine structure of the feather showing it to be identical in every detail to a modern bird wing feather. The feather came to be known as *Archaeopteryx* which means "ancient wing."

A few years later, a nearly complete and feathered fossilized skeleton of *Archaeopteryx* was discovered and was described by Richard Owen in 1863. Owen was an influential naturalist who coined the word "dinosaur" and was the first to recognize them as a distinct taxonomic group. Owen declared *Archaeopteryx* to be "unequivocally a bird," albeit an unusual one with a long bony tail, teeth, and claws on its wings.[4]

The ardent evolutionist Thomas Huxley, known as "Darwin's bulldog," was the first to propose in 1868 that birds evolved from theropod ("beast footed") dinosaurs. The theropods are a dinosaur suborder characterized by

1. University of California Museum of Paleontology – Berkley, "Are Birds Really Dinosaurs?" accessed October 25, 2018, http://www.ucmp.berkeley.edu/diapsids/avians.html.
2. Dustin Welbourne, "There's No Such Thing As Reptiles Any More — and Here's Why," The Conversation, October 14, 2014, http://theconversation.com/theres-no-such-thing-as-reptiles-any-more-and-heres-why-31355.
3. Of course, this is merely sediment from Noah's Flood, a matter of a few thousand years ago.
4. P. Shipman, *Taking Wing: Archaeopteryx and the Evolution of Bird Flight* (New York: Simon and Schuster, 1998), p. 28.

walking on two legs (e.g., *Tyrannosaurus rex*), each bearing three toes. In this respect, theropods are indeed similar to birds.

Huxley based his argument on comparing the skeletal structure of a raven-sized *Archaeopteryx* fossil to that of a chicken-sized theropod dinosaur fossil called *Compsognathus*. In fact, some of the early discovered specimens of *Archaeopteryx* were initially misclassified as *Compsognathus*. Huxley viewed *Archaeopteryx* as a transitional stage between dinosaurs and birds, providing an eagerly sought after "missing link" to support Darwin's evolutionary speculations.

Huxley's idea of the theropod origin of birds by way of *Compsognathus* soon fell out of favor, however, as evolutionists pointed out that *Compsognathus* was a contemporary of *Archaeopteryx*, having been found in the same strata, and thus was unlikely to be its ancestor. Many argued that the similarity between the two was just a case of "convergent" evolution, whereby two unrelated creatures independently evolve similar structures.

In 1913, evolutionist Robert Broom proposed that a "230-million-year old" thecodont reptile known as *Euparkeria* was the real ancestor of both dinosaurs and birds. Thecodonts are quadrupedal (some say partly bipedal) reptiles that have teeth mounted in deep sockets in their jaw from which they get their name. Thecodonts were similar to crocodiles and are considered by many evolutionists to be "archosaurs" that evolved into true dinosaurs.

This idea of the thecodont ancestry of birds was strongly promoted by Gerhard Heilmann in his seminal book *The Origin of Birds,* published in 1926, and became the prevailing view for nearly 50 years. Thecodontia is now generally considered to be an obsolete taxon and the word *thecodont* is used more as an anatomical term for socketed teeth, which could conceivably apply to almost any toothed dinosaur, pterosaur, crocodilian, or mammal.

Starting in the 1970s, evolutionist John Ostrom published several papers arguing once again that *Archaeopteryx* and the birds really did evolve from theropod dinosaurs. This time, the favored theropod ancestor was one of Ostrom's own discoveries, a "110 million-year old" dromaeosaur known as *Deinonychus*.

But since *Deinonychus* is believed to have lived about 108 to 115 million years ago, it would seem to be an unlikely candidate for being ancestral to essentially modern-looking "130 million-year-old" fossil birds found in great numbers in the Jehol Biota of Northern China,[5] to say nothing of

---

5. L.M. Chiappe and M. Qingjin, *Birds of Stone: Chinese Avian Fossils from the Age of Dinosaurs* (Baltimore MD: Johns Hopkins University Press, 2016).

the "150 million-year-old" bird *Archaeopteryx*. None the less, the theropod origin of birds and the notion that birds are in fact dinosaurs has remained the prevailing and unassailable dogma among most evolutionists.

Similarities between Birds and Dinosaurs

One of the most striking similarities between birds and many dinosaurs is the orientation of the three fused bones (ilium, ischium, and pubis) that make up the hip bone. In mammals, amphibians, and all the living orders of reptiles, the pubic bone is oriented *anteriorly* (nearer to the front of the body or head), the ischium *posteriorly* (nearer to the rear of the body), and the ilium *dorsally* (upper side or the back of an animal), while in birds at least part of the pubic bone is oriented more posteriorly near the ischium (figure 1).

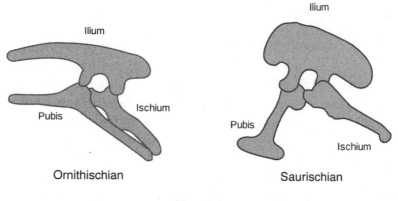

Figure 1

There is a major group of dinosaurs known as the bird-hipped dinosaurs (Ornithischians) that have a bird-like hip structure. But amazingly, evolutionists do not believe that the bird-hipped dinosaurs evolved into birds! They believe birds evolved from the other major group of dinosaurs known as the lizard-hipped (Saurischian) dinosaurs that had hips similar to reptiles and mammals!

The reason given for abandoning the bird-hipped dinosaurs as the ancestors of birds is that they are considered to be too specialized to have evolved into birds. The bird-hipped dinosaurs generally have exotic appendages such as bony plates, spikes, horns, armor plates, and other frills. Dinosaurs such as *Stegosaurus*, *Triceratops*, *Pachycephalosaurus*, and *Ankylosaurs* are examples of bird-hipped dinosaurs. By comparison, the lizard-hipped dinosaurs like the theropods are much plainer in appearance, and thus evolutionists find them easier to imagine evolving into birds.

Evolutionists claim many other skeletal similarities between birds and dinosaurs, but in many cases these similarities are shared by other vertebrates including mammals, reptiles, and amphibians. For example, birds and some dinosaurs have large orbits (eye sockets) but so do such diverse animals as the tarsier, slow loris, gibbon, tree frogs, and geckos. Like birds, theropod dinosaurs walked on three toes, but then so does the rhinoceros and the three-toed sloth. Like birds, most dinosaurs were digitigrade, meaning they walked on their toes with the heels held high off the ground, but then so do all cats and dogs as well as most other mammals.

Finally, unlike any living bird, some fossil birds had teeth, but these were mostly flightless swimmers such as the Hesperornithiformes and some flying fish eaters such as the Icthyornithiformes. In any event, the presence of teeth in some fossil birds does not necessarily show a relationship of birds to reptiles, as even some reptiles lack teeth.

What Is Distinctive About a Bird?

How then do birds differ from reptiles in general, and dinosaurs in particular. We must be aware that evolutionists have a strong evolutionary bias and attempt to argue that almost any seemingly distinctive feature of birds can be found in some form in dinosaurs. This is further confused by the evolutionary assumption that birds themselves are dinosaurs.

Birds Are "Warm Blooded"

All vertebrates produce body heat as a result of metabolism and muscle contraction. Those that produce primarily their own heat are called *endotherms*, while those that mainly gain heat through their ambient environment are called *ectotherms*. Vertebrates that regulate their body temperature within a narrow range, independent of external temperatures, are called homeothermic. Birds are homeothermic endotherms having a normal temperature between 106°F and 110°F, which is higher than most mammals.

There are no living homeothermic reptiles, but many evolutionists believe that dinosaurs were endothermic, with some even arguing they were homeothermic,[6] but the evidence for this is less than compelling. It is argued that the large body size of many dinosaurs might have served to conserve and stabilize body temperatures.

Some say possibly dinosaurs were more physically active than once thought, which might favor endothermy. The microscopic structure

---

6.   Robert T. Bakker, "Anatomical and Ecological Evidence of Endothermy in Dinosaurs," *Nature*, 1972, 238(5359): 81–85, Bibcode:1972Natur.238...81B, doi:10.1038/238081a0.

(histology) of dinosaur bone is often sighted as empirical evidence for endothermy in dinosaurs, but this is at best inconclusive. Bone histology (the study of the microscopic anatomy of the cells) varies during the life of a vertebrate and does not always correlate with endothermy.[7] One skeletal characteristic of warm-blooded animals, including birds, is the presence of scroll-like bones in the nose called nasal conchae (turbinates), which warm the inspired air. Dinosaurs appear to lack such structures, which would be consistent with dinosaurs being cold-blooded like all other living reptiles.[8]

Bone Fusion

A distinctive feature of the bird skeleton is that it is lightweight yet sturdy. In many flying birds, their bones weigh less than their feathers! This remarkable combination of light weight and strength in the bird skeleton is partly the result of a high level of bone fusion. For example, many of the bones of the fingers and hand are fused together, providing strength to the outer wing. Most of the bird's thoracic vertebrae are fused, forming a rigid backbone required to support the back and wings of the bird during flight. The fused lumbar and sacral vertebrae of the bird's lower back are in turn fused with the ilium, ischium, and pubic bones of the hip girdle to form a strong but lightweight bony structure called the *synsacrum* (figure 2). It might be

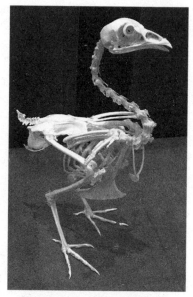

Figure 2. Chicken skeleton showing balance point at knee. The femur is internal.

noted that the bird Archaeopteryx is unusual for showing a lesser degree of bone fusion than most birds.

Pneumatic Bones

Birds are well known to have hollow bones, but "hollow" is an inadequate description of the bones of the unique avian skeleton. Without the marrow,

7. University of California Museum of Paleontology – Berkley, "The Evidence for Endothermy in Dinosaurs," accessed October 25, 2018, http://www.ucmp.berkeley.edu/diapsids/endothermy.html.
8. J. Ruben, *Science*, 1996, 273:1204–1207.

nearly all bones in the mammalian skeleton may also be said to be "hollow." The distinctive thing about the skeleton of most birds is that the bones are pneumatized, meaning they have large air spaces in many of their bones. The thin walls of these pneumatic bones are often supported by elaborate internal bony struts. Humans and other mammals have pneumatized bones in the facial part of their skull known as sinuses, and some dinosaurs such as sauropods are said to have had pneumatized bones in their very long necks, making them lighter in weight. But birds have pneumatized bones throughout their bodies.

The unique structure of avian pneumatic bones might make the bones lighter to aid in flight, but the most important function of pneumatic bones in birds is that their air spaces are in communication with the bird's respiratory system. Birds require so much oxygen for the high metabolic demands of flight that their lungs open into several air sacs scattered throughout the body which in turn expand out into some bones, making birds sort of bags of wind.

Unique Avian Respiratory System

Birds have a unique respiratory system that is the most efficient of all vertebrates. This is important because birds, unlike reptiles, have a high metabolic rate which requires efficient respiration. In addition, many migratory birds and birds of prey fly at high altitudes, which few other vertebrates could survive.

For example, a commercial aircraft collided with a Ruppell's griffon vulture at an altitude of over 37,000 feet, and the common crane and barheaded geese have been observed flying above the Himalayas at altitudes in excess of 30,000 feet.[9] At high altitude, the relative percentage of oxygen in the air remains the same (21%), but there is proportionately fewer of all air molecules, including oxygen, making breathing more difficult.

The structure of the avian lung is unique among all vertebrates, and though relatively small in size, it is the most efficient vertebrate lung. Birds do not have tidal respiration, like mammals and reptiles, where air is alternately inhaled and exhaled from the lung; rather, airflow in the avian lung is continuous and unidirectional. This results from the fact that birds do not exchange oxygen and carbon dioxide in blind-ending alveoli like the alveolar lung of mammals and reptiles, but rather they exchange gasses in flow-through tubular structures called parabronchi.

---

9.   Mark Carwardine, *Animal Records* (New York: Sterling, 2008), p. 124.

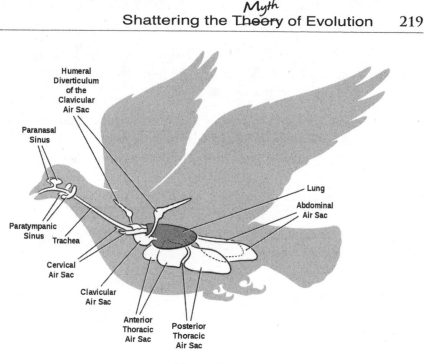

Figure 3

In parabronchial lungs, air from the trachea enters the lungs through the bronchi where it then passes through numerous tubular parabronchi where gas exchange occurs. Air exits from the lungs' parabronchi into nine air sacs arranged throughout the bird's body (figure 3).

The largest of these air sacs is the abdominal air sac, which occupies a space made available by the posterior orientation of the avian pubic bones. There is no gas exchange in the air sacs; rather, the air sacs function something like a bellows to move the air through the lungs. From the air sacs, air once again enters the lungs and passes through parabronchi to exit the lungs into the bronchi and trachea. Thus, as a result of unidirectional airflow both in and out through parabronchi, gas exchange in the lungs can occur both on inhalation and exhalation.

One of the most unique and amazing things about the avian respiratory system is that birds do not have a diaphragm. The diaphragm is a dome-shaped muscle that separates the thorax from the abdomen and is the primary muscle used in breathing by mammals and reptiles. When the dome of the diaphragm muscle flattens during contraction, it creates negative pressure in the lung causing it to expand with inspired air. During expiration, the elastic nature of the lung causes it to become smaller in size, expelling the air.

In birds, the special air sacs that fill almost every available space in the bird's body act in a bellows-like fashion to move air in and out of the lung, while the lung itself does not change in size.

- During inspiration, muscles pull the sternum down and forward while their uniquely hinged ribs move forward, causing the air sacs to expand, creating a negative pressure in the air sacs that brings air into the lungs.
- On expiration, the sternum is pulled up and back while the ribs move back.
- Even the bodily movements of birds, such as walking and flying, ventilate the air sacs.

The important point is that birds move air in and out of their lungs with numerous muscles acting on air sacs attached to the lungs, rather than by expanding and contracting the lung itself with a diaphragm.

How Did Dinosaurs Breathe?

Both mammals and reptiles have muscular diaphragms and tidal respiration, but the lungs of reptiles are less efficient than mammals because they have fewer alveoli and less surface area for gas exchange. What sort of lungs then did dinosaurs have? Lungs and diaphragms are soft tissues and thus are only infrequently encountered in a permineralized state in fossils. But fossil evidence suggests that theropod dinosaurs (the kind believed to have evolved into birds) had bellows-like septate lungs that were ventilated by a hepatic-piston diaphragm much like living crocodiles and alligators.[10]

Thus, dinosaurs, unlike birds, would apparently have expanded and contracted their lungs while breathing, and oxygenating the blood only on inhalation.

Bird Wings

All birds have wings except for the extinct moa and elephant birds. Wings may be specially suited for flapping flight, gliding, swimming, or balance when running. In flapping flight, a bird needs powerful muscles to move its wings both up and down. Indeed, the largest muscles in the bird are the breast muscles involved in moving the wings during flight and can comprise up to nearly a third of the bird's total body weight. The powerful pectoralis muscles bring the wings down in flapping flight much as our own

---

10. Ruben et al, *Science*, 1999, 283:514–516.

muscles bring our arms down.

But muscles can only pull by contraction, they can't push, so this raises the question of how the bird powerfully elevates its wing during flapping flight. There is no room to locate a muscle the size of the pectoralis above the wing on a bird's body in order to pull the wing up. Moreover,

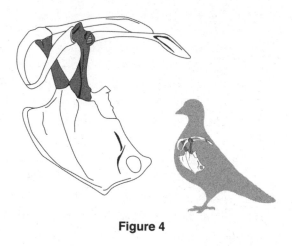

Figure 4

such a muscle in this location would be aerodynamically unsuitable.

This problem is solved by the large supracoracoideus muscle, located in the chest deep to the pectoralis muscle, which elevates the wing by means of a tendon attached to the humerus that passes through a pulley-like structure in the bird's shoulder called the triosseal canal (figure 4). Thus, the tendon of the supracoracoideus acts to raise the wing like a halyard on a sailboat raises the sail. In most flying birds, the powerful pectoralis and supracoracoideus muscles attach to a keeled sternum (breastbone), which is also unique to birds.

Bird Legs?

Do birds have knees? About halfway down a bird's leg there is a bend that might be a knee, except that it bends the wrong way (see figure 2). This is not the bird's knee but rather the bird's ankle. Thus, from this bend to the tip of the toes is the bird's foot. And from this bend to the bird's body is that part of the leg ("drumstick") that extends from the ankle to the knee.

So, the knee is not visible in an intact bird because it is just inside the bird's body. This means that all of the bird's femur (the thigh bone) with its associated muscles are inside the bird's body as well! As a result, birds walk from their knees on down rather than from their hips. There is no other vertebrate quite like this — including dinosaurs.

If we attempted to walk like a bird we would have to stand on our tiptoes with our heels held high above the ground and then bend down until our knees touched our chest. We could not walk this way, to say nothing of run, yet the ostrich can reach a speed of up to 45 miles an hour running this way — faster than a race horse.

It's All About Balance

What advantage could there possibly be for a bird to have its femur inside of its body? As we shall see, the obvious advantage of this arrangement is balance. If a creature walks on two legs, as opposed to four, the body must be balanced on the legs. This is a special problem if the body is not oriented vertically above the legs (like humans) but sets on the legs at an angle to the ground, as is the case with most bipedal birds and dinosaurs.

The fulcrum, or balance point, must be located where the legs emerge from the body. The balance point for bipedal dinosaurs is the head of their femur where it articulates with the hip bones of the pelvis. Since bipedal dinosaurs held their heavy muscular tail off the ground, the tail behind the hip counterbalanced the thorax, neck, and head in front of the hip. So, a primary function of the bipedal dinosaur tail was balance.

In contrast to bipedal dinosaurs, living birds and most fossil birds have very short tails (not counting the tail feathers) with both movable and fused vertebrae forming a short tail called the *pygostyle*. In the case of birds, there is very little weight behind the head of the femur where it articulates with the hip (synsacrum).

If a bird tried to walk from the hip like bipedal dinosaurs, it would fall forward on its beak. This is prevented by the highly flexed orientation of the femurs which brings the knees of the bird up and well forward of the head of the femur. Thus, in birds, the fulcrum of balance is the knee rather than the hip. It follows then that it should be possible to tell if a fossil is a bird or bipedal dinosaur by observing where the balance point would have to be — at the hip joint, or at the knee joint.

Bony Bird Tails vs. Bony Dinosaur Tails

Some extinct birds like Archaeopteryx had a long bony tail which has led them to be misidentified as dinosaurs. But there is a clear difference between the bony tails of fossil birds and those of bipedal dinosaurs. For example, compare the tail of Archaeopteryx with that of the theropod dinosaur Compsognathus, with which Archaeopteryx has been confused.

Theropod dinosaurs had muscular tails much like an alligator. This is evident from the fact that the tail vertebrae of such dinosaurs have bony projections that served as attachments and levers for the powerful tail muscles. On the dorsal side of the vertebrae are neural spines and on the ventral side are haemal spines (chevrons). The vertebrae of many dinosaur tails also bore laterally facing transverse processes for the attachment of ligaments and muscles. Whatever else bipedal dinosaurs did with their heavy muscular tail, balance while walking or standing was clearly important. Without a heavy tail they would have fallen headfirst.

By contrast, fossil bird tail vertebrae are much less robust than those of dinosaurs, and lack bony attachments for muscles such as dorsal and haemal spines. Indeed, there is evidence that the feathers of the bony bird tail anchored directly on the vertebrae much like flight feathers attach by means of ligaments to the wing bones in modern birds.

This suggests that the bony tails of birds had very little if any muscle, except at their base, and would have acted like a flexible spring pole with attached feathers. So, whether birds had bony tails like some extinct birds or lacked bony tails like most birds, the bird tail is too lightweight to counter-balance the body from the hip in the manner of bipedal dinosaurs. Thus, in birds, the fulcrum or balance is moved forward from the hip by means of an internal flexed thigh to the knee.

Feathers are for the Birds

Feathers have long been considered to be a unique feature of birds, much like hair is a unique feature of mammals. But this has been called into question now that birds are considered to be dinosaurs. After all, if birds are dinosaurs, then at least some dinosaurs are birds and would be expected to have feathers as all birds do. Indeed, some evolutionists believe all dinosaurs may have had some sort of feathers or "protofeathers" and most believe that at least the theropod dinosaurs had feathers.

For many years, evolutionists insisted that bird feathers evolved from frayed reptile scales and even argued that scales and feathers are very similar structures. This idea was never well supported by evidence and has now been largely abandoned by evolutionists.

Based on studies of the embryonic development of feathers, evolutionists now say feathers evolved from tubular structures in the skin which became feather follicles. This sounds like the long-refuted recapitulation myth (see chapter 25 in this volume), where developing embryos were believed to go through stages of their evolutionary history. But while developing feather follicles tell us something about their embryology, they don't necessarily tell us anything about their evolution.

Why Feathers on a Dinosaur?

A big challenge for evolutionists is why would feathers have evolved on dino-saurs? What would be the selective advantage of a reptile evolving feathers?

Some, assuming dinosaurs were warm blooded, speculate feathers evolved for conserving body heat. Others speculate that feathers evolved with their colors for sexual attraction. Still others speculate that feathers evolved for flight, but most of the "feathered" true dinosaurs would have been clearly incapable of flight.

Other less-complicated structures could have met all these needs. For example, body fat is a relatively simple but effective thermal insulator. Reptiles such as snakes show a wide variety of colors and patterns in their scales. The pterodactyls were dinosaur-like reptiles that flew with relatively simple membranes of skin like bats.

Feathers are one of the most complex structures found in the vertebrate skin. The feather follicles which produce the feathers are similar in many ways to hair follicles, but the feathers themselves are far more complex than hair. Like hair, and unlike reptilian scales or scutes, feathers grow out of tubular follicles in the skin.

All growth and development occur in a growth collar at the base of the follicle, after which programmed cell death quickly produces the fully mature dead keratinized structure of the feather. The feather emerges from its follicle rolled up like a cylinder inside of a tubular shell and is known as a pin feather. When the shell of the pin feather breaks off, the feather unfolds and interlocks in a very complex way to reveal the mature feather.

Birds produce many different types of feathers, but the typical pennaceous feather consists of a rachis (shaft) with branching barbs that make up the two feather vanes. Each barb looks like a miniature feather with its own branching barbules. The anterior barbules on one side of the barb have several tiny little hooklets, while the posterior barbules on the other side have a ridge called the dorsal flange (figure 5).

The anterior barbules of each barb overlap with the posterior barbules of the adjacent barb. The hooklets of the anterior barbules hook onto the dorsal flange of the posterior barbules locking the barbs together in the manner of a very precise and sophisticated form of a zipper.

Feather Arrangement

If feathers are to serve in flight they can't just be packed together like hairs on a mammal. Flight requires that feathers have a precise left/right positional symmetry. Thus, the feathers are arranged in a pattern of rows called *pterylae* in which the feathers on one side of the bird are in a precise mirror image arrangement of the feathers on the other side. But this in itself is still

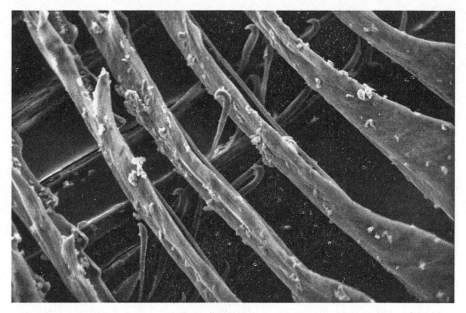

Figure 5

not sufficient for the demands of flight — the feathers must also molt and regrow in precise left/right matched pairs so as not to leave the bird aerodynamically unbalanced!

Feathers Are High Maintenance

Since feathers are subject to being ruffled from the disconnecting of their hooklets and flanges, they require a great deal of maintenance in the form of preening. Preening also removes dirt and parasites from the bird's plumage. Most birds spend an average of 9% of each day on feather maintenance, with some spending up to 25% of the day preening.[11] Preening not only requires a whole suite of learned and instinctual behaviors, but also requires special organs such as the beak. When birds preen, they use their beak to grasp each feather at its base and then slide their beak down the length of the shaft to the tip of the feather.

Most birds have a special gland located above the base of the tail called the preen gland (uropygial gland). The preen gland secretes an oily material that the bird picks up with its beak (thanks to a very flexible neck) and

11. Peter Cotgreave and Dale H. Clayton, "Comparative Analysis of Time Spent Grooming by Birds in Relation To Parasite Load," *Behaviour*, 1994, 131 (3): 171–187. doi:10.1163/156853994X00424. ISSN 0005-7959.

preens into its feathers. This serves to oil the feathers and make them water-proof. Birds lacking such glands (or other waterproofing provisions), such as the Florida Anhinga, are unable to fly when their feathers are wet due to the increased weight. Even though the Anhinga has a wing span of over three and one-half feet, it must stand in the sun with wings outstretched to dry out before it is capable of flight.

Did Real Dinosaurs Have Feathers?

There are numerous publications claiming to report evidence of feathers, or at least "protofeathers" on dinosaurs. Again, it all gets very confusing because evolutionists consider birds to be dinosaurs and birds certainly do have feathers. Claims of feathered dinosaurs have been largely confined to theropod dinosaurs where all of the families are said to have at least fine filamentous structures on their skin believed to be "protofeathers," while others are said to have true pennaceous feathers.[12] But there is no compelling evidence that the fine filaments seen on some dinosaurs are feathers of any kind, and may actually be evidence of collagen fibers in ligaments and skin.[13] Five families of theropod dinosaurs are claimed to have true pennaceous feathers like modern birds.

- The theropod family Ornithomimosauria is claimed to have pennaceous feathers but the fossil evidence only consists of some marks on bony surfaces thought to be attachment points for feathers, but no actual feathers.
- The Troodontidae family of theropods is also claimed to have pennaceous feathers but there are no published examples of such feathers, just the assumption that *Troodon* must have had feathers because it has some birdlike features.
- The "theropod" families (or clades) Oviraptosauria, Dromaeosauridae, and Avialae do indeed have well developed pennaceous feathers, but all three appear to be in fact birds and not dinosaurs.

Oviraptosauria

The *Oviraptors* have a pygostyle (short tail made of fused bones) like all modern birds and most fossil birds. Their rib cage has several distinctive features of birds including bony uncinate processes that keep the rib cage rigid,

---

12. D. Zelenitsky et al., "Feathered Non-avian Dinosaurs from North America Provide Insight into Wing Origins," *Science* 338:510-514 (2012).
13. A. Feduccia et al., "Do Feathered Dinosaurs Exist?," J Morphol 266:125–16.

which is consistent with the unique fixed lung manner of avian respiration. The beak of Oviraptors is toothless like all modern birds, and some fossils have been found in what appears to be a nesting position on eggs.

Dromaeosauridae

The Dromaeosaurs first appear in the mid-Jurassic fossil record about "167 million years" ago and have many of the characteristics of birds, including being covered in pennaceous feathers including large aerodynamic wing feathers. They had long arms (wings) that could be folded against the body and, like Archaeopteryx, three long fingers ending in claws. Their tails were long with bony vertebrae lacking dorsal spines, haemal spines, and transverse processes for muscle attachment.

Such a tail contrasts sharply with the tails of true theropod dinosaurs that are heavily muscled. If one examines a fossil of a complete and articulated Dromaeosaur skeleton such as *Zhenyuanlong*, it is clear that to balance they would need to have walked from the knee like modern birds, rather than from the hip like theropod dinosaurs.

Avialae

The clade of "theropod dinosaurs" known as Avialae clearly have pennaceous feathers, but this shouldn't come as a surprise because the Avialae are in fact birds. All living birds, for example, would be considered members of Avialae, but avialans have also been found as fossils in the late Jurassic Tiaojishan of China that evolutionists claim to be about 160 million years old.[14] This is as old or older, by secular reckoning, than most of the theropod nonavian dinosaurs that are believed to be evolutionary ancestors of birds!

Conclusion

Birds have many distinctive features that distinguish them from dinosaurs. Birds are homeothermic with a high metabolic rate and high body core temperature. Birds have a unique high efficiency flow-through respiratory system with no diaphragm muscle. Birds have a high degree of bone fusion with lightweight pneumatic bones supported within by numerous bony struts. Birds have highly flexed thighs that are located inside their body,

---

14. Y.-Q. Liu, H.-W. Kuang, X.-J. Jiang, N. Peng, H. Xu, H.-Y. Sun , "Timing of the Earliest Known Feathered Dinosaurs and Transitional Pterosaurs Older than the Jehol Biota," *Palaeogeography, Palaeoclimatology, Palaeoecology.* (2012), 323–325: 1–12. doi:10.1016/j.palaeo.2012.01.017.

bringing their balance fulcrum forward to their internal knee. As a result, birds balance and walk from the knee, not the hip as the bipedal dinosaurs did.

Finally, feathers appear to be as unique to birds as hairs are to mammals. Fossilized impressions of dinosaur skin reveal scutes, like on the alligator, not imbricated scales like lizards or feathers like birds.

> Then God said, "Let the waters abound with an abundance of living creatures, and let birds fly above the earth across the face of the firmament of the heavens." So God created great sea creatures and every living thing that moves, with which the waters abounded, according to their kind, and every winged bird according to its kind. And God saw that it was good. And God blessed them, saying, "Be fruitful and multiply, and fill the waters in the seas, and let birds multiply on the earth" (Genesis 1:20–22).[15]

---

15. Scripture in this chapter is from the New King James Version (NKJV) of the Bible.

> *Darwin argued that absence of these intermediate forms resulted from imperfection in the geologic record. In this way, the absence of evidence of fossilized intermediate forms was not evidence that they never existed, only that they did not fossilize or had just not been found yet.*

19

WHAT ABOUT THE MISSING LINKS LIKE LUCY, NEANDERTHALS, AND HOMO ERECTUS THAT PROVE HUMAN EVOLUTION?

DR. DAVID A. DEWITT received a BS in biochemistry from Michigan State University and a PhD in neurosciences from Case Western Reserve University. Currently professor of biology and chair of the Department of Biology and Chemistry at Liberty University, he is active in teaching and research. He teaches upper-level courses in cell biology and human biological variation. He has authored and coauthored several articles in peer-reviewed journals such as *Brain Research, Neurotoxicology, Journal of Alzheimer Disease*, and *Experimental Neurology*. He also wrote *Unraveling the Origins Controversy*, which answers many of the most challenging questions in the origins debate. He has presented research at both national and international meetings on creation–evolution issues. He is a member of the Society for Neuroscience, the Creation Research Society, and has served as chair of the biology section of the Virginia Academy of Sciences.

Several years ago, I saw a museum display set up with an empty case. The curator had not yet finished preparing the large fossil specimen. However, the case was ready and awaiting placement of the specimen. In the meantime, a prankster made a small label for the empty display case: THE MISSING LINK. The implication was that the case was empty because the "missing link" was still missing.

While media reports often proclaim a new fossil as a "missing link" that has been found, scientists tend to avoid the use of the term. Evolutionists view species as part of a branching tree with ancestors and descendants existing at the same time and multiple species diverging off from the same ancestor. In contrast, a "missing link" implies a chain where one species gives rise to the next in a continuous, linear chain. This is why evolutionists will say "humans and chimpanzees share a common ancestor" rather than "humans evolved from chimpanzees."

Clearly, a gulf exists between chimpanzees and modern humans, and several "missing links" have been used to plug the gap. Notably, Australopithecines, Neanderthals, and *Homo erectus* play prominent roles in this regard. However, as will be discussed below, they do not provide the evidence needed to support evolution.

What Are "Missing Links"?

Although Darwin did not use the phrase "missing link" in *Origin of Species,* the concept is nonetheless present.[1] Chapter 9 of *Origin of Species* was titled "On the Imperfection of the Geological Record." In it, Darwin discussed both the lack of what he called "intermediate varieties" in the fossil record as well as explaining why he thought they were absent. He wrote:

> The main cause, however, of *innumerable intermediate links not now occurring everywhere* throughout nature depends on the very process of natural selection, through which new varieties continually take the places of and exterminate their parent-forms. But just in proportion as this process of extermination has acted on an enormous scale, *so must the number of intermediate varieties, which have formerly existed on the earth, be truly enormous.* Why then is not every geological formation and every stratum full of such intermediate links? Geology assuredly does not reveal any such

---

1. Darwin did not use "missing link." In chapter 9, he spoke of "innumerable transitional links" and gave reasons "why such links do not commonly occur." Therefore, he spoke of transitional links and their absence, which is equivalent to "missing link."

finely graduated organic chain; and this, perhaps, is the most obvious and gravest objection which can be urged against my theory. The explanation lies, as I believe, in the extreme imperfection of the geological record (emphasis added).

Properly understood, *a missing link is a transitional intermediate between two types of organisms that has yet to be found.* Darwin acknowledged that his proposed model of evolution by natural selection required a huge number of transitional intermediates. Indeed, the process of various species arising from common ancestors means that there should be intermediates, some of which will be selected against. This means that if a giraffe ancestor had a short neck, we would expect medium-neck giraffes existed as well as long-necked ones. Or, if whales evolved from land-dwelling wolf-like creatures, there would be intermediates with short legs before the whales with no legs. If all living things had evolved from common ancestors, then the number of previously existing intermediate varieties would be quite enormous.[2] So where are all of the intermediates?

Darwin argued that absence of these intermediate forms resulted from imperfection in the geologic record. In this way, the absence of evidence of fossilized intermediate forms was not evidence that they never existed, only that they did not fossilize or had just not been found yet. This argument received a tremendous boost in 1863 with the discovery of a fossil named *archaeopteryx*. It appeared that this fossil bird with feathers, a bony tail, and teeth was exactly the kind of transitional intermediate between reptiles and birds that Darwin predicted should exist. This looked like a missing link that had been found, confirming Darwin's theory of evolution. Even if archaeopteryx were a missing link that was found (it is not), there would still be perhaps millions more which have still not been found.

What Are Genealogical Transitions?

Intuitively, we quickly identify patterns or relationships and also fill in gaps. God designed the human brain with this ability, which helps us perform a variety of daily functions. For one, recognizing patterns and relationships allows us to make predictions and understand cause and effect. Of course, we are not perfect at this and sometimes can be fooled. An example of how

---

2.   Gould and Eldridge proposed "punctuated equilibrium" as an explanation for the lack of transitional varieties in the fossil record. With long periods of stasis and short periods of rapid change, the intermediates existed for a short time relative to the endpoints. Since so few organisms ever become fossils, it is unlikely the intermediates will be found in favor of the more abundant static forms.

we can be fooled is by confusing a *morphological* transition with a *genealogical* transition.

A *morphological* transition is intermediate in *form*. Archaeopteryx is an example of a morphological transition because it has characteristics usually associated with different types of organisms. For example, it has feathers like a bird, but it has teeth, a bony tail, and a wing claw, which are more typically associated with reptiles (even though other birds were known to have these features).

Another example is the duck-billed platypus, which is a mammal. Although it has hair and nurses its young with milk, it also has a bill like a duck, webbed feet, and lays eggs. In both of these cases, the organism has a mixture of characteristics which make them appear to be a transitional intermediate. However, they are not the type of intermediate that is required by evolutionary thought.

In some ways, a motorcycle is a morphological transition between a bicycle and a car. Similarly, a spork is a morphological transition between a spoon and a fork, and a splayd is a morphological transition between a spoon, fork, and knife. Regardless of whether we are talking about these man-made objects or the organisms mentioned above, they *appear* to be intermediates when in reality they are just unique. There is no relationship between these organisms and the ones they are purported to be transitions between.

A *genealogical* transition is a transition within a created kind of organisms. Creationists recognize a created kind as a group of organisms that are related to each other through the few ancestors that were on Noah's Ark or that were originally created during the creation week. For example, all of the various dog breeds as well as foxes, coyotes, and wolves are part of the "dog kind." In some cases, the created kinds may even include organisms

Figure 1. An example of how items can be placed on a chart and give an impression of relationship and evolution. In A, the spork gives rise to both the spoon and the fork. In B, the spoon evolves into the fork with the spork as a transitional intermediate. The reality is that each is a separate type. Adapted from a figure provided courtesy of Daniel Howell.

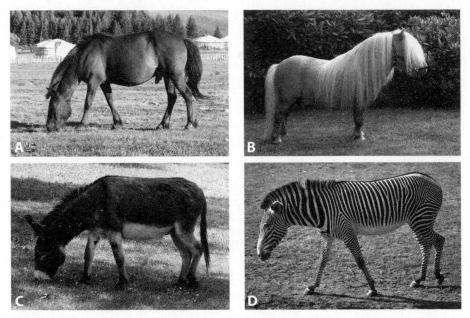

Figure 2. Representatives of the horse kind include A) the Mongolian horse, B) the Shetland pony, C) the donkey, and D) the zebra. Horses and zebras can crossbreed as can horses and donkeys and donkeys and zebras. Although horses, zebras, and donkeys are considered different species, they are likely from the same created kind.

that are distinct species. Lions, tigers, cheetah's, and panthers are part of the cat kind, whereas horses, donkeys, and zebras are part of the horse kind.

One way that a created kind is determined is through breeding. Since horses can cross with zebras and donkeys (and donkeys with zebras) to produce viable offspring, these organisms comprise a created kind. However, dogs can cross with neither horses nor cats, demonstrating that these are each distinct created kinds.

Of course, a wide range of variation can exist within a kind, which is best demonstrated by the amazing array of dog breeds. Nonetheless, different dog breeds are able to cross to produce a "Doodleman pincher" (cross between a Doberman and a poodle) or a Labradoodle (cross between a Labrador and a poodle). If we look within a created kind, we may be able to demonstrate genealogical transitions for things like increasing beak length, but the same does not hold for the origin of feathers.

What about Neanderthals?

Archaeological evidence indicates that Neanderthals hunted and trapped prey, used fire, built boats, made jewelry, made and used musical instruments, and cared for injured. Most importantly, they buried their dead. From a behavioral standpoint, Neanderthals did the same things that modern humans did.

Neanderthal skeletons had a few differences which distinguish them from modern humans. Many of the differences appear to be adaptations to a cold climate. For example, Neanderthals were shorter and stockier than modern humans with wide noses. This is not surprising, considering that the remains tend to be found across Eurasia, particularly in the north.

Other differences in the skull include a prominent brow ridge, weak chin, long face, enlarged cranial capacity, and an occipital bun (protrusion in the back of the skull). Fossil Neanderthals show a range of variation with some specimens having pronounced features, while others much less so. These unique features of Neanderthals were noted from their first discovery, leading to the conclusion by some that they were a unique species.

Initial DNA evidence supported the unique status of Neanderthals. Analysis of the control region of mitochondrial DNA showed a significant number of nucleotide differences to modern humans. However, analysis of additional Neanderthal specimens showed that Neanderthals varied from each other at the same sites in the mtDNA control region that modern humans vary from each other. This suggested that Neanderthals and modern humans may have shared a common gene pool.

That conclusion was reinforced in 2010 when the full Neanderthal genome was sequenced. Importantly, 2.5% of an average non-African modern human genome is comprised of Neanderthal DNA, demonstrating that the effects of interbreeding was significant enough to be persistent and widespread. This result conclusively demonstrates that Neanderthals and modern humans did in fact interbreed.

Additionally, DNA sequences obtained from specimens found in a cave in Denisova, Siberia, indicated that these individuals interbred with both Neanderthals and modern humans and their DNA sequences can be found in people today from Melanesia and to a lesser extent in Southeast Asia.

Taken together, Neanderthal behavior (including tool use and burial of the dead), skeletal features, and DNA sequences that support interbreeding, all suggest that Neanderthals and modern humans were part of the same created kind. This would make Neanderthals descendants of Adam and Eve just like us. All of this makes Neanderthals a very poor example of a missing link.

Neanderthal status as a missing link has been further undermined by research on another fossil hominid, *Homo heidelbergensis*. *H. heidelbergensis* skulls are much larger even than Neanderthals. Initially, this specimen was believed to be a common ancestor between Neanderthals and modern humans. With a much more robust skull and a larger brow ridge, *H. heidelbergensis* seemed to fit the bill as a Neanderthal ancestor.

However, with overlapping timeframes in addition to a range of skull variation that overlaps Neanderthals, some researchers are questioning the distinct status of *H. heidelbergensis* and are now considering that it may not be distinct from Neanderthals.

What about Australopithecines?

The first Australopithecine fossils were discovered by Donald Johansen in the early 1970s. The partially complete skeleton (~40% complete) was nicknamed "Lucy" as a tribute to the song "Lucy in the Sky with Diamonds" by the Beatles.

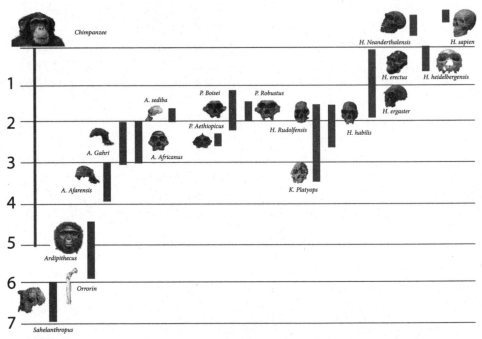

Million years ago

Figure 3. A typical chart showing various hominid fossils and the range of their timespan according to evolutionary theory. Frequently such charts have connecting lines showing which type gave rise to the next. The layout of this chart without connections highlights a major problem for evolutionists. There are several different hominids in the 1–3 million year range and many of these are contemporary with H ergaster/erectus. As more fossils have been found, evolutionists are increasingly unsure which ones (if any) are actual ancestors to man.

Since the initial discovery, numerous other Australopithecine fossils have been found, including Selam. Although a juvenile specimen, Selam is an extremely important fossil because it is essentially a complete skeleton. Indeed, some of Selam's bones had never previously been found. All of these newly found features were consistent with the conclusion that Australopithecines were just an extinct ape.

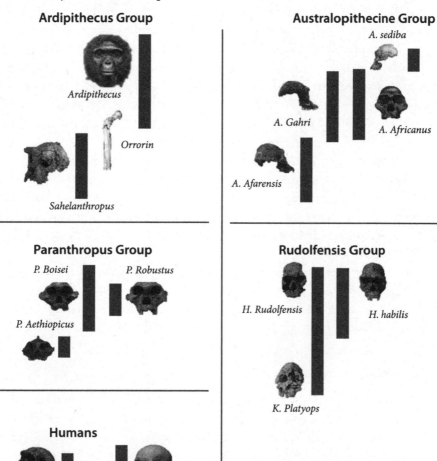

Figure 4. The same information from Figure 3 with a different layout. Notice how they can be distributed into clustered groups that demonstrate a range of variation. These likely represent distinct create kinds. In addition to humans, there may have been four different extinct ape kinds.

These include curved fingers, an ape-like hyoid, ape-like neck and shoulder blade, and chimp-sized brain. Importantly, although Selam was first reported in 2004, scientists have not reported on the feet and toes of Selam. It is likely that the feet would be chimpanzee like and thus provide even more evidence that *Australopithecines* probably did not walk upright as humans do, reducing their significance to the origin of man.

Australopithecus Sediba is another important Australopithecine fossil. This fossil is important because of its more recent evolutionary date and some cranial features like tooth enamel that are like humans. Even so, *A. sediba* has strange features as well as massive arms with oversized hands. Upon its discovery in 2010 by Berger, *A. sediba* was supposed to link humans to Australopithecines. The subsequent discovery that *A. sediba* may actually be a hodgepodge of different organisms, including human, has called into question whether this is even a legitimate taxon.

Although Lucy and the other Australopithecine fossils have many ape-like features, they are also quite distinct from living apes as well. While creationists can rightly argue that Australopithecines did not walk habitually upright, it would be a mistake to insist that they were chimpanzees. Lucy's pelvis is far more human-like than a chimpanzee's pelvis is, but it is still not really like a human pelvis.

The best conclusion regarding Australopithecines is that they represent an extinct type of ape. Instead of pigeonholing this specimen into a category with existing apes (chimpanzee, gorilla, orangutan), the evidence suggests that it is different enough to consider a separate created kind for this extinct ape.

What about Homo erectus?

In 1891, Eugene Dubois found the femur, skull cap, and a few teeth. These were found on the island of Java in Indonesia and was nicknamed "Java Man." As other more complete skeletons were found, they collectively became known as *H. erectus*. These specimens are widespread and have been found throughout Africa and Asia.

Another important fossil skull of *H. erectus* is "Peking Man," which was found in China. *Homo erectus* has similar body proportions to modern humans with relatively longer legs and shorter arms than apes and fossils like the Australopithecines. Anatomically, *H. erectus* clearly were bipedal and had prominent brow ridges.

H. erectus is quite puzzling to evolutionary scientists because it is difficult to explain the distribution (across Africa and into Southeast Asia) as well as the temporal range. Secular dating methods suggest a range of 1.8 million years ago to less than 50,000 years ago. Scientists have reclassified the supposed older fossils from Africa as *Homo ergaster*. However, this raises another conundrum.

Although *H. ergaster*, is supposedly much older than *H. erectus*, modern humans share features in common with *H. ergaster* where they both differ from *H. erectus*. This does not fit the expected pattern because organisms should not share traits with an ancient ancestor not shared with the more recent ancestor.

Further complicating the picture is a diminutive skeleton found on the island of Flores which was nicknamed "the Hobbit." In many ways, the fossil *Homo Floresiensis* is similar to *H. erectus*. The skeleton is very small (about 3 feet 6 inches) with a small brain case. In spite of the small brain, these individuals made stone tools, built boats, and likely used fire.

Although most assume that *H. Floresiensis* was descended from *H. erectus*, some of the features on the Hobbit appear to be more primitive. However, the small stature and developmental differences should not be ruled out as contributing to the differences. The possibility remains that the range of variation for *H. erectus* should be expanded to include *H. Floresiensis*.

Paleoanthropologists are unsure of the role *H. erectus* plays in human origins as more data has come to light. For example, evolutionists do not know whether *H. erectus* is a direct ancestor to our species or *part* of our species. The finding of Dmanisi Skull 5 in particular caused more confusion on the status of *H. erectus*. The Dmanisi skull, with a small braincase, brow ridge, long face, large jaw, and large teeth possessed a rather unexpected combination. Not only so, the skulls that were found had a range of trait variation so large that if they had been found separately, scientists would have classified them as different species. Instead, the Dmanisi skulls support a range of variation of humans that includes Neanderthals, *H. erectus*, and modern man.

What about Ardipithecus Ramidus?

Scientists who discover fossil hominids generally focus on what makes their fossil unique with a goal of fitting it somewhere on the human evolutionary tree. The range of variation of traits is often overlooked. If variation is taken into account, we might conclude that there are humans and several extinct apes each with their own range of variation.

An example of an extinct ape kind is *Ardipithecus Ramidus*. This fossil with a tiny braincase, opposable big toe, and long arms with massive hands was allegedly one of our first ancestors to walk habitually upright. The primary evidence for an upright gait comes from the pelvis, even though this bone was so fragmented as to be virtually unrecognizable. Many other features of the skeleton are more consistent with an arboreal lifestyle much like the modern orangutan. Indeed, the long arms and exceptionally long hands are more consistent with spending considerable time in trees.

How Should Creationists View Human Origins?

During the creation week, God made a wide array of creatures that were blessed to reproduce "after its kind." This means that within each kind was a range of variation that would also allow for adaptation as environmental conditions warranted. Typically, charts of human evolution show individual hominids with a timeframe when they allegedly lived.

Paleoanthropologists often focus on what makes a particular fossil different in the hopes of naming a new species. Another way to look at the same data is to consider the range of variation that may represent a kind. For example, although there are several different Australopithecine species, they may simply be part of the same kind. While fossils found in various parts of the world may have differences from each other, nonetheless, they are part of the same kind. This would mean that the hominid fossils would either be human descendants of Adam and Eve or an extinct ape.

Conclusion

God made man in his image. Adam and Eve, the first man and woman, disobeyed God's command and this disobedience brought death to all men. "For the wages of sin is death, but the gift of God is eternal life in Christ Jesus our Lord" (Romans 6:23; NIV). God did not treat us as our sins deserve but provided His only begotten Son, Jesus Christ, to pay the penalty for sin on our behalf. Through faith in Him, we become God's children and inherit the gift of eternal life.

> *Since there is much more prestige in finding an ancestor of man than an ancestor of living apes (or worse yet, merely an extinct ape), there is immense pressure on paleoanthropologists to declare almost any ape fossil to be a 'hominid.'*

20 WHAT ABOUT HUMAN EVOLUTION?

DR. DAVID MENTON has written numerous articles in technical and scientific journals dealing with bone, wound healing, and the epidermal barrier function and biomechanics of skin. He is also a member of the American Association of Anatomists and a Member of Sigma Xi. His honors include Silver Award for Basic Research from the American Academy of Dermatology, and profiles in *American Men and Women of Science — A Biographical Directory of Today's Leaders in Physical, Biological and Related Sciences* for almost two decades. Shortly after his retirement from Washington University School of Medicine in St. Louis, MO, Dr. Menton joined Answers in Genesis as a speaker, researcher, and contributor of articles to *Answers Magazine* and chapters of several multi-author books.

Human evolution is one of the most hotly debated subjects when entering the debate over Genesis versus the naturalistic view of evolution. Many Christians struggle to answer this question adequately.

Perhaps the most bitter pill to swallow for any Christian who attempts to "make peace" with Darwin is the presumed ape ancestry of man. Even many Christians who uncritically accept evolution as "God's way of creating" try to somehow elevate the origin of man, or at least his soul, above that of the beasts.

Evolutionists attempt to soften the blow by assuring us that man didn't exactly evolve from apes (tailless monkeys) but rather from *apelike* creatures. This is mere semantics, however, as many of the presumed apelike ancestors of man are apes and have scientific names, which include the word *pithecus* (derived from the Greek, meaning "ape").

The much-touted "human ancestor" commonly known as "Lucy," for example, has the scientific name *Australopithecus afarensis* (meaning "southern *ape* from the Afar triangle of Ethiopia"). But what does the Bible say about the origin of man, and what exactly is the scientific evidence that evolutionists claim for our ape ancestry?

Biblical Starting Assumptions

God tells us that on the same day He made all animals that walk on the earth (the sixth day), He created man separately in His own image with the intent that man would have dominion over every other living thing on earth (Genesis 1:26–28). From this it is clear that there is no animal that is man's equal, and certainly none his ancestor.

Thus, when God paraded the animals by Adam for him to name, He observed that "for Adam there was not found an help meet for him" (Genesis 2:20).[1] Jesus confirmed this uniqueness of men and women when He declared that marriage is to be between a man and a woman because "from the beginning of the creation God made them male and female" (Mark 10:6). This leaves no room for prehumans or for billions of years of cosmic evolution prior to man's appearance on the earth. Adam chose the very name "Eve" for his wife because he recognized that she would be "the mother of all living" (Genesis 3:20). The Apostle Paul stated clearly that man is not an animal: "All flesh is not the same flesh: but there is one kind of flesh of men, another flesh of beasts, another of fishes, and another of birds" (1 Corinthians 15:39).

---

1.   Scripture in this chapter is from the King James Version (KJV) of the Bible.

Evolutionary Starting Assumptions

The only permissible question is, "From which apes did man evolve?"

While Bible-believing Christians stand on the foundation that God's Word is true and that man's ancestry goes back only to a fully human Adam and Eve, evolutionists begin with the assumption that man has, in fact, evolved from apes. No paleoanthropologists (those who study the fossil evidence for man's origin) would dare to seriously raise the question, "*Did* man evolve from apes?" The only permissible question is, "From *which* apes did man evolve?"

Since evolutionists generally do not believe that man evolved from any ape that is now living, they look to fossils of humans and apes to provide them with their desired evidence. Specifically, they look for any anatomical feature that looks "intermediate" (between that of apes and man). Fossil apes having such features are declared to be ancestral to man (or at least collateral relatives) and are called *hominids*.

Living apes, on the other hand, are not considered to be hominids, but rather are called *hominoids* because they are only similar to humans but did not evolve into them. Nonetheless, evolutionists are willing to accept mere similarities between the fossilized bones of extinct apes and the bones of living men as "proof " of our ape ancestry.

What Is the Evidence for Human Evolution?

Though many similarities may be cited between living apes and humans, the only historical evidence that could support the ape ancestry of man must come from fossils. Unfortunately, the fossil record of man and apes is very sparse. Approximately 95 percent of all known fossils are marine invertebrates, about 4.7 percent are algae and plants, about 0.2 percent are insects and other invertebrates, and only about 0.1 percent are vertebrates (animals with bones). Finally, only the smallest imaginable fraction of vertebrate fossils consists of primates (humans, apes, monkeys, and lemurs).

Because of the rarity of fossil hominids, even many of those who specialize in the evolution of man have never actually seen an original hominid fossil, and far fewer have ever had the opportunity to handle or study one. Most scientific papers on human evolution are based on casts of original specimens (or even on published photos, measurements, and descriptions of them). Access to original fossil hominids is strictly limited by those who discovered them and is often confined to a few favored evolutionists who agree with the discoverers' interpretation of the fossil.

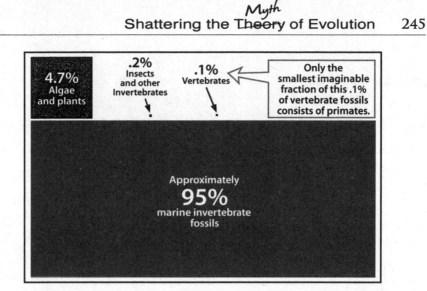

Since there is much more prestige in finding an ancestor of man than an ancestor of living apes (or worse yet, merely an extinct ape), there is immense pressure on paleoanthropologists to declare almost any ape fossil to be a "hominid." As a result, the living apes have pretty much been left to find their own ancestors.

Many students in our schools are taught human evolution (often in the social studies class!) by teachers having little knowledge of human anatomy, to say nothing of ape anatomy. But it is useless to consider the fossil evidence for the evolution of man from apes without first understanding the basic anatomical and functional differences between human and ape skeletons.

Jaws and Teeth

Because of their relative hardness, teeth and jaw fragments are the most frequently found primate fossils. Thus, much of the evidence for the ape ancestry of man is based on similarities of teeth and jaws.

In contrast to man, apes tend to have incisor and canine teeth that are relatively larger than their molars. Ape teeth usually have thin enamel (the hardest surface layer of the tooth), while humans generally have thicker enamel. Finally, the jaws tend to be more U-shaped in apes and more parabolic in man.

The problem in declaring a fossil ape to be a human ancestor (i.e., a hominid) on the basis of certain humanlike features of the teeth is that some living apes have these same features and they are not considered to be ancestors of man. Some species of modern baboons, for example, have relatively small canines and incisors and relatively large molars. While most apes do have thin enamel, some apes, such as the orangutans, have relatively thick enamel. Clearly, teeth tell us more about an animal's diet and feeding habits than its supposed evolution. Nonetheless, thick enamel is one of the most commonly cited criteria for declaring an ape fossil to be a hominid.

Artistic imagination has been used to illustrate entire "apemen" from nothing more than a single tooth. In the early 1920s, the "apeman" *Hesperopithecus* (which consisted of a single tooth) was pictured in the *London Illustrated News* complete with the tooth's wife, children, domestic animals, and cave! Experts used this tooth, known as "Nebraska man," as proof for human evolution during the time of the Scopes trial in 1925. In 1927, parts of the skeleton were discovered together with the teeth, and Nebraska man was found to really be an extinct peccary (wild pig)!

Skulls

Skulls are perhaps the most interesting primate fossils because they house the brain and give us an opportunity, with the help of imaginative artists, to look our presumed ancestors in the face. The human skull is easily distinguished from all living apes, though there are, of course, similarities.

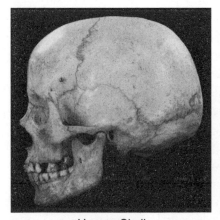

Human Skull

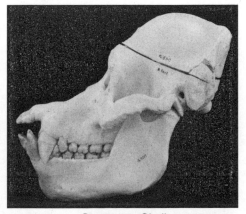

Orangutan Skull

The vault of the skull is large in humans because of their relatively large brain compared to apes. Even so, the size of the normal adult human brain varies over nearly a threefold range. These differences in size in the human brain do not correlate with intelligence. Adult apes have brains that are generally smaller than even the smallest of adult human brains, and of course they are not even remotely comparable in intelligence.

Perhaps the best way to distinguish an ape skull from a human skull is to examine it from a side view. From this perspective, the face of the human is nearly vertical, while that of the ape slopes forward from its upper face to its chin. From a side view, the bony socket of the eye (the *orbit*) of an ape is obscured by its broad, flat upper face. Humans, on the other hand, have a more curved upper face and forehead, clearly revealing the orbit of the eye from a side view.

Another distinctive feature of the human skull is the nose bone that our glasses rest on. Apes do not have protruding nasal bones and would have great difficulty wearing glasses.

Leg Bones

The most eagerly sought-after evidence in fossil hominids is any anatomical feature that might suggest *bipedality* (the ability to walk on two legs). Since humans walk on two legs, any evidence of bipedality in fossil apes is considered by evolutionists to be compelling evidence for human ancestry. But we should bear in mind that the way an ape walks on two legs is entirely different from the way man walks on two legs. The distinctive human gait requires the complex integration of many skeletal and muscular features in our hips, legs, and feet. Thus, evolutionists closely examine the hipbones (*pelvis*), thighbones (*femur*), leg bones (*tibia* and *fibula*), and foot bones of fossil apes in an effort to detect any anatomical features that might suggest bipedality.

Evolutionists are particularly interested in the angle at which the femur and the tibia meet at the knee (called the *carrying angle*). Humans are able to keep their weight over their feet while walking because their femurs converge toward the knees, forming a carrying angle of approximately nine degrees with the tibia (in other words, we're sort of knock-kneed). In contrast, chimps and gorillas have widely separated, straight legs with a carrying angle of essentially zero degrees. These animals manage to keep their weight over their feet when walking by swinging their body from side to side in the familiar "ape walk."

Evolutionists assume that fossil apes with a high carrying angle (human-like) were bipedal and thus evolved into man. Certain *australopithecines* (apelike creatures) are considered to have walked like us and thus to be our ancestors largely because they had a high carrying angle. But high carrying angles are not confined to humans — they are also found on some modern apes that walk gracefully on tree limbs and only clumsily on the ground.

Living apes with a high carrying angle (values comparable to man) include such apes as the orangutan and spider monkey — both adept tree climbers and capable of only an apelike bipedal gait on the ground. The point is that there are *living* tree-dwelling apes and monkeys with some of the same anatomical features that evolutionists consider to be definitive evidence for bipedality, yet none of these animals walks like man and no one suggests they are our ancestors or descendants.

Foot Bones

The human foot is unique and not even close to the appearance or function of the ape foot. The big toe of the human foot is in-line with the foot and does not jut out to the side like an ape's. Human toe bones are relatively straight, rather than curved and grasping like ape toes.

While walking, the heel of the human foot hits the ground first and then the weight distribution spreads from the heel along the outer margin of the foot up to the base of the little toe. From the little toe it spreads inward across the base of the toes and finally pushes off from the big toe. No ape has a foot or push-off like that of a human, and thus, no ape is capable of walking with our distinctive human stride or making human footprints.

Hipbones

The pelvis (hipbones) plays a critically important role in walking, and the characteristic human gait requires a pelvis that is distinctly different from that of the apes. Indeed, one only has to examine the pelvis to determine if an ape has the ability to walk like a man.

The part of the hipbones that we can feel just under our belt is called the iliac blade. Viewed from above, these blades are curved forward like the handles of a steering yolk on an airplane. The iliac blades of the ape, in contrast, project straight out to the side like the handlebars of a scooter. It is simply not possible to walk like a human with an apelike pelvis. On this feature alone one can easily distinguish apes from humans.

Only Three Ways to Make an "Apeman"

Knowing from Scripture that God didn't create any apemen, there are only three ways for the evolutionist to create one:

1. Combine ape fossil bones with human fossil bones and declare the two to be one individual — a real "apeman."
2. Emphasize certain humanlike qualities of fossilized ape bones, and with imagination upgrade apes to be more humanlike.
3. Emphasize certain apelike qualities of fossilized human bones, and with imagination downgrade humans to be more apelike.

These three approaches account for *all* of the attempts by evolutionists to fill the unbridgeable gap between apes and men with fossil apemen.

Combining Men and Apes

The most famous example of an apeman proven to be a combination of ape and human bones is Piltdown man. In 1912, Charles Dawson, a medical doctor and an amateur paleontologist, discovered a mandible (lower jawbone) and part of a skull in a

gravel pit near Piltdown, England. The jawbone was apelike, but had teeth that showed wear similar to the human pattern. The skull, on the other hand, was very humanlike. These two specimens were combined to form what was called "Dawn man," which was calculated to be 500,000 years old.

The whole thing turned out to be an elaborate hoax. The skull was indeed human (about 500 years old), while the jaw was that of a modern female orangutan whose teeth had been obviously filed to crudely resemble the human wear pattern. Indeed, the long ape canine tooth was filed down so far that it exposed the pulp chamber, which was then filled in to hide the mischief. It would seem that any competent scientist examining this tooth would have concluded that it was either a hoax or the world's first root canal! The success of this hoax for over 50 years, in spite of the careful scrutiny of the best authorities in the world, led the human evolutionist Sir Solly Zuckerman to declare: "It is doubtful if there is any science at all in the search for man's fossil ancestry."[2]

---

2. S. Zuckerman, *Beyond the Ivory Tower* (London: Weidenfeld & Nicolson, 1970), p. 64.

Making Man Out of Apes

Many apemen are merely apes that evolutionists have attempted to upscale to fill the gap between apes and men. These include all the australopithecines, as well as a host of other extinct apes such as *Ardipithecus, Orrorin, Sahelanthropus*, and *Kenyanthropus*. All have obviously ape skulls, ape pelvises, and ape hands and feet. Nevertheless, *australopithecines* (especially *Australopithecus afarensis*) are often portrayed as having hands and feet identical to modern man; a ramrod-straight, upright posture; and a human gait.

The best-known specimen of *A. afarensis* is the fossil commonly known as "Lucy." A life-like mannequin of "Lucy" in the *Living World* exhibit at the St. Louis Zoo shows a hairy, humanlike female body with human hands and feet but with an obviously apelike head. The three-foot-tall Lucy stands erect in a deeply pensive pose with her right forefinger curled under her chin, her eyes gazing off into the distance as if she were contemplating the mind of Newton.

Few visitors are aware that this is a gross misrepresentation of what is known about the fossil ape *Australopithecus afarensis*. These apes are known to be long-armed knuckle-walkers with locking wrists. Both the hands and feet of this creature are clearly apelike. Paleoanthropologists Jack Stern and Randall Sussman[3] have reported that the hands of this species are "surprisingly similar to hands found in the small end of the pygmy chimpanzee–common chimpanzee range." They report that the feet, like the hands, are "long, curved and heavily muscled" much like those of living tree-dwelling primates. The authors conclude that no living primate has such hands and feet "for any purpose other than to meet the demands of full or part-time arboreal (tree-dwelling) life."

Despite evidence to the contrary, evolutionists and museums continue to portray Lucy (*A. afarensis*) with virtually human feet (though some are finally showing the hands with long, curved fingers).

Making Apes Out of Man

In an effort to fill the gap between apes and men, certain fossil *men* have been declared to be "apelike" and thus, ancestral to at least "modern" man. You might say this latter effort seeks to make a "monkey" out of man! Human fossils that are claimed to be "apemen" are generally classified under the genus *Homo* (meaning "man"). These include *Homo erectus, Homo heidelbergensis*, and *Homo neanderthalensis*.

---

3.   *American Journal of Physical Anthropology* 60:279–317, 1983.

The story of how Neanderthal man was demoted to an apeman provides much insight into the methods of evolutionists.

The best-known human fossils are of Cro-Magnon man (whose marvelous paintings are found on the walls of caves in France) and Neanderthal man. Both are clearly human and have long been classified as *Homo sapiens*. In recent years, however, Neanderthal man has been downgraded to a different species — *Homo neanderthalensis*. The story of how Neanderthal man was demoted to an apeman provides much insight into the methods of evolutionists.

Neanderthal man was first discovered in 1856 by workmen digging in a limestone cave in the Neander valley near Dusseldorf, Germany. The fossil bones were examined by an anatomist (Professor Schaafhausen) who concluded that they were human.

At first, not much attention was given to these finds, but with the publication of Darwin's *Origin of Species* in 1859, the search began for the imagined "apelike ancestors" of man. Darwinians argued that Neanderthal man was an apelike creature, while many critical of Darwin (like the great anatomist Rudolph Virchow) argued that Neanderthals were human in every respect, though some appeared to be suffering from rickets or arthritis.

Over 300 Neanderthal specimens have now been found scattered throughout most of the world, including Belgium, China, Central and North Africa, Iraq, the Czech Republic, Hungary, Greece, northwestern Europe, and the Middle East. This group of people was characterized by prominent eyebrow ridges (like modern Australian Aborigines), a low forehead, a long, narrow skull, a protruding upper jaw, and a strong lower jaw with a short chin. They were deep-chested, large-boned individuals with a powerful build. It should be emphasized, however, that none of these features fall outside the range of normal human anatomy. Interestingly, the brain size (based on cranial capacity) of Neanderthal man was actually *larger* than average for that of modern man, though this is rarely emphasized.

Most of the misconceptions about Neanderthal man resulted from the claims of the Frenchman Marcelin Boule who, in 1908, studied two Neanderthal skeletons that were found in France (LeMoustier and La Chapelle-aux- Saints). Boule declared Neanderthal men to be anatomically and intellectually inferior brutes who were more closely related to apes than humans. He asserted that they had a slumped posture, a "monkey-like" arrangement of certain spinal vertebrae, and he even claimed that their feet were of a "grasping type" (like those of gorillas and chimpanzees). Boule concluded that Neanderthal man could not have walked erectly, but rather must have walked in a clumsy fashion. These highly biased and inaccurate views prevailed and were even expanded by many other evolutionists up to the mid-1950s.

In 1957, the anatomists William Straus and A.J. Cave examined one of the French Neanderthals (La Chapelle-aux-Saints) and determined that the individual suffered from severe arthritis (as suggested by Virchow nearly 100 years earlier), which had affected the vertebrae and bent the posture. The jaw also had been affected. These observations are consistent with the Ice Age climate in which Neanderthals had lived. They may well have sought shelter in caves, and this, together with poor diet and lack of sunlight, could easily have led to diseases that affect the bones, such as rickets.

In addition to anatomical evidence, there is a growing body of cultural evidence for the fully human status of Neanderthals. They buried their dead and had elaborate funeral customs that included arranging the body and covering it with flowers. They made a variety of stone tools and worked with skins and leather. A wood flute was recently discovered among Neanderthal remains. There is even evidence that suggests that Neanderthals engaged in medical care. Some Neanderthal specimens show evidence of survival to old age despite numerous wounds, broken bones, blindness, and disease. This suggests that these individuals were cared for and nurtured by others who showed human compassion.

Still, efforts continue to be made to somehow dehumanize Neanderthal man. There is, in fact, nothing about Neanderthals that is in any way inferior to modern man. One of the world's foremost authorities on Neanderthal man, Erik Trinkaus, concludes: "Detailed comparisons of Neandertal skeletal remains with those of modern humans have shown that there is nothing in Neandertal anatomy that conclusively indicates locomotor, manipulative, intellectual, or linguistic abilities inferior to those of modern humans."[4]

What about Homo naledi — a Practical Example?

It is not convincing that *H. naledi* is human, even though others claim to recognize it at the status of "near human." Looking at the fossils and skull reconstruction, *H. naledi* had a sloped lower face and a very robust mandible that bears little resemblance to humans. It also has a small cranium. The proximal and medial phalanges of the hand are even more curved than *Au. afarensis*, suggesting an ape-like creature.

Dr. Elizabeth Mitchell writes of *naledi*:

---

4. *Natural History* 87:10, 1978.

Despite all the media articles and Berger's implication that *Homo naledi* is a glorious mosaic of incipient humanity superimposed on an australopithecine base, the data presented in the study reveals what is most likely an ape. Perhaps a glorious example of ape diversity in the world God created, but not an ape stepping up the evolutionary ladder reaching for human-ness. The fragmentary nature of most fossils, including these, can make definitive identification difficult, but the extremely small braincase — assuming the composite reconstruction is accurate — and the sloped ape-like face, the jaw, the shoulder, the curved fingers and toes, the rib cage, and flared pelvis all are consistent with an australopithecine variant.[5]

The skull and most bones are distinctly ape. Thus, it is really a case of an ape dressed up like a human.

Conclusion

Why then are there continued efforts to make apes out of man and man out of apes? In one of the most remarkably frank and candid assessments of the whole subject and the methodology of paleoanthropology, Dr. David Pilbeam (a distinguished professor of anthropology) suggested the following:

Perhaps generations of students of human evolution, including myself, have been flailing about in the dark; that our data base is too sparse, too slippery, for it to be able to mold our theories. Rather the theories are more statements about us and ideology than about the past. Paleoanthropology reveals more about how humans view themselves than it does about how humans came about. But that is heresy.[6]

Oh, that these heretical words were printed as a warning on every textbook, magazine, newspaper article, and statue that presumes to deal with the bestial origin of man!

No, we are not descended from apes. Rather, God created man as the crown of His creation on day 6. We are a special creation of God, made in His image, to bring Him glory. What a revolution this truth would make if our evolutionized culture truly understood it!

5.   Elizabeth Mitchell, "Is *Homo naledi* a New Species of Human Ancestor?" *Answers in Depth,* Answers in Genesis, September 12, 2015, https://answersingenesis.org/human-evolution/homo-naledi-new-species-human-ancestor/.

6.   *American Scientist* 66:379, 1978.

> *Well, I'm going to let you in on a secret as to why creationists rarely take notice of these alleged missing links. It is because the evolutionists are digging in the wrong place — just like the bad guys in Indiana Jones.*

21

DIGGING FOR "MISSING LINKS" IN THE WRONG PLACE

BODIE HODGE is a News Anchor for *Answers News*, a popular world famous news program from Answers in Genesis including Ken Ham and Georgia Purdom. Bodie has spoken on four continents and has a multitude of his works translated in various foreign languages.

I n the movie *Indiana Jones and the Raiders of the Lost Ark*, there was a medallion that ultimately gave calculated directions to the precise location where the Ark of the Covenant was hidden — a lost, buried city. On both sides, the medallion was engraved with calculations for making a staff on which to attach the medallion.

Indiana Jones had the medallion, but the "bad guys," led by a man named Belloq, had an imprint of just one side of the medallion. The bad guys didn't know that the rest of the calculation was on the opposite side of the medallion. Upon realizing this, Indiana Jones says, "Belloq's staff is too long. They are digging in the wrong place!"[1]

So why is this significant?

Evolutionary Diggings . . . in the Wrong Place Too?

Each year there are many headlines, books, technical articles, and videos about another supposed missing link — a supposed link between a land mammal and whale,[2] a dinosaur and bird,[3] an ape and human,[4] and so forth. Usually, these are quite easy to refute by anatomical features.

For example, alleged missing links turn out to be anything but — for example, either ape, human, or a fake (e.g., Piltdown man[5]) or dinosaur, bird, or a fake (e.g., Archaeoraptor[6]).

Nevertheless, these alleged missing links rarely make creationists cringe. I think it frustrates some of the evolutionists because they think they have

1. "They're Digging in the Wrong Place," *Indiana Jones and the Raiders of the Lost Ark*, directed by Steven Spielberg (Los Angeles, CA: Pictures, 1981).
2. Terry Mortenson, "Fossil Evidence of Whale Evolution?" Answers in Genesis, March 25, 2014, https://answersingenesis.org/aquatic-animals/fossil-evidence-of-whale-evolution/.
3. David Menton, "Did Dinosaurs Turn into Birds?" *The New Answers Book 1*, Ken Ham, gen. ed. (Green Forest, AR: Master Books, 2006), p. 296–305, https://answersingenesis.org/dinosaurs/feathers/did-dinosaurs-turn-into-birds/.
4. David Menton, "Did Humans Really Evolve from Apelike Creatures?" *The New Answers Book 2*, Ken Ham, gen. ed. (Green Forest, AR: Master Books, 2008), p. 83–93, https://answersingenesis.org/human-evolution/ape-man/did-humans-really-evolve-from-apelike-creatures/.
5. Monty White, "The Piltdown Man Fraud," Answers in Genesis, November 24, 2003, https://answersingenesis.org/human-evolution/piltdown-man/the-piltdown-man-fraud/.
6. Editors, "Archaeoraptor Hoax Update — National Geographic Recants!" Answers in Genesis, March 2, 2000, https://answersingenesis.org/human-evolution/piltdown-man/the-piltdown-man-fraud/.

found some sort of knock-out evidence that they interpret as support for evolution. But creationists rarely bat an eye.

Well, I'm going to let you in on a secret as to why creationists rarely take notice of these alleged missing links. It is because the evolutionists are digging in the wrong place — just like the bad guys in *Indiana Jones*. When you don't have the correct information, you can miss the mark significantly.

What Do You Mean by "Digging in the Wrong Place"?

Essentially, the geologic rock layers (strata) are listed in the following charts.

Typically, evolutionists are searching for alleged human missing links in the upper strata like Pleistocene and Pliocene (bolded). Of course, there are exceptions to this.

In a general sense, evolutionists look for alleged dinosaur-to-bird missing links in the Cretaceous and Paleocene (bolded). Once again, there are exceptions to this, too.

But here is the problem. The rock layers from Cambrian to Miocene — at least mapped in the mountains of Ararat (Genesis 8:4) — were from

	Rock layer		Rock layer		Rock layer
1	Recent	1	Recent	1	Recent
2	Pleistocene	2	**Pleistocene**	2	Pleistocene
3	Pliocene	3	**Pliocene**	3	Pliocene
4	Miocene	4	Miocene	4	Miocene
5	Oligocene	5	Oligocene	5	Oligocene
6	Eocene	6	Eocene	6	Eocene
7	Paleocene	7	Paleocene	7	**Paleocene**
8	Cretaceous	8	Cretaceous	8	**Cretaceous**
9	Jurassic	9	Jurassic	9	Jurassic
10	Triassic	10	Triassic	10	Triassic
11	Permian	11	Permian	11	Permian
12	Pennsylvanian	12	Pennsylvanian	12	Pennsylvanian
13	Mississippian	13	Mississippian	13	Mississippian
14	Devonian	14	Devonian	14	Devonian
15	Silurian	15	Silurian	15	Silurian
16	Ordovician	16	Ordovician	16	Ordovician
17	Cambrian	17	Cambrian	17	Cambrian
18	Precambrian	18	Precambrian	18	Precambrian

the Flood.[7] Miocene and Eocene rock is intricately part of the makeup of the mountains of Ararat, as is Cretaceous and Triassic (many times inverted, lying above the Miocene and Eocene). Since that time, the upper strata are post-Flood strata — such as Ice Age layers[8] and recent volcanic flows.[9] I understand creationists debate about tertiary sediment (Paleocene through Miocene) and encourage you to study this further.[10]

The table shows the biblical timescale of the geologic layers in the region of the mountains of Ararat.

So when evolutionists say they found a transitional form between an ape and a human in Pliocene rock, creationists hardly flinch. Evolutionists are looking at the rock strata and the age of the earth[11] incorrectly because humans were around long before that rock was ever laid down! Furthermore, humans existed when the Cambrian rock was laid down during the Flood. To go one more step, mankind had dominated the earth for over 1,600 years[12] *before* the Cambrian rock was laid down!

When someone says that they found a transitional form between a dinosaur and a bird in the Paleocene, again, creationists hardly think twice. Both

---

7. I'm denoting these bolded layers as Flood because Miocene, Eocene, Cretaceous, and Triassic sediments are found in the makeup of the Mountains of Ararat (formed by the 150th day of the Flood), so these specific layers were indeed Flood layers. Even if other Miocene-Paleocene were post-Flood layers, the article's same point is made. Though there is debate on tertiary sediment elsewhere in the world being Flood or post-Flood, it is not for this article (see footnote 4). Y. Yilmaz, "Alochthonous Terranes in the Tethyan Middle East: Anatolia and the Surrounding Regions," *Philosophical Transactions of the Royal Society* A 331 (1990): 611–624; G.C. Schmidt, "A Review of Permian and Mesozoic Formations Exposed Near the Turkey/Iraq Border at Harbol," *Bulletin of the Mineral Research and Exploration Institute* 62 (1964): 103–119.
8. Mike Oard, "Where Does the Ice Age Fit?" *The New Answers Book 1*, Ken Ham, gen. ed. (Green Forest AR: Master Books, 2006), p. 207–219, https://answersingenesis.org/environmental-science/ice-age/where-does-the-ice-age-fit/.
9. Andrew Snelling, "Volcanoes — Windows Into Earth's Past," Answers In Genesis, July 1, 2010, https://answersingenesis.org/geology/natural-features/volcanoes-windows-into-earths-past/.
10. The debate over the Flood/Post-Flood boundary is an ongoing debate in creationist literature. I suggest starting with the discussion here: Andrew Snelling, *Earth's Catastrophic Past* (Green Forest, AR: Master Books, 2010), https://answersingenesis.org/store/sku/10-3-124/; and the Institute for Creation Research's Column Project led by Dr. Tim Clarey, including http://www.icr.org/article/10779/.
11. Bodie Hodge, "How Old Is The Earth?" *The New Answers Book 2*, Ken Ham, gen. ed. (Green Forest AR: Master Books, 2008), p. 41–52, https://answersingenesis.org/age-of-the-earth/how-old-is-the-earth/.
12. Bodie Hodge, "Ancient Patriarchs in Genesis," Answers in Genesis, January, 20, 2009, https://answersingenesis.org/bible-characters/ancient-patriarchs-in-genesis/.

specimens died the same year in the same Flood[13] and are not related. This is why finding feathers in the rock layers "before the dinosaurs" is not a problem for creationists.[14] Nor is it a problem when we find theropod dinosaurs (which supposedly evolved into birds in the evolutionary story) that had eaten birds in lower Cretaceous rock.[15] Birds were made on day 5, which is a day before the dinosaurs; land animals, like dinosaurs, were made on day 6.[16] Having both buried in Flood sediment isn't a big deal.

	Rock layer	Timeline
1	Recent	Post-Flood
2	Pleistocene	Post-Flood
3	Pliocene	Post-Flood
4	Miocene	**Flood**
5	Oligocene	Flood
6	Eocene	**Flood**
7	Paleocene	Flood
8	Cretaceous	**Flood**
9	Jurassic	Flood
10	Triassic	**Flood**
11	Permian	Flood
12	Pennsylvanian	Flood
13	Mississippian	Flood
14	Devonian	Flood
15	Silurian	Flood
16	Ordovician	Flood
17	Cambrian	Flood
18	Precambrian	Pre-Flood

13. For more about the Flood, see Ken Ham and Bodie Hodge, *A Flood of Evidence* (Green Forest, AR: Master Books, 2016).
14. Jeff Hecht, "Reptile Grew Feather-Like Structures Before Dinosaurs," *New Scientist* 2857 (2012), 8. When these feathers were found, the researchers arbitrarily and without warrant said they attach to a pre-dinosaur reptile (in the evolutionary view). However, the feathers would have attached to this reptile in an anatomically impossible way. This proves the feathers were not part of the reptile.
15. Lida Xing et al., "Abdominal Contents from Two Large Early Cretaceous Compsognathids (Dinosauria: Theropoda) Demonstrate Feeding on Confuciusornithids and Dromaeosaurids," *PLOS*, August 29, 2012, doi:10.1371/journal.pone.0044012.
16. Ken Ham, "What Really Happened to the Dinosaurs?" *The New Answers Book 1* (Green Forest, AR: Master Books, 2006), p. 149–176, https://answersingenesis.org/dinosaurs/when-did-dinosaurs-live/what-really-happened-to-the-dinosaurs/.

Indeed Digging in the Wrong Place . . .

If evolutionists want to get creationists to take notice, then they need to find all these alleged transitional forms in the pre-Cambrian (essentially pre-Flood) rocks. But keep in mind that we had over 1,600 years of erosion and rock strata where people and animals *did coexist* before the Flood.

Consider the evolutionists for a moment. Would they be convinced if a researcher found a body of a person preserved from the Mount St. Helens eruption[17] and claimed it was the earliest human ancestor? Not at all, because that sediment came from a catastrophe that happened well *after* people were around. It is the same with the Flood and post-Flood sediment. It was formed *after* people, birds, whales, and all other creatures were around.

The point is that evolutionists keep digging in the wrong place, yet they wonder why we hardly take notice. Well . . . this is why.

So Why Don't Evolutionists Look at Flood Rock and Recognize It as "Flood Rock"?

Biblical creationists presuppose the Bible's truth and subsequently the true history of the earth — including Noah's Flood. Evolutionists have presuppositions too, albeit, false ones, but presuppositions nonetheless. This is why when evolutionists look at Flood rock they unwittingly believe that the rock was actually laid down slowly and gradually over long ages. I suggest they have been indoctrinated to believe such stories as gradual rock accumulation over millions of years which has never been observed or repeated. Thus, the concept of millions of years is not in the realm of science but interpretation.

Nevertheless, God and His Word are the ultimate standard, and any standard — man's opinion — that opposes God and His Word is a lesser standard — a false authority fallacy. But the battle is about worldview. The evolutionists have a false worldview about rock layers from the Flood. It is this false worldview that drives their conclusions in hopes of finding missing links.

A correct worldview can help researchers get back on the right track and have a correct understanding of Flood rock and evidences. Let God be true and every man be found a liar (Romans 3:4).

---

17. Steve Austin, "Why Is Mount St. Helens Important to the Origins Controversy?" *The New Answers Book 3*, Ken Ham, gen. ed. (Green Forest, AR, 2010: Master Books, 2010), p. 251–260, https://answersingenesis.org/geology/mount-st-helens/why-is-mount-st-helens-important-to-the-origins-controversy/.

> *However, the scientists didn't know if that's actually how the millions of small DNA fragments of the chimp genome were arranged — were they really in the correct places? They just assumed it was correct based on evolutionary assumptions.*

22 Do Humans and Chimps Share a Common Ancestor?

As a former biology professor with a PhD in molecular genetics, **DR. GEORGIA PURDOM** has the experience necessary to make scientific concepts understandable to a wide variety of people. She has given both general and in-depth presentations and is a regular speaker in the Creation Museum Speaker Series. In addition, she has been a speaker at many Answers in Genesis conferences. Dr. Purdom has published papers in the *2008 and 2013 Proceedings of the International Conference on Creationism* and *Answers Research Journal*. In addition, she has numerous lay-friendly and semi-technical articles in *Answers* magazine and on the AiG website. Dr. Purdom's expertise in natural selection was crucial in her design of the "Natural Selection Is Not Evolution" exhibit at the Creation Museum. She also has research interests in speciation of animals after Noah's Flood and design features in DNA.

W e're probably all familiar with the iconic image of man's supposed evolution from an ape-like creature. On the far left is a small chimp that, over the course of millions of years, gets larger, walks upright and loses hair, and on the far right we have man as the final product (at least for now).

On the surface it looks rather simple and straightforward and, to many, believable. But does it reflect reality or is it just another evolution story?

Biblical History

According to God's Word, man and chimps were separate creations by God. In Genesis 1:24–25, we read of God creating the land animals by His spoken word according to their kind (which would include the kind that chimps belong to). In Genesis 1:26–27, we read of the creation of man and woman as not only separate creations from the animals but also as unique creatures because they alone were made in the image of God. They were told to have dominion over the animals and take care of God's creation.

So clearly, from a biblical perspective, man didn't evolve from any creature. Man (Adam) was made from the dust of the ground (Genesis 2:7) and woman (Eve) was made from a rib from his side (Genesis 2:22). This is very different from the evolution story and both cannot be correct.

Does Genetics Confirm Biblical or Evolutionary History?

From TV shows to zoo signs to textbooks and more, we often hear or read that human and chimp DNA is 98–99% the same and that this proves our shared ancestry. But is that true? Surprisingly, even the evolutionists would agree it's false. In a telling article entitled, "Relative Differences: The Myth of 1%," the author (an evolutionist) wrote, "Genomewise [referring to the DNA inside the nucleus of the cell], humans and chimpanzees are quite similar, but studies are showing that they are not as similar as many tend to believe."[1]

Another evolutionist stated, "It is now clear that the genetic differences between humans and chimpanzees are far more extensive than previously thought; their genomes are not 98% or 99% identical."[2] So just how similar is human and chimp DNA?

At the Sequence Level

DNA is composed of four bases — adenine (A), guanine (G), thymine (T), and cytosine (C) — arranged in a unique order inside every living organism

---

1. Joe Cohen, "Relative Differences: The Myth of 1%," *Science* 316 (2007): 1836.
2. Todd Preuss, "Human Brain Evolution: From Gene Discovery to Phenotype Discovery," *PNAS* 109 (2012): 10709–10716.

on the planet. The completed human genome sequence was published in 2000 after many challenging years of trying to assemble the largest jigsaw puzzle on the planet!

Think of it like this. Scientists were trying to put together an enormous puzzle with millions of small DNA fragments (the puzzle pieces) with essentially no idea how they fit together. They lacked the standard picture found on the front of the puzzle box.

When it came time to sequence and assemble the chimp genome, scientists decided to save time and money and use the genome of the closest living "relative" of chimps — humans — as the picture on the front of the puzzle box (so to speak). They took the sequences of the chimp genome and matched them up to similar sequences in the human genome. In places they even added and "corrected" the chimp DNA sequence with human DNA sequence resulting in a very "humanized" chimp genome![3]

However, the scientists didn't know if that's actually how the millions of small DNA fragments of the chimp genome were arranged — were they really in the correct places? They just assumed it was correct based on evolutionary assumptions.

The 98–99% similarity figure comes from comparing only DNA between humans and chimps that aligns (figure 1). This is sequence that is similar enough (although not a 100% match) that a computer program aligns them. And within this aligned region there is only one type of difference that evolutionists typically count and believe is significant for the obvious physical differences between humans and chimps. These differences are called substitutions.

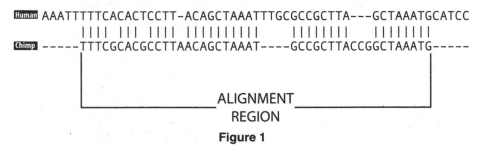

Figure 1

For example, human DNA might have a T but chimp DNA in the same location has a G (figure 2). Evolutionary ideas propose that the common ancestor of humans and chimps likely had a G in that position but in the

---

3.   Jeffrey P. Tomkins, *More Than a Monkey: The Human-Chimp DNA Similarity Myth* (Createspace Independent Pub., 2012), p. 16.

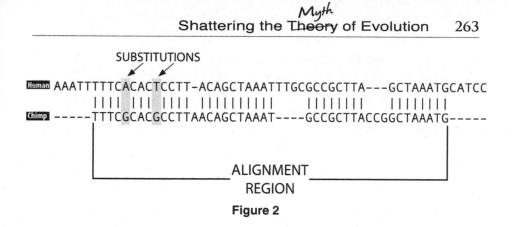

Figure 2

line that eventually led to humans a mutation occurred which changed the G to T. These types of differences account for the often touted 1–2% difference between human and chimp DNA.[4]

What about the other differences within the aligned DNA, like gaps where whole sections of human DNA have no match to the sequence in chimp DNA (and vice versa)? (figure 3). There are other differences as well that total approximately a 16% difference.[5] That's 480 million base differences![6] What about the DNA that is not alignable? There are millions of bases of DNA outside the aligned regions in human DNA that have no match in chimp DNA and vice versa. Approximately 4% of human DNA has no alignment to chimp DNA.[7] That's a glaring 20% total difference between human and chimp DNA.

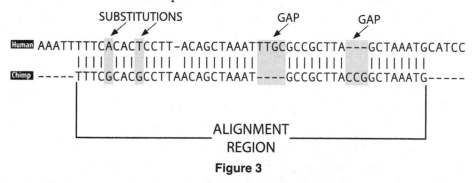

Figure 3

4. Jeffrey P. Tomkins, "Comprehensive Analysis of Chimpanzee and Human Chromosomes Reveals Average DNA Similarity of 70%," *Answers Research Journal* 6 (2013): 63–69.
5. Jeffrey P. Tomkins, "Comparison of 18,000 De Novo Assembled Chimpanzee Contigs to the Human Genome Yields Average BLASTN Alignment Identities of 84%," *Answers Research Journal* 11 (2018): 205–209.
6. Both chimps and humans have approximately 3 billion base pairs in their genome; 0.16 x 3 billion = 480 million.
7. Jeffrey P. Tomkins (2018) Ibid.

If there are so many other differences, why are they not counted? Because there's not enough time. Evolution works by slow, random processes, and in order to account for that many differences in the DNA there would need to be more time since humans and chimps shared a common ancestor.

The current timeframe of 6 million years is simply not enough. In addition, even if there was more time and those many mutations could occur, they don't do what evolution needs them to do. Mutations don't cause the gain of novel traits — the gain of genetic information necessary to go from one kind of organism to another. They simply degrade or slightly alter *pre-existing* DNA and thus, *pre-existing* traits (see chapter 15 for more information on mutations).

In summary, there are too many DNA differences between humans and chimps for them to have shared a common ancestor several million years ago. And even if more time were possible, mutations simply cannot make the changes necessary for one kind of organism to evolve into a completely different kind of organism.

At the Expression Level

DNA is more than just a sequence of bases. It's a library that encodes the information on how to produce all the proteins necessary for each living organism. Genes are distinct sequences of DNA that encode the information for making the proteins, but there is also a lot of regulatory information encoded in the DNA for when, where, how much, and under what conditions those proteins are produced. The sequences are said to regulate the expression of the genes.

But it's even more complex than that! There are chemical tags that modify DNA and influence how the genes express the proteins (figure 4). The chemical tags are referred to as epigenetic markers because they exist outside of (epi-) the actual sequence of DNA (-genetics). The markers have been shown to be heritable between parent and offspring.

Let me use an analogy to explain. The following sentence can have two very different meanings, depending on the punctuation used. "A woman, without her man, is nothing" or "A woman: Without her, man is nothing." Perhaps it's a silly illustration, but it gets the point across.

The words of both sentences are the same, but the meaning is different because of the punctuation. The same is true for DNA and its chemical tags. The sequence of DNA can be identical but produce different results based on the presence or absence of epigenetic markers. So, if humans and chimps

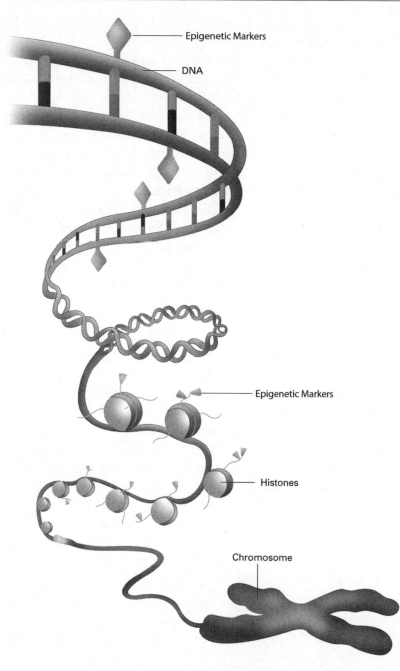

Figure 4
Image Credit: National Institute of General Medical Sciences/
NATIONAL INSTITUTES OF HEALTH/Science Source

share a common ancestor and these chemical tags are heritable, they should have similar epigenetic markers, right?

They should but they don't. One study compared human and chimp epigenetic markers in neutrophils.[8] Neutrophils (a type of white blood cell) were chosen because this cell type is so similar in humans and chimps. The scientists discovered differences in thousands of places.[9] Some epigenetic markers were in humans and not chimps and vice versa.[10]

Another study showed major differences between human and chimp epigenetic markers in brain cells.[11] Over 1,000 genes had major differences, and many times those differences led to increased expression of those genes in humans.[12] The research also showed that abnormal patterns of epigenetic markers in humans typically lead to disease.[13] So how could these markers change and evolve over time if so little change is tolerated well?

As with the sequence level, there are too many differences at the epigenetic level between humans and chimps for them to have shared a common ancestor several million years ago.

At the "Mistake" Level

Did you know that only 2% of human DNA codes for proteins and the other 98% is considered "junk?" Many evolutionists are convinced that "junk" DNA is a leftover from an organism's evolutionary past, a type of genetic fossil that is no longer utilized.

One type of "junk" DNA is pseudogenes that are believed to be imperfect copies of functional genes ("false" genes). The pseudogenes are thought to have encoded functional proteins at some point in the evolutionary history of the organism, but have accumulated mutations to the point that they no longer produce those proteins.

When evolutionists compare pseudogenes among organisms, they believe that similar mutations or "mistakes" are evidence of their common ancestry. Basically, the mistake happened in a common ancestor and was

---

8.   David I.K. Martin et al., "Phyloepigenomic Comparison of Great Apes Reveals a Correlation Between Somatic and Germline Methylation States," *Genome Research* 21 (2011): 2049–2057.

9.   Ibid.

10.   Ibid.

11.   Jia Zeng et al., "Divergent Whole-Genome Methylation Maps of Human and Chimpanzee Brains Reveal Epigenetic Basis of Human Regulatory Evolution," *The American Journal of Human Genetics* 91 (2012): 455–465.

12.   Ibid.

13.   Ibid.

passed down to all those organisms that evolved from that ancestor. The more shared mistakes, the closer the evolutionary relationship of the organisms being compared (figure 5).

Two main problems arise when drawing this conclusion from shared mistakes in pseudogenes. First, scientists are discovering that many pseudogenes are actually functional. One group of researchers stated, "But, definitely, the so-called pseudogenes are really functional, not to be considered any more as just "junk" or "fossil" DNA.[14]

One great example of this is the human beta-globin pseudogene (HBBP1). Humans and primates have several beta-globin genes that produce proteins composing hemoglobin (the protein in red blood cells responsible for carrying oxygen (figure 6). Both humans and primates share the same "mistakes" in the beta-globin pseudogene which is claimed to support their common ancestry.

However, it has been discovered that the beta-globin pseudogene is transcribed (from DNA to RNA) and that the RNA transcript is expressed in many different human cell types.[15] Although the RNA is never translated into a protein, the RNA appears to regulate other genes (regulatory RNAs are common).[16] There are also many active sites within the pseudogene that appear to be involved with regulation, likely of the other beta-globin genes.[17]

In addition, a mutation in the beta-globin pseudogene has been associated with a form of thalassemia (blood disorder).[18] So rather than being a nonfunctional leftover from our evolutionary past, the beta-globin pseudogene appears to be functional and important. We are not observing shared "mistakes" in the pseudogene due to common ancestry but rather shared design that is important for both humans and primates.

Second, comparisons of pseudogene sequences often only include selected regions in order to make the shared "mistakes" and thus, shared ancestry argument stronger. A good example of this can be found with the GULO pseudogene. The GULO gene encodes a protein necessary for the synthesis of Vitamin C. A few animals produce a functional GULO protein, but many mammals and birds (including humans and primates) have

---

14. Yan-Zi Wen et al., "Pseudogenes Are Not Pseudo Any More," *RNA Biology* 9 (2012): 27–32.
15. Jeffrey P. Tomkins, "The Human Beta-Globin Pseudogene Is Non-variable and Functional," *Answers Research Journal* 6 (2013): 293–301.
16. Ibid.
17. Ibid.
18. Ibid.

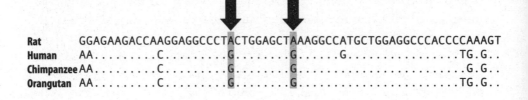

Rat   GGAGAAGACCAAGGAGGCCCTACTGGAGCTAAAGGCCATGCTGGAGGCCCACCCCAAAGT
Human   AA.........C.........G.........G.....G..............TG.G..
Chimpanzee AA.........C.........G.........G.....................G.G..
Orangutan   AA.........C.........G.........G...................TG.G..

Rat   GGTAGCCCACTACCCCGTAGAGGTGCGCTTCACCCGAGGCGATGACATTCTGCTGAGCCC
Human   ...GT.........TG..G.G...A.........T.-.A.........C..A........
Chimpanzee ...GT.........TG..G.G.C.A.........T.-.A.........C..A........
Orangutan   ...GT.........G..G.G....A-.A.........G.C..A........

Rat   CTGCTTCCAGAGGGACAGCTGCTACATGAACATCATTATGTACAG
Human   ..........T.......C.....C.........ACC......
Chimpanzee ..........C.......C.....C.........ACC......
Orangutan   ..........CA.......C...TC.........ACC......

Figure 5. The first three arrows show supposed shared "mistakes" in a human, chimp, and orangutan pseudogene as compared to the functional gene in rats. The last two arrows show "mistakes" that only appear in humans and chimps and are not found in orangutans. This supposedly supports the idea that humans and chimps are more closely related because they have more shared "mistakes" than humans and orangutans. Figure adapted from Figure 1A, Yuriko Ohta, et al., "Random nucleotide substitutions in primate nonfunctional gene for L-gulono-γ-lactone oxidase, the missing enzyme in L-absorbic acid biosynthesis," Biochimica et Biophysica Acta 1472 (1999): 408-411.

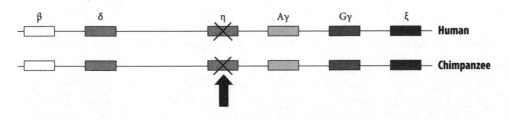

Figure 6. Humans and chimps have similar β-globin functional genes and also a similar pseudogene.

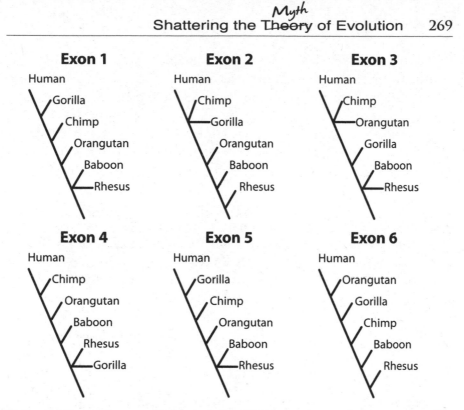

Figure 7. Depending on which exon in the GULO pseudogene is compared, a different evolutionary tree forms. For exons 1 and 5, humans are more closely related to gorillas. For exon 6, humans are more closely related to orangutans. For exons 2–4, humans are more closely related to chimps.

mutations in the GULO gene and cannot make Vitamin C. Both humans and primates share the same "mistakes" in the GULO pseudogene that is claimed to support their common ancestry.

However, the gorilla GULO pseudogene is actually more similar (87%) to the human GULO pseudogene (when comparing the whole gene and its regulatory region) than chimp (84%) to human.[19] In fact, depending on what part of the GULO pseudogene is compared, a different evolutionary tree "grows" (figure 7[20]). In some cases, humans were more closely related to gorillas or orangutans than to chimps.[21] If humans and chimps suppos-

19. Jeffrey P. Tomkins, "The human GULO pseudogene- evidence for evolutionary discontinuity and genetic entropy," *Answers Research Journal* 7 (2014): 91-101.
20. Figure 7 is adapted from Figure 4 of Jeffrey P. Tomkins, "The Human GULO Pseudogene — Evidence for Evolutionary Discontinuity and Genetic Entropy," online, *Answers Research Journal* 7 (2014): 91–101, available at https://answersingenesis.org/genetics/human-gulo-pseudogene-evidence-evolutionary-discontinuity-and-genetic-entropy/. Accessed 1/15/2019.
21. Ibid.

edly have the closest shared ancestry, why doesn't the evidence consistently bear that out? Because these differences in the GULO pseudogene between humans and chimps are not shared "mistakes" and, therefore, not evidence of shared ancestry.

As with the sequence and expression levels, there are too many differences even at the supposed "mistake" level between humans and chimps for them to have shared a common ancestor several million years ago.

Conclusion

The biblical account of creation and the evolution story are mutually exclusive when it comes to the origin of man. The Bible makes it clear that man and woman were distinct creations by God and made in His image. Genetic evidence, just like the fossil evidence, confirms that man and chimps do not share a common ancestor and, therefore, confirms and is consistent with the biblical account of creation.

Beyond the science for overturning the evolutionary story of mankind's origin, there is a more significant reason why knowing our origins is important. Paul shares in Romans 5:15,

> But the free gift is not like the trespass. For if many died through *one man's* trespass, much more have the grace of God and the free gift by the grace of that *one man Jesus Christ* abounded for many (emphasis mine).[22]

And in 1 Corinthians 15:21–22, "For as by *a man* came death, by *a man* has come also the resurrection of the dead. For as in *Adam* all die, so also in *Christ* shall all be made alive" (emphasis mine). In both passages Paul talks about "one man," "a man," and Adam as bringing death into this world. We know from Genesis 3 that Adam and Eve ate from the tree of knowledge of good and evil which God had told them not to eat from.

The punishment for Adam's sin was suffering and death for mankind (Genesis 3:19; Romans 5:12) and all of creation (Romans 8:22). That is the bad news in Genesis and why all humans have a sin problem. But Paul also shares the good news that the solution to sin and our salvation is found in the "one man Jesus Christ." The sinless, perfect Son of God took the punishment for sin by dying on the Cross. He then resurrected, showing His power over death and Satan (Genesis 3:15; 1 Corinthians 15:3–4). Our origins matter because the Gospel is rooted in the history of Genesis.

---

22. Scripture in this chapter is from the English Standard Version (ESV) of the Bible.

> *To put it bluntly and truthfully, human chromosome 2 cannot be the result of a fusion of two chromosomes in the ancestor to humans. The evolution story is nothing more than wishful thinking.*

23 IS HUMAN CHROMOSOME 2 THE RESULT OF A FUSION THAT SUPPORTS SHARED ANCESTRY WITH APES?

DR. GEORGIA PURDOM holds a PhD in molecular genetics from Ohio State University. Her specialty is cellular and molecular biology. Dr. Purdom's graduate work focused on genetic regulation of factors important for bone remodeling. Her scientific research focuses on the roles of natural selection and mutation in microbial populations. She seeks to understand the original, created, "very good" roles of bacteria in the pre-Fall world, and genetic mechanisms that have led to their adaptations and pathogenicity in a post-Fall world. As a scientist, a wife, and a mother, Dr. Purdom also has a passion to help women understand the importance of Genesis. She has appeared as a speaker at the Answers for Women conferences offering a wide variety of speakers on topics relevant to women, one of the largest conferences hosted by AiG.

To begin this chapter, I have to tell you a story. It's the evolution story to explain why humans and chimps have a different number of chromosomes. You see, if we have shared ancestry it seems odd that we don't have the same number of chromosomes.

The Evolution Story

Chimps have 24 pairs of chromosomes, but humans only have 23 pairs. Early analyses of human and chimp chromosomes based on staining the chromosomes showed similar banding patterns for human chromosome 2 and chimp chromosomes 12 and 13 (figure 1).[1]

Chromosome 2 (human)

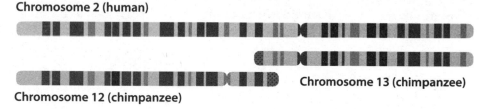

Chromosome 13 (chimpanzee)

Chromosome 12 (chimpanzee)

Figure 1

Evolutionists postulated that human chromosome 2 resulted from an end-to-end fusion of chimp chromosomes 12 and 13 (figure 2). In fact, evolutionists were so convinced of their story that they renamed the chimp chromosomes 2A (formerly chromosome 12) and 2B (formerly chromosome 13), reflecting their belief that what we observe in humans is a chromosome fusion that has happened at some point in the past as we evolved from a shared ancestor with the apes.

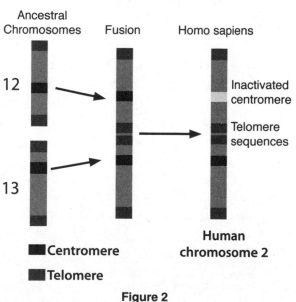

Figure 2

1. Jorge J. Yunis and Om Prakash, "The Origin of Man: A Chromosomal Pictorial Legacy," *Science* 215 (1982): p. 1525–1530.

Evolutionists are so enamored with this story that Dr. Ken Miller, molecular biologist and professor of biology at Brown University, in a presentation stated, "If we don't find it [a fused chromosome in humans] then the case for common ancestry for our species might be refuted."[2] The problem is that banding patterns can only give us a general comparison of the chromosomes and not a really detailed one.

You've probably heard the phrase, "We've come a long way, baby," and we have since the days of chromosome staining. It's now possible to sequence the DNA of human and chimp chromosomes and compare the actual sequence of the DNA rather than just banding patterns. So, what did these much more direct and detailed comparisons show? Well, according to evolutionists, it showed definitively that humans and apes shared a common ancestor. Dr. Miller stated in an interview,

> Is there any question to explain these facts [referring to the supposed DNA sequence similarities between human chromosome 2 and chimp chromosomes 2A and 2B] — and these are facts, this is not hypothesis or conjecture — any way to explain these facts in light of the view that our species was uniquely designed or intelligently created? The answer is no. You can only explain this by evolutionary common ancestry.[3]

Dr. Francis Collins, head of the National Institute of Health, wrote, "The fusion that occurred as we evolved from the apes has left its DNA imprint here. It is very difficult to understand this observation without postulating a common ancestor."[4] These scientists are overwhelmingly convinced that human chromosome 2 is the result of a fusion and that it proves human and chimp shared ancestry, so should we just throw in the towel and admit that evolution is true and biblical creation is false?

No, what we need to do is take a closer look at the evidence. The Bible is true[5] so nothing in science can contradict that truth. The reality is that direct DNA sequence comparisons show that the evolution story of fusion and shared ancestry is nothing more than a fairy tale.

2. Ken Miller, "Ken Miller Human Chromosome 2 Genome," published November 2007, https://www.youtube.com/watch?v=8FGYzZOZxMw.
3. Kenneth Chang, "The Mistakes That Argue for Evolution," *New York Times*, July 6, 2009, https://tierneylab.blogs.nytimes.com/2009/07/06/the-mistakes-that-argue-for-evolution/.
4. Francis S. Collins, *The Language of God* (New York: Free Press, 2006), p. 138.
5. Ken Ham and Bodie Hodge, *How Do We Know the Bible Is True?* Volume 1 (Green Forest, AR: Master Books, 2011), p. 15–24 .

Where Are the Telomeres?

Telomeres are DNA sequences typically found at the ends of chromosomes. They are kind of like aglets — the small sheaths of plastic found at the end of shoelaces that keep shoelaces from unraveling. When DNA replication occurs, it does not go all the way to the ends of the chromosomes. Telomeres are repetitive sequences that contain no functional information. Even though some of the telomere sequence might be missing in the newly replicated chromosome, the sequences between the telomeres that contain genes, regulatory sequences, etc. are protected.

Telomeres have specific repetitive sequences associated with them and should be readily identifiable in approximately the middle of human chromosome 2 if a fusion of two chromosomes in an ancestor to humans has occurred. What does the sequence show? It certainly doesn't show any telomeres (figure 3).

A group of evolutionary scientists researching the proposed fusion stated, "If the fusion occurred within the telomeric repeat arrays less than ~6 Mya, why are the arrays at the fusion site so degenerate?"[6] What should be thousands and thousands of bases in length, is only several hundred.[7] Why at the supposed fusion site do they not find much repetitive telomeric DNA sequence? Easy — human chromosome 2 is not the result of a fusion, instead God created

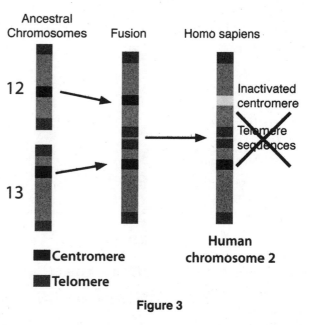

Figure 3

---

6. Yuxin Fan et al., "Genomic Structure and Evolution of the Ancestral Chromosome Fusion Site in 2q13-2q14.1 and Paralogous Regions on Other Human Chromosomes," *Genome Research* 12 (2002): p. 1651–1662.

7. Jeffrey Tomkins and Jerry Bergman, "The Chromosome 2 Fusion Model of Human Evolution, Part 2: Re-analysis of the Genomic Data," *Journal of Creation* 25 (2011): p. 111–117.

chimps and humans on day 6 of creation week and they were created as separate kinds, have different numbers of chromosomes, and do not share a common ancestor.

Instead of being telomeres, the sequences at the supposed fusion site are interstitial telomeric repeats that are found throughout chromosomes and not specific to human chromosome 2.[8] These sequences have recently been shown to play a regulatory role in the transcription of DNA into RNA, an intermediate step in the process of protein production.[9]

Where Is the Second Centromere?

Centromeres are DNA sequences typically found near the middle of the chromosomes. Each chromosome has only one, and they serve as a binding region for microtubules (long tubes that act and look like rope) that pull chromosomes apart during cell division. They too have specific repetitive sequences associated with them and should be readily identifiable. If human chromosome 2 is the result of a fusion, then it should have two centromeres, albeit one centromere should be non-functional but still identifiable. What does the sequence show? Again, it doesn't show a second centromere (figure 4).

The area in which evolutionary scientists postulated the centromere is located should be several hundred thousand bases in length. Yet, just like the alleged fusion location, the area is very small

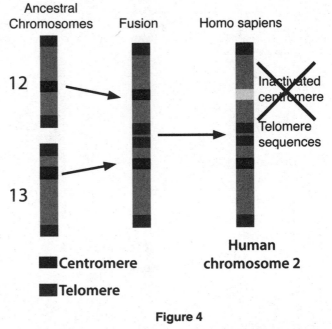

Figure 4

8. Jeffrey P. Tomkins, "Combinatorial Genomic Data Refute the Human Chromosome 2 Evolutionary Fusion and Build a Model of Functional Design for Interstitial Telomeric Repeats," in *Proceedings of the Eighth International Conference on Creationism*, J.H. Whitmore, ed. (Pittsburgh, PA: Creation Science Fellowship, 2018), p. 222–228.
9. Ibid.

(one-tenth the size of a real centromere) and muddled.[10] Many of the repetitive sequences found there are not specific to centromeres and are found scattered throughout chromosomes.[11]

In addition, the alleged second centromere itself is located inside a gene (ANKRD30BL). Centromeres are never located inside genes! Once again, we see evidence that human chromosome 2 is not the result of a fusion, giving more support for humans and chimps being separate creations of God and not sharing common ancestry. The evolutionary story is becoming more myth and less fact.

What's a Gene Doing There?

While analyses of the supposed fusion point may not have shown any telomeres, it did show something very interesting — a gene! Now you might be thinking, "So what, there's lots of genes in chromosomes." True, but remember, telomeres don't have functional information, which means they certainly don't contain any genes. If two chromosomes fused to become human chromosome 2, not only should we find telomeric sequences (which we don't) there shouldn't be genes anywhere near the fusion point yet that's exactly what we see.

The gene, known as DDX11L2, is a RNA helicase gene that alters RNA structure to allow RNA to be translated into a protein.[12] This gene has been shown to be expressed in at least 255 various cell and/or tissue types, showing it has a lot of activity in the human body.[13] The alleged fusion site is a promoter (initiates transcription of the gene) inside the DDX11L2 gene[14] (figure 5).

Not only do telomeres not have genes, but it's impossible to create a gene by fusing the ends of chromosomes! In addition to the gene, there are more areas surrounding the proposed fusion site that show very dissimilar DNA sequence between humans and chimps.[15] To put it bluntly and truthfully, human chromosome 2 cannot be the result of a fusion of two

10. Jeffrey P. Tomkins, "Debunking the Debunkers: A Response to Criticism and Obfuscation Regarding Refutation of the Human Chromosome 2 Fusion," *Answers Research Journal* 10 (2017): 45–54.
11. Jeffrey Tomkins and Jerry Bergman, "The Chromosome 2 Fusion Model of Human Evolution, Part 2: Re-analysis of the Genomic Data," *Journal of Creation* 25 (2011): p. 111–117.
12. Jeffrey P. Tomkins, "Alleged Human Chromosome 2 'Fusion Site' Encodes an Active DNA Binding Domain Inside a Complex and Highly Expressed Gene-negating Fusion," *Answers Research Journal* 6 (2013): p. 367–375.
13. Ibid.
14. Ibid.
15. Ibid.

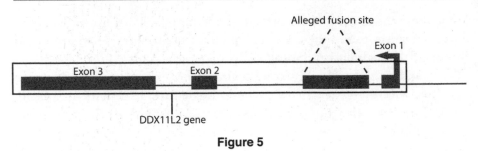

Figure 5

chromosomes in the ancestor to humans. The evolution story is nothing more than wishful thinking.

Conclusion

Do you think if evolutionary scientists were confronted with all this evidence showing human chromosome 2 can't possibly be the result of a fusion, they would change their mind? Dr. Ken Miller in a presentation stated, "You know what, if we don't find it [a fused chromosome in humans], evolution is wrong. We don't share a common ancestor."[16] That's a pretty dogmatic statement! He's saying that he would completely dismiss the idea that humans and chimps share a common ancestor based on just this one piece of evidence. I know for a fact that he does have knowledge of the information presented in this chapter, yet he still believes humans and chimps share a common ancestor. Why hasn't he changed his mind?

Because the creation/evolution issue has never been about the evidence. Romans 1:20 makes it obvious that the evidence is clear, "For his invisible attributes, namely, his eternal power and divine nature, have been clearly perceived, ever since the creation of the world, in the things that have been made. So they are without excuse."[17] People can know from creation that God is the Creator. However, Paul also tells us in Romans 1:18, "For the wrath of God is revealed from heaven against all ungodliness and unrighteousness of men, who by their unrighteousness suppress the truth." People suppress the truth in unrighteousness.

Instead, this is a worldview issue. The only way we can know about the unobservable past is through information provided by an eyewitness account of someone who was there. The real question is, who do we trust for knowing about the past? Man, who wasn't there during the supposed

16. Ken Miller, "How to Shut Up Pesky Creationists," published September 2007, https://www.youtube.com/watch?v=dK3O6KYPmEw.
17. Scripture in this chapter is from the English Standard Version (ESV) of the Bible.

millions and billions of years of earth history, or God, who was an eyewitness and inspired man to write it down (2 Timothy 3:16)? God's Word makes it clear in Genesis that land animals and man were created on day 6 of creation week (Genesis 1:24–25).

God created all the animals and then God created man (male and female), and God made man unique because He made man in His image (Genesis 1:26–27). Observable science in the present confirms the biblical account of creation is true.

> *Vestigial organs are popularly supposed to be useless evolutionary leftovers. But they are not. So-called vestigial structures and behaviors are not footprints of evolution. But they are footprints of a different sort.*

ARE VESTIGIAL ORGANS EVIDENCE OF AN EVOLUTIONARY PAST?

DR. TOMMY MITCHELL has worked with Answers in Genesis for the past 13 years and has authored a number of articles and contributed chapters to numerous books. As a scientist, physician, and father, Dr. Mitchell seeks to provide solid answers from the Bible to equip people to stand in the face of personal tragedy and popular evolutionary misinformation. Using communication skills developed over many years of medical practice, he is able to connect with people at all educational levels and unveil the truth that can change their lives. In addition to his role as speaker and writer, Dr. Mitchell serves the ministry as both speaker liaison and technical liaison.

Drumbeaters for an evolutionary worldview claim you can find some of the best evidence for evolution in your own body. The "vestigial" structures showcased by the human body, they say, are footprints of our evolutionary past. The term *vestigial* can simply refer to a remnant of a more robust structure. The word acquired its evolutionary application a few decades after Darwin popularized his belief that many organs had lost their original functions as they were passed down through the ages to newly evolved species that no longer needed them.

The list of supposed vestigial leftovers has changed over time as structures that were "obviously" useless were discovered to have important functions while other anatomical mysteries of unknown function were discovered. Sometimes, even after clear demonstration of a structure's functionality, the label sticks. Catchy-sounding claims, it seems, are more popular and memorable than truth.

Observational science has never demonstrated any mechanism by which a living organism can acquire the genetic information to evolve into a new, different kind of organism. Nor do we observe nascent organs (new complex organs doing a new function) forming. Nevertheless, evolutionary proponents claim that the existence of vestigial organs (supposed old organs that no longer do a function) can only be understood through an evolutionary worldview.

Since evolutionary processes should presumably allow only useful structures to evolve and get passed along, the existence of useless organs can only make sense, supposedly, if they once served an important role in an evolutionary ancestor and then got handed down as so much extra baggage. This chapter will focus on the latter aspect of the argument.

Unknown Functions

All so-called vestigial organs can be easily understood within a biblical worldview. God created the world and filled it with life about 6,000 years ago. He designed all living things to reproduce and vary within their created kinds. Humans did not evolve from animals. Adam and Eve, the first two humans, were His most special creation.

God pronounced that all His creation was "very good" at the end of creation week. While structures have degenerated during 6,000 years of sin's curse, it would not be reasonable to think that God included any useless parts in any of the living things He made "good" in the beginning.

Scientists have discovered functions for many anatomic structures previously thought to be useless. An example in humans would be the thymus gland. A collection of lymphatic tissue in the chest, medical professionals used to get very concerned if the thymus gland in a child, seen on x-ray, was larger than they expected it to be. It was once common practice to irradiate enlarged thymus glands in children. Now we know that the thymus gland is important for the maturation of the immune system's T-lymphocytes.

An example from the animal world is the adipose fin. Found on the backs of some fish between the dorsal and tail fins, the small adipose fin was considered a useless vestigial organ. Hatcheries commonly clip it to track the salmon they produce. A few years ago, it was discovered that the adipose fin is richly innervated, suggesting that it is an important mechano-sensory organ that helps fish navigate turbulent waters. Clipping the adipose fin may potentially decrease the survival of fish encountering difficult conditions in the wild.

Small but Significant

As the wise Designer, God placed similar ("homologous") forms of many organs in different kinds of living things. Homologous structures might be smaller or less impressive in a human than, say, in an ape. We humans have, for instance, sparse body hair, not fur. But this is not evidence that those homologues came from a common evolutionary ancestor, only that a common design does not need to be as robust in the human to serve its designated purpose.

The Tailbone

Our tailbone is a classic example of supposed baggage from a bygone evolutionary time. Let's examine that assertion. From the third to seventh week of development, the lower part of the curled C-shaped human embryo resembles a tail. This part of the embryo contains around a dozen segments. These segments are *not* vertebrae, and they were *not* destined in a more primitive evolutionary path to become a tail!

The segments contain *somites*, blocks of cells that will differentiate into muscle, bone, and cartilage. Part of this material even forms the fibrous supports for the spinal nerves that reach out to the lower part of the body. Once this elongated segmented part of the embryo has fulfilled all its functions, most of the somites disappear. In their place, in the maturing baby, we see the 3 to 5 tiny vertebrae that fuse together to form the coccyx, the "tail-end" of our vertebral column.

The human embryo does not re-play the supposed evolutionary history of vertebrates. It never has a "tail" in the sense that a dog or monkey does.

What appears to the uninformed to be a "tail" is, as we have seen, a collection of raw material that follows a carefully choreographed plan written in the human genome to form many vital structures, including, finally, the "tailbone."

The human coccyx — tailbone — is a critically important attachment point for muscles that keep our pelvic organs in place. God designed human beings to walk upright. Some muscles of the pelvis, attached by sturdy connective tissue to the coccyx, form a sling that supports all the pelvic organs in the optimal orientation to allow bladder and bowel control. If those supporting tissues begin to stretch and weaken with age, the pelvic organs can herniate downward, giving some people a distressingly inconvenient taste of what life would be like without a tailbone.

Outer Ear Muscles

Just as we humans are not equipped to wag our tails, most of us are unable to wiggle our ears. We do have muscles attached to our outer ears. Nevertheless, we cannot — like a rabbit or a dog — flatten our ears against our head in fear or make them stand up and reorient themselves to monitor interesting sounds. Evolutionists tell us that our outer ear muscles are vestigial remnants of the ancestry we share with our floppy-eared furry friends.

So, are outer ear muscles without function? Actually, no. Electrical activity in the outer ear muscles spikes in response to sudden noise, on the side from which the noise originates. Stimulation of the ear muscles triggers a reflex shifting of the eyes toward the source of the sound. In addition, the ear's outer edge curls slightly. Our outer ears are shaped and placed to help us determine the direction from which sounds originate. Thus, while we cannot reorient our ears to point toward a sound's origin, stimulation of the outer ear muscles does serve to instantly draw our attention toward the source of a sound.

Goosebumps and Body Hair

Goosebumps and the hair that covers most of our skin are another popular item on the list of human evolutionary baggage. In response to a chill or strong emotion, goosebumps form when tiny muscles tug on our hair follicles, making even sparse hair stand up taller. The simultaneous tug on the skin makes little bumps pop up. Because we don't have fur or feathers to fluff up for insulation or to make ourselves look fearsome, evolutionists claim goosebumps are useless proofs of our evolutionary past.

But are goosebumps, the fine hair covering most of our skin, and the hair follicles and tiny muscles attached to them really useless to us? Not at all! When muscles tug on our hair follicles, they help the protective oil produced by follicles' sebaceous glands ooze out onto the skin. Their combined muscle action generates a little extra heat on a cold day. And inside every hair follicle are epithelial cells that can be recruited to speed up wound healing. Without this supply of epithelial cells, even minor wounds would have to slowly heal from the edges inward.

Furthermore, our hair follicles are attached to sensitive nerve endings, and when strong emotions prompt our fine hairs to stand up, they are more easily touched, increasing our sensitivity to the brush of danger. There is certainly nothing useless about goosebumps and body hair, and they are not the proof of an evolutionary past.

The Appendix

The appendix is found in humans and some, but not all, mammalian animals. Our appendix is a worm-like structure attached to the caecum. This is the part of the digestive tract where the small intestine ends and the large intestine begins. When Darwin considered the human appendix, comparing it to the long and much more impressive appendix of an orangutan, he decided that our appendix was nothing but a useless rudiment leftover from our supposed vegetarian evolutionary ancestors. Following Darwin's line of thinking, and knowing that the appendix can become inflamed, many surgeons in the modern age have routinely removed the normal appendix during the course of surgery for other problems.

A biblical worldview would have led 20th-century doctors to assume that the appendix had some function as yet to be determined. Alas, the popular evolutionary worldview led to the assumption that the appendix was unimportant, resulting in its casual routine removal. Well, it turns out that the appendix is actually an important part of the immune system. The appendix forms early in gestation, and by the 17th week of life, a large population of lymphocytes has taken up residence in the appendix of the human fetus.

Lymphocytes are cells of the immune system. The white blood cells that make antibodies are lymphocytes. Antibodies are molecules designed to recognize and stick to invaders, like bacteria or viruses. Once an antibody sticks to an invader, it is destroyed by other lymphocytes. The fact that even the normal appendix of an adult is packed with lymphocytes should have long ago been a clue to the appendix's important role in the immune system. After all, the gut is the part of our body where many microbes from outside are introduced to the immune system that protects us on the inside. What better place to install a special collection of guardians of the gut?

The appendix, we have learned, is a reservoir for the "good" bacteria that help protect the gut from overpopulation by "bad" bacteria. Colonies of desirable bacteria, known as biofilms, readily form on the mucous lining of the bowel, especially in the appendix. Furthermore, the lymphocytes that live in the normal appendix include a type that is pre-programmed to respond to threats. These lymphocytes help protect the "good" bacteria sequestered in the appendix from destruction, making them available to re-seed the gut with the "good" bacteria needed to protect it.

Does this really work? Apparently, it does. People without an appendix, it turns out, are statistically more vulnerable to a dangerous recurrent *Clostridium difficile* infection of the digestive tract. When God designed our perfect bodies, He was aware that man would sin and bring ruin to His perfect creation. The immune system He designed equipped us to confront the challenges that would come. And the appendix was not useless but instead an important part of the immune system He made to protect us.

Degeneration and Loss

Once sin entered God's perfect creation, problems began to crop up. Sickness, debilitating problems of aging, and death became the norm in human lives. Mutations — errors — began to accumulate within the genomes of all living things. Mutations resulting in loss of genetic information may result in degeneration of the structures dependent on the affected genes. This is one way that a structure can lose some of its robustness and functionality in whatever part of the population is affected by the inherited mutations.

The blind cavefish is a great example of how mutation can cause a loss of function. These Mexican tetras can be either sighted or blind. The blind ones live in subterranean darkness. Mexican tetras have a mutation that causes those that live in dark caves to be blind.

In fish populations that dwell in the light, a molecule masks the effect of this particular mutation. (This is an example of an *epigenetic* effect — a factor outside of the genes themselves that controls how genes get expressed.) The Mexican tetras that live in subterranean caves have what could be called "vestigial" eyes — degenerated remnants of eyes in tiny eye sockets. Blind cavefish illustrate loss of function, but not evolution.

Palmaris Longus Muscle

Anatomic structures may lose function or even disappear entirely. Anatomists know that there are a lot of variations within the human species. That is not evidence that some of us our more evolved than others! Let's examine the example of the palmaris longus muscle.

The palmaris longus is a muscle you can do without. It is located in the wrist with several other muscles that flex the wrist. Ten to 15% of people are missing the palmaris longus in one or both wrists. To see whether you have one or not, flex your wrist while touching your pinkie to your thumb. If you have a palmaris longus, you will see a tight, raised band extending down into your hand. This band — the tendon of the palmaris longus muscle — attaches to a strong, flat layer of connective tissue in your palm. Because you can easily do without it, surgeons often harvest the palmaris longus for tendon grafts when repairing injuries elsewhere in the body.

Just because you can do without something doesn't mean you inherited it as an evolutionary leftover. Many movements we make involve multiple muscles working together. Even though the role of palmaris longus in wrist flexion is small, it is not insignificant. Furthermore, the palmaris longus makes a substantial contribution to thumb strength when moving it away from the palm and then toward the pinkie. (Try it, and watch your palmaris longus tense, if you have one!) Studies show that athletes who excel at sports demanding great grip strength are more likely to have a palmaris longus. Thus, while you can get along fine without a palmaris longus, it is useful to those who have it.

Palmar Grasp Reflex

What daddy doesn't love to touch the palm of his newborn son or daughter and feel him or her tightly grip his finger! "How strong!" he proudly exclaims. Surely the palmar grasp reflex of a newborn baby is the most endearing item on the vestigial list. A primate animal newborn's grip on its mother keeps it from falling to the ground as she scampers about. But human mothers do not swing through trees with their clinging newborns, and human mothers don't have fur for a baby to grasp even if they did. Therefore, evolutionists consider the human palmar grasp reflex, as well as the equivalent foot-curling (plantar) reflex, to be vestiges of our evolutionary past.

These grasp reflexes have nothing to do with evolution, however. They are the result of normal spinal reflexes that are in place in a baby long before birth. They represent an intermediate stage of neurological development, a maturation process that continues for several months after birth. As neuronal connections form in a growing baby's nervous system, the brain begins inhibiting these particular reflexes. The reflexes eventually disappear altogether, replaced by the ability to manipulate objects, balance, and walk.

Infant grasp reflexes are expressions of a normal stage in neurological matu-ration. They do not reveal our "inner monkey."

Conclusion

The word *vestige* comes from the Latin word for *footprint*. Vestigial organs are popularly supposed to be useless evolutionary leftovers. But they are not. So-called vestigial structures and behaviors are not footprints of evolution. But they are footprints of a different sort. Some are footprints of the degen-eration sin has brought into the biological world in the 6,000 years since God created us. Others are the footprints of the intricate development of the human embryo and the finely engineered designs of our Designer, the Creator God of the Bible.

> *Yet it is not just the gullible public who have imbibed their dose of fabricated, over-simplified evolutionary evidence from textbooks and the popular media.*

25

WHAT ABOUT HAECKEL'S FAKED EMBRYOS? HOW DO THEY RELATE TO ABORTION?

DR. ELIZABETH MITCHELL received a BS in chemistry from Furman University, graduating from Vanderbilt University School of Medicine, then earning board certification and fellowship in the American College of Obstetrics and Gynecology. As a researcher and speaker, Dr. Mitchell currently contributes dozens of articles on a wide variety of topics to *Answers Magazine*, Answers In Depth, and Answers in Genesis' website. She is also a contributor to the very popular multi-volume *The New Answers Book* series.

An evolutionary worldview is not just a belief about origins in an unseen past long ago and far, far away. An evolutionary worldview shapes decisions we make in the present, even the life-and-death decisions about the lives of the unborn.

Millions of Years and Modern Morality

To see how evolutionary claims about life's supposed origins millions of years ago guide decisions affecting the lives of millions of unborn children in the present, we need to look back to the 19th century. There we find Ernst Haeckel, a German zoology professor who lived at the same time as Charles Darwin.

Haeckel's work with embryos expanded upon, popularized, and supposedly proved Darwinian claims that vertebrate embryos develop through stages that rapidly re-run their evolutionary past. And in this modern world of legalized, sanitized, authorized abortions, it seems logical to some that if a pregnancy could be ended while the unborn was still resembling an early evolutionary animal stage, then abortion would have no more moral significance than catching a fish or gigging (spearing) a frog.

Big Words and Bold Claims

This scientific belief — that human embryos pass through a fish stage, an amphibian stage, a reptile stage, and so forth — is called the "biogenetic law," not that it is a law of science; it is just a name. It is summed up in the catchy claim, "Ontogeny recapitulates phylogeny." So what does that mean?

- *Ontogeny* refers to embryonic development.
- *Phylogeny* refers to stacking up the various categories of animals in their supposed order of evolution from simpler to more complex.
- *Recapitulates* means "repeats."

In other words, the "biogenetic law" claims that developing embryos re-play their evolutionary past. Since embryology is observable, and phylogeny is unobservable, "recapitulation theory" — another name for the "biogenetic law" — was and sadly still is seen as scientific evidence of an evolutionary past. It is not that "recapitulation theory" is a proper *theory* in science, again, like "biogenetic law" it's just a name given to this idea.

To acquire scientific proof of this supposed "biogenetic law," Haeckel published sketches of embryos he claimed to observe. Well, sort of. What he actually published were drawings of embryos that were substantially altered to line up with his beliefs. A skilled illustrator, Haeckel placed his sketches of embryos from various animal groups side by side to show their similarities.

Yet many of these similarities were his own fabrications. Not mere exaggerations, Haeckel blatantly falsified his drawings. Some he simply copied over and over. Some he re-sized. Inconvenient bulges — the initial stages of growth — were eliminated if they did not suit his purposes.

For instance, he removed limb buds known to be present to prove the limbless-ness of all the embryos at a certain stage. Haeckel fabricated a fiction and foisted it off on his own generation and generations yet unborn to support an evolutionary worldview.

Fiction, Fraud, or Teaching Tool?

Now Haeckel was not the only scientist studying embryos at the time. And the reality that he'd been playing fast and loose with the facts was soon recognized by the scientific community. Despite this, however, Haeckel's now legendary claim became embedded in both the public mind and the scientific educational system more rapidly and firmly than could have been achieved with the modern Internet to perpetuate it. Ernst Haeckel has gone down in history as one of the most well-known scientific fraudsters of all time.

The so-called "biogenetic law" he "proved" has long been acknowledged as false by evolutionary scientists. Nevertheless, the tenacity of Haeckel's illustrated claims is shown by their appearance in modern textbooks and even in the 21st-century thinking of those who should know better.

Just as urban legends recur with the modern public, never fully put to rest because people want to believe them, so recapitulation theory — even the bogus artwork that supports it — has continued to pop up in textbooks for over a century. Evolutionist Steven J. Gould, in the year 2000, decried this "mindless recycling that has led to the persistence of these drawings in a large number, if not a majority, of modern textbooks!"[1]

Yet it is not just the gullible public who have imbibed their dose of fabricated, over-simplified evolutionary evidence from textbooks and the popular media. Real scientists also have trouble letting go of "recapitulation theory" — now crafted into a more modernized version of the discredited "biogenetic law."

Haeckel's idea has been just too attractive for many evolutionists to abandon. For instance, Ernst Mayr's modification, laid out in "Recapitulation Reinterpreted: the Somatic Program," appeared in 1994 in the *Quarterly*

---

1.   Stephen Jay Gould, "*Abscheulich!* (Atrocious!)," *Natural History* 109 no. 2 (2000): 44–45.

Review of Biology. He wrote that despite "the disrepute into which Haeckel's claims had fallen . . . every embryologist knew that there was a valid aspect to the claim of recapitulation."[2]

A 2012 paper coauthored by Richard Lenski, "Ontogeny Tends to Recapitulate Phylogeny in Digital Organisms," notes that Mayr's "sentiment is still widely held today, and the idea that ontogeny recapitulates phylogeny in some form has its modern proponents."[3]

The key difference between Haeckel's version and its more modern versions is one of degree. Haeckel claimed that the sequential stages of a vertebrate embryo's development resembled the *adult* forms of the animal phyla in their evolutionary history.

However, honest observation shows that developing embryos do not resemble the adults on any proposed evolutionary tree of life. Therefore, a modified form of the theory holds that an embryo only resembles the *embryos* of its evolutionary ancestors, not the adults.

A more radical retrofitting of Haeckel's claims maintains that Haeckel intended recapitulation theory to apply only to individual traits, rather than to entire embryonic stages. Noting that Haeckel's own writings reveal he knew early embryos from different phyla have a lot of differences, his modern apologists have written that "Haeckel's own views on art stressed the primacy of interpretation over pure observation."[4] Thus, Haeckel's fraudulent artwork has been sanitized and re-defined as a helpful teaching tool! Such is the demand for evolutionary propaganda.

Evolutionary Baby Steps?

In embryology, we often see an anatomical structure re-shape itself, step by step, into a form more in line with its destiny in the mature animal or human. Other embryologic structures form, serve their purpose, and then disappear altogether. Such observable steps in the development of an embryo are the sort Haeckel's modern apologists refer to in their effort to show that Haeckel, at some level, had the right idea.

However, these intermediate embryologic forms are not *evolutionary intermediates.* They are observable *developmental intermediates* that allow the embryo's cells to differentiate and take their proper places. Structures in the

---

2. Ernst Mayr, "Recapitulation Reinterpreted: the Somatic Program," *Quarterly Review of Biology* 69, no. 2 (June 1994): 223–232.
3. J. Clune et al., "Ontogeny Tends to Recapitulate Phylogeny in Digital Organisms," *The American Naturalist* 180, no. 3 (2012): E54–E63.
4. M. Richardson and G. Keuck, "Haeckel's ABC of Evolution and Development," *Biological Reviews of the Cambridge Philosophical Society* 77, no. 4 (2002): 495–528.

embryo provide scaffolds for other structures, stimulate the development of subsequent stages in anatomical formation, act as place-holders for coming anatomical attractions, and in countless ways follow the highly structured plan choreographed by the organism's DNA. There is no evolutionary experimentation or randomness, no testing of evolving traits by natural selection.

Embryonic development is directed by the blueprint in an embryo's DNA. And that DNA is specific — a human's DNA, a chimp's DNA, a frog's DNA, a fish's DNA. At no time in science do we see DNA of one creature mutating to produce new information that can change the organism into a new kind, not even by the summation of millions of baby steps. Neither do we see, through studying embryonic development, a replay of evolutionary development.

Truth or Consequences

Perhaps nowhere has Haeckel's fiction done more irreversible damage than in the lives of the unborn and young women who have chosen to destroy them. Faced with an unwanted pregnancy, at a time fraught with emotional vulnerability and fear, a pregnant woman can be assured — using Haeckel's popular pseudoscientific fiction — that early abortion does not really destroy a person because her pregnancy is only at a fish stage.

Evolutionist Christopher Hitchens in his book *God Is Not Great: How Religion Poisons Everything* was still spouting this nonsense in 2007 when he wrote:

> As with evolution in general, therefore, in utero we see a microcosm of nature and evolution itself. In the first place we begin as tiny forms that are amphibian, before gradually developing lungs and brains (and growing and shedding that now useless coat of fur) and then struggling out and breathing fresh air after a somewhat difficult transition.[5]

Thus, just as evolutionary proponents claim that human ancestors passed through many stages in which they were not yet human, so Haeckel's recapitulation theory is used to support the idea that a developing baby passes through many stages in which it is not human and therefore can conveniently be destroyed without the guilt and taint of having murdered a real child.

---

5. Christopher Hitchens. *God Is Not Great: How Religion Poisons Everything* (New York: Twelve, 2007), p. 212.

Twisting Haeckel's Fishy Tale

The claim most commonly used to support the notion that a developing baby replays our fishy ancestry before taking on human form is the presence of our infamous "gill slits."

The poorly named "gill slits" in human embryos are not gills or slits. They are folds of tissue destined to develop into various anatomical parts of the head and neck. At no time in the human embryo do they have either a function or a structure remotely resembling gills. They don't even turn into anything having to do with lungs or breathing! And never in the course of development does a human embryo absorb oxygen from the surrounding water as fish do with gills.

Was Haeckel unaware of these facts? Could his biases have been the result of ignorance? No. Although, according to evolutionist Steven Jay Gould, "in Haeckel's evolutionary reading, the human gills slits *are* (literally) the adult features of an ancestor" (emphasis in original),[6] in later writings Haeckel did not ascribe a respiratory function to these gill slits in the non-fish embryo. Nevertheless, he still maintained that there were actual gill slits and gill arches in the non-fish embryos. Haeckel wrote in 1892:

> We never meet with a Reptile, Bird or Mammal which at any period of actual life breathes through gills, and the gill-arches and openings which do exist in the embryos are, during the course of their ontogeny, changed into entirely different structures, viz. into parts of the jaw-apparatus and the organ of hearing.[7]

In 1903, Haeckel wrote of the "total loss of respiratory gills," saying that "in the embryos of amniotes there is never even a trace of gill lamellae, of real respiratory organs, on the gill arches."[8] Thus, Haeckel knew the truth about gill slits and still chose to use them to perpetuate his beliefs by falsifying scientific observations.

Haeckel's legacy includes the fish claims used to assuage the guilt of those who prefer the fiction that the destruction of an "inconvenient"

---

6. Stephen Jay Gould, *Ontogeny and Phylogeny* (Cambridge, MA: Belknap Press, 1977), p. 7.
7. Ernst Haeckel, *The History of Creation* [translation of the 8th German Edition of *Natürliche Schöpfungsgeschichte*], ed. E.R. Lankester (London: Kegan Paul, 1892). Quoted in M. Richardson and G. Keuck, "Haeckel's ABC of Evolution and Development," *Biological Reviews of the Cambridge Philosophical Society* 77, no. 4 (2002): 495–528.
8. Ernst Haeckel, *Anthropogenie oder Entwickelungsgeschichte des Menschen*; Quoted in M. Richardson and G. Keuck, "Haeckel's ABC of Evolution and Development," *Biological Reviews of the Cambridge Philosophical Society* 77, no. 4 (2002): 495–528.

unborn baby bearing the marks of its evolutionary past is not the killing of a human being at all.

Those Fishy Gill Slits

Gill slits is a misleading name — like "biogenetic law" or "recapitulation theory." These folds are neither gills nor slits. Another popular name, *branchial arches*, is just as deceptive, because *branchial* comes from the Greek word for "gills."

A better name is *pharyngeal arches,* meaning "arch-shaped folds near the throat." (*Pharyngeal* is the scientific word for things having to do with the throat. When you say you have a sore throat, your doctor says you have pharyngitis.) The creases between the folds are called *pharyngeal clefts*, and the undersides of the folds are called *pharyngeal pouches.*

These pouches and clefts are not connected by an opening as actual gill slits would be. Each fold morphs into specific structures, none of which are ever used for breathing. The outer and middle ear as well as the bones, muscles, nerves, and glands of the jaw and neck, and even the immune system's thymus gland develop from these folds as tissues differentiate in compliance with human DNA. Only superficially and at the most simplistic level do these important folds ever resemble gills. Mammalian pharyngeal arches are no more related to gills — ancestrally or otherwise — than stars are to streetlights.

Some embryology textbooks have adopted non-deceptive terminology. Nevertheless, the meaning-packed terms *gill slits* and *gill-like structures* persist. Even texts that refer to these folds by correct names sometimes perpetuate the powerful gill slit myth. For instance, Mader's *Biology* (2007 edition) correctly describes the ultimate anatomic destiny of each pharyngeal arch component and then asks:

> Why should terrestrial vertebrates develop and then modify such structures like pharyngeal pouches that have lost their original function? The most likely explanation is that fishes are ancestral to other vertebrate groups.[9]

A later 2016 edition of Sylvia Mader's *Biology* textbook with Michael Windelspecht also includes redrawn versions of Haeckel's faked embryos.[10]

---

9.   Sylvia Mader, *Biology*, 9th ed. (New York: McGraw-Hill, 2007), p. 97.
10. Sylvia Mader and Michael Windelspecht, *Biology*, 12th edition, (New York: McGraw-Hill, 2016), p. 274.

Another defender of Haeckel includes Donald Prothero's textbook in 2013 called *Bringing Fossils to Life*.[11]

What "lost original function"? No one has ever documented that pharyngeal pouches in the embryos of terrestrial vertebrates function as gills or that adult terrestrial vertebrates ever had gills.

Preserved in textbooks and the media, the fishy ancestral myth persists. Our unseen and unverified fishy past still surfaces regularly in the popular assumption that the pouches/folds/slits, or whatever-they-get-called, are leftovers from a fish ancestor.

Inside the Human Body, a popular 2011 BBC1 program hosted by Dr. Michael Mosley, provides a typical example. The program featured a state-of-the-art high-quality video of human embryonic development called "Anatomical Clues to Human Evolution from Fish."[12]

The video was produced by digitally splicing scans taken in early pregnancy. Mosley interpreted developing features, including "gill-like structures," as anatomical proof of fish in our evolutionary past.[13]

Built on Haeckel's fishy and fraudulent foundation, is it any wonder that an abortionist today can draw on such pseudo-science to justify the murder of an unborn human being? It's time for educators, scientists, the media, and the public to put aside Haeckel's fraudulent images and his ideas. We must not supply pseudoscientific propaganda to purveyors of legalized murder.

---

11. Donald Prothero, *Bringing Fossils to Life*, 3rd edition (New York: Columbia University Press, 2013), p. 29.
12. https://www.bbc.co.uk/news/health-13278255.
13. https://answersingenesis.org/human-body/vestigial-organs/vestigial-hiccups-folding-fish-eyes-and-other-fables/.

> *Like many, Trotsky probably did not realize that the precious few instances of the name 'God' did not appear in the first edition of* Origin of Species. *These references were added later, and many suspect that this was done to influence church members to adopt Darwinism.*

26 WHAT ARE THE MORAL IMPLICATIONS OF THE RELIGION OF EVOLUTION?

BODIE HODGE has been actively engaged in apologetics for nearly 20 years, teaching kids from junior high to adult prior to joining Answers in Genesis. His ability to utilize his science background with biblical authority has been a unique teaching experience. From his experience with kids and family books to more higher level philosophy and biblical debate, Bodie has intrigued audiences and readers even though he has suffered two massive heart attacks and survived them by the grace of God.

I f God and His Word are not the authority . . . then by default . . . who is? *Man* is. When people reject God and His Word as the ultimate authority, then man is attempting to elevate his or her thoughts (collectively or individually) to a position of authority *over* God and His Word.

Introduction: Man's Authority or God's Authority . . . Two Religions

So often, people claim that "Christians are religious and the enlightened unbelievers who reject God are *not* religious." Don't be deceived by such a statement. For these nonbelievers are indeed religious . . . *very* religious, whether they realize it or not — for they have bought into the religion of humanism.

Humanism is the religion that elevates man to be greater than God. Humanism, in a broad sense, encompasses any thought or worldview that rejects God and the 66 books of His Word in part or in whole; hence *all* non-biblical religions have humanistic roots. There are also those that *mix* aspects of humanism with the Bible. Many of these religions (e.g., Mormons, Islam, Judaism, etc.) openly borrow from the Bible, but they also have mixed *human* elements into their religion where they take some of man's ideas to supersede many parts of the Bible, perhaps in subtle ways.[1]

There are many forms of humanism, but secular forms of humanism have become one of the most popular today. Variant forms of secular humanism include atheism, agnosticism, non-theism, Darwinism, and the like. Each shares a belief in an evolutionary worldview with man as the centered authority over God.

Humanism organizations can also receive a tax-exempt status (the same as a Christian church in the United States and the United Kingdom) and they even have religious documents like the *Humanist Manifesto*. Surprisingly, this religion has free rein in state schools, museums, and media under the guise of neutrality, seeking to fool people into thinking it is not a "religion."[2]

---

1. For example: in Islam, Muhammad's words in the Koran are taken as a higher authority than God's Word (the Bible); in Mormonism, they have changed nearly 4,000 verses of the Bible to conform to Mormon teachings and add the words of Joseph Smith and later prophets as superior to God's Word; in Judaism, they accept a portion of God's Word (the Old Testament) but by human standards, they reject a large portion of God's Word (the New Testament) as well as the ultimate Passover lamb, Jesus Christ.
2. Although the U.S. Supreme Court says that religion is not to be taught in the classroom, this one seems to be allowed.

Humanism and "Good"

Christians are often confronted with the claim that a humanistic worldview will help society become "better."[3] Even the first *Humanist Manifesto*, of which belief in evolution is a subset, declared: "The goal of humanism is a free and universal society in which people voluntarily and intelligently co-operate for the common good."

But can such a statement be true? For starters, what do the authors mean by "good"? They have no legitimate foundation for such a concept, since one person's "good" can be another's "evil." To have some objective standard (not a relative standard), they must *borrow* from the absolute and true teachings of God in the Bible.

Beyond that, does evolutionary humanism really teach a future of prosperity and a common good? Since death is the "hero" in an evolutionary framework, then it makes one wonder. What has been the result of evolutionary thinking in the past century (20th century)? Perhaps this could be a test of what is to come.

Let's first look at the death estimates due to aggressive conflicts stemming from leaders with evolutionary worldviews, beginning in the 1900s, to see the hints of what this "next level" looks like. See the chart on the following pages.

Charles Darwin's view of molecules-to-man evolution was catapulted into societies around the world in the mid-to-late 1800s. Evolutionary teachings influenced Karl Marx, Leon Trotsky, Adolf Hitler, Pol Pot, Mao Zedong, Joseph Stalin, Vladimir Lenin, and many others. Let's take a closer look at some of these people and events and examine the evolutionary influence and repercussions.

World War I and II, Hitler, Nazis, and the Holocaust

Most historians would point to the assassination of Archduke Francis Ferdinand on June 18, 1914, as the event that triggered World War I (WWI). But tensions were already high, considering the state of Europe at the time. Darwinian sentiment was brewing in Germany. Darwin once said:

> At some future period, not very distant as measured by centuries, the civilized races of man will almost certainly exterminate and replace the savage races throughout the world. At the same

---

3. One can always ask the question, by what standard do they mean "better?" God *is* that standard, so they refute themselves when they speak of things being better or worse. In their own professed worldview, it is merely arbitrary for something to be "better" or "worse."

time the anthropomorphous apes . . . will no doubt be extermi-
nated. The break between man and his nearest allies will then be
wider, for it will intervene between man in a more civilized state,
as we may hope, even than the Caucasian, and some ape as low
as a baboon, instead of as now between the negro or Australian
[Aborigine] and the gorilla.[4]

Darwin viewed the "Caucasian" (white-skinned Europeans) as the dominant "race" in his evolutionary worldview. To many evolutionists at the
time, mankind had evolved from ape-like creatures that had more hair, dark
skin, dark eyes, etc. Therefore, more "evolved" meant less body hair, blond
hair, blue eyes, etc. Later, in Hitler's era, Nazi Germany practiced *Lebens-
born*, which was a controversial program, the details of which have not been
entirely brought to light. Many claim it was a breeding program that tried
to evolve the "master race" further — more on this below.

But the German sentiment prior to WWI was very much bent on con-
quering for the purpose of expanding their territory and their "race." An
encyclopedia entry from 1936 states:

In discussions of the background of the war much has been
said of Pan-Germanism, which was the spirit of national con-
sciousness carried to the extreme limit. The Pan-Germans, who
included not only militarists, but historians, scientists, educators
and statesmen, conceived the German people, no matter where
they located, as permanently retaining their nationality. The
most ambitious of this group believed that it was their mission
of Germans to extend their kultur (culture) over the world, and
to accomplish this by conquest if necessary. In this connection
the theory was advanced that the German was a superior being,
destined to dominate other peoples, most of whom were thought
of as decadent.[5]

Germany had been buying into Darwin's model of evolution and saw themselves as the superior "race," destined to dominate the world, and their
actions were the consequence of their worldview. This view set the stage for
Hitler and the Nazi party and paved the road to WWII.

4. Charles Darwin, *The Descent of Man* (New York: A.L. Burt, 1874, 2nd ed.), p. 178.
5. *The American Educator Encyclopedia* (Chicago, IL: The United Educators, Inc., 1936), p.
    3914 under entry "World War."

Table 1 — Estimated deaths as a result of an evolutionary worldview

Who/What?	Specific event and estimated dead	Total Estimates
Pre-Hitler Germany/ Hitler and the Nazis	WWI: 8,500,000[1] WWII: 70 million[2] [Holocaust: 17,000,000][3]	95,000,000
Leon Trotsky and Vladimir Lenin	Bolshevik revolution and Russian Civil War: 15,000,000[4]	15,000,000
Joseph Stalin	20,000,000[5]	20,000,000
Mao Zedong	14,000,000–20,000,000[6]	Median estimate: 17,000,000
Korean War	2,500,000?[7]	~2,500,000
Vietnam War (1959–1975)	4,000,000– 5,000,000 Vietnamese, 1,500,000– 2,000,000 Lao and Cambodians[8]	Medians of each and excludes French, Australia, and U.S. losses: 6,250,000
Pol Pot (Saloth Sar)	750,000–1,700,000[9]	Median estimate: 1,225,000
Abortion to children[10]	China estimates from 1971– 2006: 300,000,000[11] USSR estimates from 1954– 1991: 280,000,000[12] US estimates 1928–2007: 26,000,000[13] France estimates 1936–2006: 5,749,731[14] United Kingdom estimates 1958–2006: 6,090,738[15] Germany estimates 1968–2007: 3,699,624[16] Etc.	621,500,000 and this excludes many other coun- tries
Grand estimate		~778,000,000

Footnotes for Table 1

1. *The World Book Encyclopedia*, Volume 21, Entry: World War II (Chicago, IL: World Book, Inc.), p. 467; such statistics may have some variance depending on source, as much of this is still in dispute.
2. Ranges from 60 to 80 million, so we are using 70 million.
3. Figures ranged from 7 to 26 million.
4. Russian Civil War, http://en.wikipedia.org/wiki/Russian_Civil_War, October 23, 2008.
5. Joseph Stalin, http://www.moreorless.au.com/killers/stalin.html, October 23, 2008.
6. Mao Tse-Tung, http://www.moreorless.au.com/killers/mao.html, October 23, 2008.
7. This one is tough to pin down and several sources have different estimates, so this is a middle of the road estimate from the sources I found.
8. Vietnam War, http://www.vietnamwar.com/, October 23, 2008.
9. Pol Pot, http://en.wikipedia.org/wiki/Pol_Pot, October 23, 2008.
10. This table only lists estimates for abortion deaths in a few countries; so, this total figure is likely very conservative as well as brief stats of other atrocities.
11. Historical abortion statistics, PR China, compiled by Wm. Robert Johnston, last updated June 4, 2008, http://www.johnstonsarchive.net/policy/abortion/ab-prchina.html.
12. Historical abortion statistics, U.S.S.R., compiled by Wm. Robert Johnston, last updated June 4, 2008, http://www.johnstonsarchive.net/policy/abortion/ab-ussr.html.
13. Historical abortion statistics, United States, compiled by Wm. Robert Johnston, last updated June 4, 2008, http://www.johnstonsarchive.net/policy/abortion/ab-unitedstates.html.
14. Historical abortion statistics, France, compiled by Wm. Robert Johnston, last updated June 4, 2008, http://www.johnstonsarchive.net/policy/abortion/ab-france.html.
15. Historical abortion statistics, United Kingdom, compiled by Wm. Robert Johnston, last updated June 4, 2008, http://www.johnstonsarchive.net/policy/abortion/ab-unitedkingdom.html.
16. Historical abortion statistics, FR Germany, compiled by Wm. Robert Johnston, last updated June 4, 2008, http://www.johnstonsarchive.net/policy/abortion/ab-frgermany.html.

Hitler and the Nazis

World War II dwarfed World War I in the total number of people who died. Racist evolutionary attitudes exploded in Germany against people groups such as Jews, Poles, and many others. Darwin's teaching on evolution and humanism heavily influenced Adolf Hitler and the Nazis.

Hitler even tried to force the Protestant church in Germany to change fundamental tenants because of his newfound faith.[6] In 1936, while Hitler was in power, an encyclopedia entry on Hitler stated:

> . . . a Hitler attempt to modify the Protestant faith failed.[7]

6. *The American Educator Encyclopedia* (Chicago, IL: The United Educators, Inc., 1936), p. 1702 under entry "Hitler."
7. *The American Educator Encyclopedia* (Chicago, IL: The United Educators, Inc., 1936), p. 1494 under entry "Germany."

His actions clearly show that he did not hold to the basic fundamentals taught in the 66 books of the Bible. Though some of his writings suggest he did believe in some form of God early on (due to his upbringing within Catholicism), his religious views moved toward atheistic humanism with his acceptance of evolution. Many atheists today try to disavow him, but actions speak louder than words.

The Alpha History site (dedicated to the history of Nazi Germany by providing documents, transcribed speeches, and so on) says:

> Contrary to popular opinion, Hitler himself was not an atheist. . . . Hitler drifted away from the church after leaving home, and his religious views in adulthood are in dispute.[8]

So this history site is not sure what his beliefs were, but they seem to be certain that he was not an atheist! If they are not sure what beliefs he held, how can they be certain he was not an atheist?[9] The fact is that many people who walk away from church become atheists (i.e., they were never believers in the first place as 1 John 2:19 indicates). And Hitler's actions were diametrically opposed to Christianity . . . but not atheism, where there is no God who sets what is right and wrong.[10]

Regardless, this refutes notions that Hitler was a Christian as some have falsely claimed. Hitler's disbelief started early. He said:

> The present system of teaching in schools permits the following absurdity: at 10 a.m. the pupils attend a lesson in the catechism, at which the creation of the world is presented to them in accordance with the teachings of the Bible; and at 11 a.m. they attend a lesson in natural science, at which they are taught the theory of evolution. Yet the two doctrines are in complete contradiction. As a child, I suffered from this contradiction, and ran my head against a wall. . . . Is there a single religion that can exist without a dogma? No, for in that case it would belong to the order of science. . . . But there have been human beings, in the baboon category, for at least three hundred thousand years. There

---

8. Religion in Nazi Germany, http://alphahistory.com/nazigermany/religion-in-nazi-germany/, April 3, 2013.
9. Romans 1 makes it clear that all people believe in God, they just suppress that knowledge, and this is also the case with any professed atheist.
10. For an extensive treatise on Hitler's (and the Nazi's) religious viewpoints, see: J. Bergman, *Hitler and the Nazi Darwinian Worldview* (Kitchener, Ontario, Canada: Joshua Press Inc., 2012).

is less distance between the man-ape and the ordinary modern man than there is between the ordinary modern man and a man like Schopenhauer. . . . It is impossible to suppose nowadays that organic life exists only on our planet.[11]

Consider this quote in his unpublished second book:

> The types of creatures on the earth are countless, and on an individual level their self-preservation instinct as well as the longing for procreation is always unlimited; however, the space in which this entire life process plays itself out is limited. It is the surface area of a precisely measured sphere on which billions and billions of individual beings struggle for life and succession. In the limitation of this living space lies the compulsion for the struggle for survival, and the struggle for survival, in turn contains the precondition for evolution.[12]

Hitler continues:

> The history of the world in the ages when humans did not yet exist was initially a representation of geological occurrences. The clash of natural forces with each other, the formation of a habitable surface on this planet, the separation of water and land, the formation of the mountains, plains, and the seas. That [was] is the history of the world during this time. Later, with the emergence of organic life, human interest focuses on the appearance and disappearance of its thousandfold forms. Man himself finally becomes visible very late, and from that point on he begins to understand the term "world history" as referring to the history of his own development — in other words, the representation of his own evolution. This development is characterized by the never-ending battle of humans against animals and also against humans themselves.[13]

Hitler fully believed Darwin as well as Darwin's precursors — such as Charles Lyell's geological ages and millions of years of history. In his statements here,

---

11. Adolf Hitler, 1941, translated by Norman Cameron and R.H. Stevens, *Hitler's Secret Conversations, 1941–1944* (The New American Library of World Literature, Inc., 1961).
12. Adolf Hitler, edited by Gerald L. Weinberg, *Hitler's Second Book* (Enigma Books, 2003), translated by Krista Smith, p. 8.
13. Ibid., p. 9.

there is no reference to God. Instead, he unreservedly flew the banner of naturalism and evolution and only mentioned God in a rare instance to win Christians to his side, just as agnostic Charles Darwin did in his book *On the Origin of Species*.[14]

One part of the Nazi party political platform's 25 points in 1920 says:

> We demand freedom of religion for all religious denominations within the state so long as they do not endanger its existence or oppose the moral senses of the Germanic race. The Party as such advocates the standpoint of a positive Christianity without binding itself confessionally to any one denomination.[15]

Clearly this "positive Christianity" was an appeal to some of Christianity's morality, but not the faith itself. Many atheists today still appeal to a "positive Christian" approach, wanting the morality of Christianity (in many respects), but not Christianity.

Christianity was under heavy attack by Hitler and the Nazis as documented from original sources prior to the end of WWII by Bruce Walker in *The Swastika against the Cross*.[16] The book clearly reveals the anti-Christian sentiment by Hitler and the Nazis and their persecution of Christianity and their attempt to make Christianity change and be subject to the Nazi state and beliefs.

In 1939–1941, the Bible was rewritten for the German people at Hitler's command, eliminating all references to Jews and made Christ out to be pro-Aryan! The Ten Commandments were replaced with these twelve[17]:

1. Honor your Fuhrer and master.
2. Keep the blood pure and your honor holy.
3. Honor God and believe in him wholeheartedly.
4. Seek out the peace of God.
5. Avoid all hypocrisy.

---

14 In the first edition of *Origin of Species*, God is not mentioned, in the sixth edition, "God" was added several times to draw Christians into this false religion. See R. Hedtke, *Secrets of the Sixth Edition* (Green Forest, AR: Master Books, 2010).

15. Nazi Party 25 Points (1920), http://alphahistory.com/nazigermany/nazi-party-25-points-1920/.

16. B. Walker, *The Swastika against the Cross* (Denver, CO: Outskirts Press, Inc., 2008).

17. Hitler rewrote the Bible and added two commandments, Pravda News Site, 8/10/2006, http://english.pravda.ru/world/europe/10-08-2006/83892-hitler-0/; Jewish References erased in newly found Nazi Bible, Daily Mail Online, August 7, 2006, http://www.dailymail.co.uk/news/article-399470/Jewish-references-erased-newly-Nazi-Bible.html.

6.   Holy is your health and life.
7.   Holy is your well-being and honor.
8.   Holy is your truth and fidelity.
9.   Honor your father and mother — your children are your aid and your example.
10. Maintain and multiply the heritage of your forefathers.
11. Be ready to help and forgive.
12. Joyously serve the people with work and sacrifice.

Hitler had *replaced* Christ in Nazi thought; and children were even taught to pray to Hitler instead of God![18] Hitler and the Nazis were not Christian, but instead were humanistic in their outlook, and any semblance of Christianity was cultic. The Nazis determined that their philosophy was the best way to bring about the common good of all humanity.

Interestingly, it was Christians alone in Germany who were unconquered by the Nazis and suffered heavily for it. Walker summarizes in his book:

> You would expect to find Christians and Nazis mortal enemies. This is, of course, exactly what happened historically. Christians, alone, proved unconquerable by the Nazis. It can be said that Christians did not succeed in stopping Hitler, but it cannot be said that they did not try, often at great loss and nearly always as true martyrs (people who could have chosen to live, but who chose to die for the sake of goodness.)[19]

Hitler and the Nazis' evolutionary views certainly helped lead Germany into WWII because they viewed the "Caucasian" as more evolved (and more specifically the Aryan peoples of the Caucasians), which to them justified their adoption of the idea that lesser "races" should be murdered in the struggle for survival. Among the first to be targeted were Jews, then Poles, Slavs, and then many others — including Christians, regardless of their heritage.

Trotsky, Lenin

Trotsky and Lenin were both notorious leaders of the USSR — and specifically the Russian revolution. Lenin, taking power in 1917, became a ruthless leader and selected Trotsky as his heir. Lenin and Trotsky held to Marxism, which was built in part on Darwinism and evolution applied to a social scheme.

18. Walker, p. 20–22.
19. Ibid., p. 88.

Karl Marx regarded Darwin's book as an "epoch-making book." With regard to Darwin's research on natural origins, Marx claimed, "The latter method is the only materialistic and, therefore, the only scientific one."[20]

Few realize or admit that Marxism, the primary idea underlying communism, is built on Darwinism and materialism (i.e., no God). In 1883, Freidrich Engels, Marx's longtime friend and collaborator, stated at Marx's funeral service, "Just as Darwin discovered the law of evolution in organic nature, so Marx discovered the law of evolution in human history."[21] Both Darwin and Marx built their ideologies on naturalism and materialism (tenants of evolutionary humanism). Trotsky once said of Darwin:

> Darwin stood for me like a mighty doorkeeper at the entrance to the temple of the universe. I was intoxicated with his minute, precise, conscientious and at the same time powerful, thought. I was the more astonished when I read . . . that he had preserved his belief in God. I absolutely declined to understand how a theory of the origin of species by way of natural selection and sexual selection and a belief in God could find room in one and the same head.[22]

Trotsky's high regard for evolution and Darwin were the foundation of his belief system. Like many, Trotsky probably did not realize that the precious few instances of the name "God" did not appear in the first edition of *Origin of Species*. These references were added later, and many suspect that this was done to influence church members to adopt Darwinism. Regardless, Trotsky may not have read much of Darwin's second book, *Descent of Man*, in which Darwin claims that man invented God:

> The same high mental faculties which first led man to believe in unseen spiritual agencies, then in fetishism, polytheism, and ultimately in monotheism, would infallibly lead him, as long as his reasoning powers remained poorly developed, to various strange superstitions and customs.[23]

20. Robert Maynard Hutchins, editor, *Great Books of the Western World*, Volume 50, Capital, Karl Marx (Chicago, IL: William Benton Publishers, 1952), footnotes on p. 166 and p. 181.

21. Gertrude Himmelfarb, *Darwin and the Darwinian Revolution* (London: Chatto & Windus, 1959), p. 348.

22. Max Eastman, *Leon Trotsky: The Portrait of a Youth* (New York: Greenberg, 1925), p. 117–118.

23. Charles Darwin, *The Descent of Man and Selection in Relation to Sex*, chapter III (Mental Powers of Man and the Lower Animals), 1871, as printed in *Great Books of the Western World*, Volume 49, Robert Hutchins, ed. (Chicago, IL: Encyclopedia Britannica, 1952), p. 303.

Vladimir Lenin picked up on Darwinism and Marxism and ruled very harshly as an evolutionist. His variant of Marxism has become known as Leninism. Regardless, the evolutionist roots of Marx, Trotsky, and Lenin were the foundation that Communism has stood on — and continues to stand on.

Stalin, Mao, and Pol Pot, to Name a Few

Perhaps the most ruthless communist leaders were Joseph Stalin, Mao Zedong, and Pol Pot. Each of these were social Darwinists, ruling three different countries — the Soviet Union, China, and Cambodia, respectively. Their reigns of terror demonstrated the end result of reducing the value of human life to that of mere animals, a Darwinistic teaching.[24] Though I could expand on each of these, you should be getting the point by now. So let's move to another key, but deadly, point in evolutionary thought.

Abortion — The War on Babies

The war on children has been one of the quietest, and yet bloodiest, in the past hundred years. In an evolutionary mindset, the unborn have been treated as though they are going through an "animal phase" and can simply be discarded.

Early evolutionist Ernst Haeckel first popularized the concept that babies in the womb are actually undergoing animal developmental stages, such as a fish stage and so on. This idea has come to be known as *ontogeny recapitulates phylogeny.* Haeckel even faked drawings of various animals' embryos and had them drawn next to human embryos looking virtually identical (see figure 1).

These drawings have been shown to be completely false.[25] Haeckel himself partially confessed as much.[26] However, this discredited idea has been used repeatedly for a hundred years! Textbooks today still use this concept (though not Haeckel's drawings), and museums around the world still teach it.

---

24. R. Hall, "Darwin's Impact — The Bloodstained Legacy of Evolution," *Creation Magazine* 27(2):46-47, March, 2005, http://www.answersingenesis.org/articles/cm/v27/n2/darwin.
25. Michael Richardson et al, *Anatomy and Embryology*, 196(2):91–106, 1997.
26. Haeckel said, "A small portion of my embryo-pictures (possibly 6 or 8 in a hundred) are really (in Dr Brass's [one of his critics] sense of the word) "falsified" — all those, namely, in which the disclosed material for inspection is so incomplete or insufficient that one is compelled in a restoration of a connected development series to fill up the gaps through hypotheses, and to reconstruct the missing members through comparative syntheses. What difficulties this task encounters, and how easily the draughts — man may blunder in it, the embryologist alone can judge." M.L. Hutchinson, "The Truth about Haeckel's Confession," *The Bible Investigator and Inquirer*, Melbourne, March 11, 1911, p. 22–24.

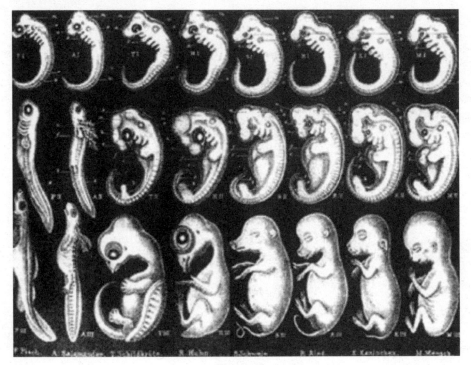

Figure 1

Through this deception, many women have been convinced that the babies they are carrying in their wombs are simply going through an animal phase and can be aborted. Author and general editor of this volume, Ken Ham, states:

> In fact, some abortion clinics in America have taken women aside to explain to them that what is being aborted is just an embryo in the fish stage of evolution, and that the embryo must not be thought of as human. These women are being fed outright lies.[27]

Evolutionary views have decreased the value of human life. Throughout the world the casualties of the war on children is staggering. Though deaths of children and the unborn did exist prior to the "evolution revolution," they have increased exponentially after the promotion of Darwinian teachings.

27. Ken Ham, *The Lie: Evolution*, chapter 8, "The Evils of Evolution" (Green Forest, AR: Master Books, 1987), p. 105.

The War on Marriage and Gender

Where many of the previous sections dealt with moral implications that openly killed millions, we need to recognize that religious views based on evolutionary ideas have penetrated into other areas of society.

Marriage is under attack. Sexual immorality is rampant. Homosexuality and sexual deviancy is guised under many names — gay, lesbian, transgender, cross dresser, gender-queer, and hosts of other names. However, the nature of the sin is still the same in God's eyes (Genesis 19:4–7; Leviticus 18:1, 22, 20:1, 13; Judges 19:22–25; Romans 1:22–32, 1 Corinthians 6:9–11; 1 Timothy 1:8–11, Jude 4–8, and Revelation 21:8, 22:15).

But if man is just a product of evolution, where we came from nothing and are returning to nothing, then why limit yourself to being moral? Only repentance from such a false religion and turning to Jesus Christ can remedy this situation (1 Corinthians 6:11).

The War on Youth: Suicide, Drugs, and School Attacks

For the privileged youth that survived the abortion holocaust, their lives have been a constant trial. Being taught that there is no meaning in life from an evolutionary worldview that has been imposed on millions of kids worldwide, the youth of today can easily put two and two together. If kids are taught they are merely rearranged atoms doing what atoms do, then why not take your life, or destroy it with drugs, or take others' lives with you (e.g., school shootings).

After all, if a student is deceived into believing the religion of evolution and views themselves as animals and everyone else as animals, then why not treat them like cockroaches. Without God, morality is relative (hence, arbitrary) and meaningless.

Conclusion

Is evolution the cause of wars and deaths? Absolutely not — both existed long before Darwin was born. Sin is the ultimate cause.[28] But an evolutionary worldview has done nothing but add fuel to the fire.

In spite of the wars, atrocities, and degraded morality caused by those who subscribed to an evolutionary worldview in recent times, there is still hope. We can end the seemingly endless atrocities against the unborn and those deemed less worthy of living, including the old and impaired.

---

28. Ken Ham, gen. ed., *The New Answers Book 1* (Green Forest, AR: Master Books, 2006), chapter 26, "Why Does God's Creation Include Death and Suffering?" p. 325-338, http://www. answersingenesis.org/articles/nab/why-does-creation-include-suffering.

In Egypt, Israelite boys were slaughtered by being thrown into the Nile at the command of Pharaoh (Exodus 1:20). And yet, by the providence of God, Moses survived and led the Israelites to safety, and the Lord later judged the Egyptians.

In Judea, under the Roman Empire, subordinate King Herod the Great commanded the slaughter of all the boys under the age of two in and around Bethlehem. And yet, by the providence of God, Jesus, the Son of God, survived and later laid down His life to bring salvation to mankind as the Prince of Peace. Herod's name, however, went down in history as an evil tyrant and murderer.

In this day and age, governments readily promote and fund the killing of children, both boys and girls, and sometimes command it, through abortion. By providence, however . . . you survived.

While we can't change the past, we can learn from it. If we are to stop this continuing bloodshed, we must get back to the Bible and realize the bankrupt religion of evolutionary humanism has led only to death — by the millions. We need to point those who think humanity is the answer to the Savior who took the sins of humanity on Himself to offer them salvation.

> *It does not say that Darwin renounced evolution. It merely says that Darwin speculated over the outcome of his ideas. He never backed away from evolution.*

 # DID DARWIN RENOUCE EVOLUTION AND GET SAVED ON HIS DEATHBED?

Having spent over 20 years as a physician, **DR. TOMMY MITCHELL** brings a unique perspective to his work and presentations with Answers in Genesis. He is currently completing a junior high anatomy curriculum series with Master Books and has authored chapters in the *Answers Books 4 Teens* series. Dr. Mitchell graduated from the University of Tennessee-Knoxville with a BA in cell biology. He then attended Vanderbilt University School of Medicine, and in 1984 received his medical degree.

It has been widely held among many sincere and well-meaning Christians that Charles Darwin on his deathbed not only renounced evolution, but also accepted Jesus Christ as his Savior. The tale of this deathbed conversion has been passed down over the years as fact. This "event" has even been used as "evidence" that evolution is false. The overzealous have, at times, boldly proclaimed, "See — even Darwin knew that this theory was not true!"

Early Reports

What is the basis for this story? As often as it is repeated, there must be credible evidence that these events actually took place, right? Surely, the tale would not have continued through the years if it were a lie? Sadly, when evidence is sought, there is little to support this story.

Charles Darwin died on April 19, 1882, and was buried in Westminster Abbey. Within days of his death, reports of a conversion experience began to circulate. The first report supposedly came in a sermon preached in South Wales by a gentleman identified as "Mr. Huntingdon."

Some weeks later there surfaced a report about a letter sent to John Eadie, a divinity professor in Glasgow, in which Darwin indicated, "He can with confidence look to Calvary."[1] Curiously, when examined, Darwin's existing correspondence (which totals over 14,000 letters) contains no communication between these two men.[2]

Lady Hope

The most often cited evidence for the alleged conversion of Darwin comes from a woman known as Lady Hope. She was born Elizabeth Reid Cotton in December 1842 and was the daughter of General Sir Arthur Cotton. She and her father were active evangelists in Kent, near Charles Darwin's home. In 1877, she married Admiral Sir James Hope and thus became Lady Hope, a title she continued to use even after remarrying Thomas Denny subsequent to Sir James's death a few years later.

While traveling in America in 1915 she attended a conference in East Northfield, Massachusetts. While there she apparently told the story of a visit she had with Darwin before his death. She recounted this tale during a devotional service and was later persuaded to write an account of this visit, which was then published in the *Watchman-Examiner*, a national Baptist magazine, on August 19, 1915.[3]

---

1. James Moore, *The Darwin Legend* (Grand Rapids: Baker Books, 1994), p. 82.
2. David Herbert, *Charles Darwin's Religious Views* (London: Hersil Publishing, 1990), p. 59.
3. Moore, p. 190.

Here, Lady Hope claimed to have visited Darwin on an autumn afternoon. She noted that Darwin had been bedridden for several months before his death, and at the time of her visit she found him sitting up in bed. Lady Hope indicated that Darwin was at the time reading the Bible, which she claimed he was always studying. When asked what he was reading he replied, "Hebrews . . . the Royal Book." Darwin also supposedly commented, "I was a young man with unformed ideas."

Lady Hope further claimed that before her departure she was asked by Darwin to return and speak to his servants in his summerhouse. When asked about the subject on which she should speak, Darwin was said to have replied "Christ Jesus!"

What Really Happened?

Unfortunately, when the full text of the report is examined, there are many inconsistencies that make the story untenable. While it is possible that Lady Hope did visit Darwin's home in late 1881, this was almost seven months before his death.[4] He was certainly not bedridden for six months before his death. Further, there was nothing to indicate that he was always studying the Bible.

On the Down House property, there was a small summerhouse, but it was too small to accommodate 30 people. There is nothing in his writings to indicate that Darwin ever asked anyone to speak about "Christ Jesus."

Further, it is fascinating what Lady Hope's story does not say. It does not say that Darwin renounced evolution. It merely says that Darwin speculated over the outcome of his ideas. He never backed away from evolution. Nor does the Lady Hope story say that Darwin actually became a Christian. The story, even if true, merely claims Darwin was reading the Bible and made a statement about Christ. Nowhere is there a claim of a saving relationship[5] with the Savior.

As soon as this story became public, the denials from Darwin's family began (as they did after every supposed "conversion story" became known). In a letter to James Howe, Darwin's son Francis wrote in 1915: "He [Darwin] could not have become openly and enthusiastically Christian without the knowledge of his family, and no such change occurred."[6]

---

4. Ibid., p. 167.
5. Bodie Hodge, "What Does It Mean to Be 'Saved'?" Answers in Genesis, April 21, 2009, https://answersingenesis.org/gospel/salvation/what-does-it-mean-to-be-saved/.
6. Ibid., p. 144.

In a letter dated May 28, 1918, Francis again writes: "Lady Hope's account of my father's views on religion is quite untrue. I have publicly accused her of falsehood, but I have not seen any reply."[7]

Darwin's daughter Henrietta wrote in 1922: "I was present at his deathbed. Lady Hope was not present during his last illness, or any illness. . . . He never recanted any of his scientific views, either then or earlier."[8]

Conclusion

Beyond these denials, if the tale were true, why did Darwin's wife Emma not rejoice in this? She was always troubled by what she perceived as the godless nature of his views. If he indeed repented, why did she not make this known? Also, if the story were credible, why did Lady Hope wait 33 years before relating it, and even then, relating it in a country across the ocean?

Given the weight of evidence, it must be concluded that Lady Hope's story is unsupportable, even if she did actually visit Darwin. There is no evidence to support that he ever became a Christian, and he never renounced evolution.

As much as we would like to believe that he died with a saving knowledge of Jesus Christ, it is much more likely that he didn't. It is unfortunate that the story continues to be promoted by many sincere people who use this in an effort to discredit evolution when many other great arguments exist, including the greatest: the Bible.

7.   Francis Darwin to [A. Le Lievre?], November 27, 1917, reprinted in Moore, p. 145.
8.   Herbert, p. 88–89.

Evolution is a religion. It's a core tenant of atheism and an attempt to explain life without God.

28 CONCLUSION

KEN HAM holds a bachelor's degree in applied science (with an emphasis on environmental biology) awarded by the Queensland Institute of Technology in Australia. He also holds a diploma of education from the University of Queensland (a graduate qualification necessary for Ken to begin his initial career as a science teacher in the public schools in Australia). In recognition of the contribution Ken has made to the church in the USA and internationally, Ken has been awarded six honorary doctorates: a Doctor of Divinity (1997) from Temple Baptist College in Cincinnati, Ohio; a Doctor of Literature (2004) from Liberty University in Lynchburg, Virginia; a Doctor of Letters (2010) from Tennessee Temple University; a Doctorate in Humane Letters from Mid-Continent University in Kentucky (2012); a Doctor of Science from Bryan College in Tennessee (2017); and a Doctor of Divinity, Mid-America Baptist Theological Seminary, Tennessee (2018).

AVERY FOLEY is a writer for Answers in Genesis from Ontario, Canada. She holds a Master of Arts in theological studies from Liberty Baptist Theological Seminary. She regularly appears as a guest newscaster on Answers News.

A s we've seen throughout this book, Christians don't need to be afraid of evolutionary teaching. It's a bankrupt philosophy that raises its "fist" at God, but ultimately fails scientifically. In reality, it's a glass house cracking into rubble. Observational science, when done correctly, will always confirm God's Word and the history recorded in it because that history is true.

Starting from the foundation of truth that is God's Word, we should never be afraid to challenge evolutionary ideas. First Corinthians 3:19 says, "For the wisdom of this world is folly with God."[1] The world may consider us foolish for not adopting what it considers to be wisdom. But when this "wisdom" ignores God's Word, it's nothing but foolishness.

In an attempt to not appear foolish in the eyes of the world, many Christians embrace evolutionary ideas and try to add them into Scripture. As this book has powerfully demonstrated, scientifically there is no justification for this attempt. Evolution simply does not satisfactorily explain what we see in the world. And yet many Christians still attempt to mix evolution with Christianity.

Really, this is nothing more than an attempt to mix the pagan religion of our day with Christianity. Evolution is a religion. It's a core tenant of atheism and an attempt to explain life without God. When Christians try to add it (along with millions of years) into the Bible, they are taking aspects of the evolutionary religion and aspects of Christianity and combining them.

It's really no different from the ancient Israelites who compromised the true religion given to them by God with the pagan beliefs, rituals, and idols of the nations around them. God judged them for their compromise then, and He is judging our compromise today!

As Christians, we need to believe God's Word — all of it. As the Apostle Paul put it, "Let God be true but every man a liar" (Romans 3:4). All of Scripture is breathed out by God (2 Timothy 3:16) and therefore carries the authority of the God who does not lie (Titus 1:2), so we can trust God and take Him at His Word.

When we don't believe God's Word and instead try to mix it with evolutionary ideas, we create major theological problems. Every major Christian doctrine is either directly or indirectly founded in the history in Genesis. If you undermine that history, you undermine the foundation for *all* of our doctrine — including the gospel message!

Scripture clearly teaches that God created a perfect world (Genesis 1:31) and that God's works are perfect (Deuteronomy 32:4). This original creation

---

1. Scripture in this chapter is from the English Standard Version (ESV) of the Bible.

was perfect, free from death and suffering. Death would be the consequence of sin, should Adam and Eve (the first two humans) choose to disobey (Genesis 2:17). They rebelled against God and their actions brought death and the curse into creation (Genesis 3:16–19; Romans 5:12). Death is a direct consequence of sin.

It's because death *is* the just penalty for sin that Jesus needed to come and die a physical death on the Cross (1 Corinthians 15:22). When Christians add millions of years and evolution into the Bible, they are really putting untold ages of death, suffering, disease, extinction, and animal carnivory before sin.

They are putting death and suffering in God's very good creation (Genesis 1:31)! No longer is death the penalty for sin. Instead of being an enemy (1 Corinthians 15:26) it becomes the very means by which God chose to create! So, if death was just part of God's creation, why did Jesus have to come and die?

Compromise with the religion of our day undermines the entire gospel message. Instead of allowing man's fallible interpretation of the evidence to determine what we believe, we need to trust the Word of our Creator. No person or scientist knows everything, or has always been there, but God not only knows everything but was there at creation and has told what happened, how it happened, and over what timeframe it happened in His Word. We would do well to remember God's words to Job:

> Where were you when I laid the foundation of the earth?
> Tell me, if you have understanding.
> Who determined its measurements — surely you know!
> Or who stretched the line upon it?
> On what were its bases sunk,
> or who laid its cornerstone,
> when the morning stars sang together
> and all the sons of God shouted for joy? (Job 38:4–7)

God's Word — not the glass house words of fallible, sinful human beings — must be our authority in all areas, including history and science! In the question of creation vs. evolution, it really comes down to a question of authority. Who will you trust? Who will your authority be? God's Word or man's word? As believers, we can settle for nothing less than God's Word being the authority in all areas.

If we can trust God with our eternal souls, we can trust him with our minds (Mark 12:30) and believe His Word over that of fallible man (humanism)!

The Genesis-Romans Road to Salvation

Genesis 1:1 — [**God made everything.**]

In the beginning, God created the heavens and the earth.

Genesis 1:31 — [**God made everything perfectly (Deuteronomy 32:4) — no death, no suffering.**]

Then God saw everything that he had made, and behold it was very good. And there was evening and there was morning, the sixth day.

Genesis 3:17–19 – [**The punishment for sin is death, and because of sin the world is no longer perfect.**]

And to Adam he said, "Because you have listened to the voice of your wife and have eaten of the tree of which I commanded you, 'You shall not eat of it,' cursed is the ground because of you; in pain you shall eat of it all the days of your life; thorns and this-tles it shall bring forth for you; and you shall eat the plants of the field. By the sweat of your face you shall eat bread, till you return to the ground, for out of it you were taken; for dust you are, and to dust you shall return."

Romans 5:12 — [**Because Adam, our mutual grandfather, sinned, we now sin, too.**]

Therefore, just as sin came into the world through one man, and death through sin, and so death spread to all men because all sinned.

Romans 3:23 — [**We need to realize that we are all sinners, including ourselves.**]

For all have sinned and fall short of the glory of God.

Romans 6:23 — [**The punishment for sin is a just punishment — death — but God came to rescue us and give the free gift of salvation by sending His Son Jesus.**]

For the wages of sin is death, but the free gift of God is eternal life in Christ Jesus our Lord.

Romans 10:9 — [To receive this free gift of salvation, you need to believe in Jesus as your risen Lord and Savior. Salvation is not by works, but by faith — see also John 3:16 and Acts 16:30–31.]

Because, if you confess with your mouth that Jesus is Lord and believe in your heart that God raised him from the dead, you will be saved.

Romans 5:1 — [Being saved, you are now justified and have peace with God.]

Therefore, since we have been justified by faith, we have peace with God through our Lord Jesus Christ.